Reinaldo Arenas

Twayne's World Authors Series
Cuban Literature

David William Foster, Editor
Arizona State University

TWAS 870

REINALDO ARENAS
Lázaro G. Carriles

Reinaldo Arenas

Francisco Soto

College of Staten Island,
City University of New York

Twayne Publishers
An Imprint of Simon & Schuster Macmillan
New York

Prentice Hall International
London • Mexico City • New Delhi • Singapore • Sydney • Toronto

Twayne's World Authors Series No. 870

Reinaldo Arenas
Francisco Soto

Copyright © 1998 by Twayne Publishers

Twayne Publishers
An Imprint of Simon & Schuster Macmillan
1633 Broadway
New York, NY 10019

Library of Congress Cataloging-in-Publication Data

Soto, Francisco, 1956–
    Reinaldo Arenas / Francisco Soto; [David William Foster, editor].
        p. cm. — (Twayne's world authors series; TWAS 870)
    Includes bibliographical references and index.
    ISBN 0-8057-4554-8
    1. Arenas, Reinaldo, 1943– —Criticism and interpretation.
    I. Foster, David William. II. Title. III. Series.
PQ7390.A72Z87   1998
863—dc21   98–21201
                                                                    CIP

This paper meets the requirements of ANSI/NISO Z3948-1992 (Permanence of Paper).

10 9 8 7 6 5 4 3 2 1

Printed in the United States of America

In loving memory of my dear friend
Saúl Rosales Jr.
(1955–1994)

Contents

Preface

Cuban writer Reinaldo Arenas (1943–1990) is considered to be one of Latin America's most innovative and provocative late twentieth-century literary voices. A prolific writer who overcame enormous persecution and censorship, Arenas wrote novels, short stories, poetry, theater, and essays. The publication of his autobiography, *Antes que anochezca* (*Before Night Falls*), in 1992 and its subsequent translation into various languages has made Arenas more internationally recognized as a major literary figure than he was during his lifetime. *Before Night Falls* boldly articulates Arenas's homoerotic adventures and misadventures. Its publication, and critical and commercial success, marks an important milestone indeed in Latin American letters, because it is the first openly homosexual autobiography ever published in an area of the world traditionally known for its machismo and homophobia.

This study is not only the first comprehensive review in English to examine and analyze the author's major works, but it is also the first to trace the articulation of homoerotic themes and issues in the Cuban writer's oeuvre. Almost all of Arenas's writings contain either implicit or explicit homosexual characters, episodes, and scenes. This study illustrates how Arenas became more daring and open in portraying homosexual themes in his work after he left Cuba in 1980.

Although Arenas's representation of homosexuality cannot be considered positive in the way that much of contemporary gay literature, such as that published in North America, strives to celebrate homosexual identity and to represent gay relationships based on mutual respect and equality, it nonetheless marks an important step in breaking the silence surrounding homosexuality in Latin America, where homosexuality continues to be a topic that is very much in the closet. In Cuba, where Arenas suffered persecution and censorship for being homosexual, policies on homosexuality have been and continue to be the focus of long-standing debates. The infamous UMAP concentration camps that were constructed in Cuba in the early 1960s specifically for the purpose of correcting "antisocial" and "deviant" homosexual behaviors led Jean-Paul Sartre to remark: "Cuba does not have Jews, but has homosexuals." As recently as a few years ago, "Sidatorios," asylums for AIDS patients isolated against their will from the rest of Cuban society, were condemned

by human rights organizations. Still, many people both inside and outside Cuba support the official government policies while others even talk
of a new openness in Cuba toward homosexuals.

Like many Latin American writers who find it impossible to separate
their literary careers from the sociopolitical realities of their countries,
Arenas was an outspoken critic of Fidel Castro's regime, a *machista* system built on a patriarchal cult of masculinity. Arenas's criticism of the
Cuban revolution was an angry cry against a system under which he,
like many others, had been persecuted for being homosexual. At first a
supporter of the Cuban revolution, Arenas turned away from the Castro
regime in the mid-1960s when the government's open persecution of
homosexuals began to escalate. His dissatisfaction with the government
deepened when his writings—transgressive, unconventional, and sup-
portive of the individual's right to self-expression—were declared anti-
revolutionary and censored. Soon afterward, Arenas was no longer permitted to publish on the island. Defiant, he secretly sent his manuscripts
abroad where they were immediately published, infuriating the Castro
regime, which on various occasions confiscated and destroyed his work
and ultimately branded him a nonperson in Cuba.

During the 1970s, while his novels were being read and praised in
Europe and Latin America, Arenas lived a picaresque life in Havana,
moving constantly and working at odd jobs simply to survive. From
1974 to 1976 he was imprisoned in El Morro, a Spanish colonial fortress
converted by the revolution into a maximum-security prison; the
charges were lascivious abuses. Finally in 1980, as a result of a bureaucratic blunder, he escaped from the island through the Mariel exodus.

After his arrival in the United States, Arenas settled in New York
City. Having been censored in Cuba for so long, the writer, as if intoxi-
cated with his newly found freedom, began to write prodigiously: novels, short stories, poetry, dramatic pieces, essays, newspaper articles.
Moreover, he reworked old manuscripts that he had managed to get out
of Cuba. For Arenas, writing was both a liberating act of self-expression
and an act of fury in which he challenged, undermined, and subverted
ideological dogmatism, especially that which attempts to silence homosexual desire. But living in exile was far from perfect. Although Arenas
was finally able to express himself freely, both as a writer and as a homosexual, he nonetheless felt despised and forsaken by the Cuban exile
community in Miami, whose reactionary politics and morality seemed
hypocritical. In exile he felt he was a ghost, a mere shadow of who he
once was. Moreover, New York City, a place in which he lived and expe-

rienced moments of happiness, became yet another nightmare as a result of the AIDS epidemic. Finally on 7 December 1990, suffering from AIDS and too sick to continue writing, Arenas committed suicide.

This book is divided into six chapters. The first five chapters analyze various texts that mark important moments in the development and articulation of homosexual themes and issues in Arenas's oeuvre. A final chapter summarizes Arenas's life and literary activity within the context of the most virulently homophobic period of Cuban history, 1959–1980.

Chapter 1 analyzes Arenas's autobiography, *Before Night Falls,* to present an overview of the writer's work, life, and times. Here I highlight how the autobiography calls attention to the sexual and political repression Arenas endured in Cuba due to the Cuban revolution's policies against homosexuals and its open hostility to any expression, either literary or individual, at variance with revolutionary morals.

Chapter 2 studies Arenas's *pentagonía,* a five-book sequence of novels—described by Arenas as both a writer's autobiography and a metaphor of Cuban history—that constitutes a unique intradependent unit within the author's oeuvre. This quintet presents the struggles and persecutions of a protean character whose life, from childhood to adulthood, spans different moments of Cuban history. In this chapter, I examine the development of a homosexual awakening on the part of the protagonist during progressive stages of his life in Cuban society.

Chapter 3 studies the two short novellas "Old Rosa" and "The Brightest Star." Each novella deals with its own particular issues of oppression, manifested during two distinct eras. My reading of both "Old Rosa" and "The Brightest Star" demonstrates that while oppression can clearly manifest itself in societies that suppress ideological pluralism (as has been the case during both Cuba's prerevolutionary and revolutionary eras), it can also present itself on a more restricted level, in one person's intolerance to accept another's expressions of difference, whether those expressions be sexual, racial, or political.

Chapter 4 studies the three stories of *Viaje a La Habana* (Journey to Havana). The chapter argues that while each story presents its own anecdote, characters, and action, the three, nonetheless, share a central theme: the search, conscious and unconscious, for a homosexual identity that ultimately represents a personal liberation. Perhaps in no other text has Arenas articulated with such passion the need for the homosexual man to accept and express himself freely in a world that censures and prohibits his conduct.

Chapter 5 studies Arenas's poetry. Although mainly recognized as a prose writer, Arenas left behind a poetic trilogy, titled *Leprosorio,* which brings together under one title three separate long poems: "El central" *(El Central: A Cuban Sugar Mill),* "Morir en junio y con la lengua afuera" (To Die in June, Gasping for Air), and "Leprosorio" (Leper Colony). In addition, in 1989 Arenas published a collection of shorter poems—sonnets and free verse poems written between 1969 and 1989—titled *Voluntad de vivir manifestándose* (The Will to Live Manifesting Itself). In this chapter, I analyze the representation of homoerotic desire in many of these poems and also show that over time these poetic texts explore and express more openly homosexual themes.

Chapter 6 summarizes Arenas's life and literary production from the historical context of the Cuban revolution and its problematic relationship with the issue of homosexuality.

I would like to point out that although each chapter focuses on those particular texts that, in my estimation, best exemplify the development of a homosexual sensibility in Arenas's works, references will also be made throughout the book to other texts that the author published during his lifetime. I am aware that a "sensibility," contrary to an idea, presents a more difficult subject for analysis; nonetheless, when I suggest a "homosexual sensibility" in Arenas's writings, I am referring to an awareness of and sensitivity to homosexual themes and issues that challenge society's heterosexist hegemony by creating a liberating space in which homosexual desire can be expressed and explored. Throughout this study, I have been very careful not to designate Arenas as a "gay" writer, not out of the belief that this type of label limits him as a writer (a rather homophobic argument, to say the least), but rather because such a label tells us nothing of the body of work he produced. Moreover, as many contemporary Latin American scholars who have begun to study the theme of homosexuality in Latin American letters have pointed out, the term "gay" does not have the same political meaning in Latin America that it does in North America, where being "gay" is more a matter of identity than of same-sex desire and sexual activity. For these reasons, I have chosen to sidestep these debates over terminology, which at the present are far from being concluded within the international homosexual and lesbian community, and rather focus my efforts on underscoring the homosexual themes and issues in Arenas's major works, carefully tracing the development of a homoerotic sensibility that becomes more progressively daring.

Finally, I have used existing English translations of Arenas's work followed by standard references. For untranslated works, I have quoted from the original Spanish and have provided my own translation without quotation marks and without comment. For essays, interviews, and other texts that are cited more for content than for style or aesthetics, I have given only my translations, followed by references to the original.

Acknowledgments

I am indebted to the College of Staten Island for the released time award I received for the 1995–1996 academic year during which I saw this project through its final phases. A special word of thanks to Mirella Affron (Vice President/Provost), Joan Hartman (Dean of Humanities), and Kathryn Talarico (Chair of the Department of Modern Languages) whose help and advice I have greatly appreciated. In addition, I am grateful to the PSC-CUNY awards for the financial support I received from 1994–1997, which assisted me with this and other projects.

I would also like to thank Elena M. Martínez whose friendship and confidence in my work have been a constant source of support. In addition, I would like to express my gratitude to Perla Rozencvaig, Dolores Koch, and the late Roberto Valero. Their encouragement over the years has given me the stimulus to continue working on Reinaldo Arenas's texts.

Finally, I thank Mark Albano without whose unwavering love I would surely sink in the quicksand of life.

Chronology

1943   Born, 16 July, near the town of Holguín (Oriente province), Cuba. Illegitimate son of Antonio Arenas Machín and Oneida Fuentes Rodríguez. Two months after his birth, the father abandons the family.

1948   Accidentally meets his father while he and his mother take a walk by the river. The mother reacts angrily by throwing stones. He would never see his father again.

1958   Joins the guerrilla rebel forces fighting against the dictatorial government of Fulgencio Batista. Spends the year in the Gibara mountains, Oriente province.

1959   With the triumph of the revolution, he is awarded a scholarship to study agricultural accounting.

1960   Summer: Takes first trip to Havana.

1961   Finishes studies in agricultural accounting and is assigned to work at the William Soler farm near Manzanillo, in the southernmost part of Cuba's Oriente province.

1962   Accepted to take part in a planning course for agricultural accounts at the University of Havana. Goes to live in Havana.

1963   Starts work at the National Library where he also begins to write his first novel *Celestino antes del alba* (*Singing from the Well*). Also begins to contribute stories and literary articles to *La Gaceta de Cuba* and *Unión,* two periodicals published by UNEAC (Cuban Writers and Artists Union).

1964   Is befriended by Virgilio Piñera and José Lezama Lima who read and react positively to the draft manuscript to *Celestino antes del alba* (*Singing from the Well*).

1965   Finishes *Celestino antes del alba*. The novel is awarded an honorable mention in the *Concurso Nacional de Novela Cirilo Villaverde* (Cirilo Villaverde National Novel Competition).

1965   Persecution of homosexuals escalates in Cuba. UMAP concentration camps are created and will remain active until 1969.

1966   Finishes *El mundo alucinate* (*The Ill-Fated Peregrinations of Fray Servando*).

1967   *Celestino antes del alba* is published in Cuba in a limited edition of 2,000 copies. Meets Jorge and Margarita Camacho while the couple visit Cuba; with their help, smuggles out the manuscripts of *Celestino antes del alba* and *El mundo alucinante*.

1968   Editions du Seuil, France, publishes *Le monde hallucinant*.

1969   *El mundo alucinante* is published in Spanish in Mexico, Editorial Diógenes.

1969   First version of *Otra vez el mar* (*Farewell to the Sea*) completed. This version will mysteriously disappear.

1970   Sent to the Manuel Sanguily Sugar Mill to cut sugarcane; *El central* is composed there.

1971   April: First National Congress on Education and Culture adopts homophobic policies.

1971   Second version of *Otra vez el mar* completed. This version is subsequently confiscated by the state security police.

1972   *Con los ojos cerrados* (*With My Eyes Closed*) is published in Uruguay, Editorial Arca.

1973   Arrested for charges of lascivious abuses and counter-revolutionary propaganda. While released on bail, escapes and is on the run from authorities for four months.

1974   January: Arrested in Lenin Park, Havana, and taken to the prison at El Morro Castle for two months. Later transferred to State Security at Villa Marista where for five months he is interrogated and finally forced to sign a confession of guilt. Returned to El Morro Castle where he spends another year behind bars.

1976   Is transferred to a rehabilitation farm in Flores, Havana province. Is released later that same year. For the next three years he constantly moves and works at odd jobs simply to survive.

1980 May 4: As a result of a bureaucratic blunder, manages to escape from Cuba through the Mariel exodus. In the United States, lives in Miami until December at which time he moves to New York City.

1981 *El central* and *Termina el desfile* (The Parade Ends) are published. Is awarded a Guggenheim scholarship to complete his novel, *Farewell to the Sea*.

1982 The following authorized editions appear: *El mundo alucinante* (*The Ill-Fated Peregrinations of Fray Servando*), *El palacio de las blanquísimas mofetas* (*The Palace of the White Skunks*), *Otra vez el mar* (*Farewell to the Sea*). *Celestino antes del alba* is reissued under the new title *Cantando en el pozo* (*Singing from the Well*). Founds the literary magazine *Mariel* which is published until 1984.

1983 Travels to Europe. Visits Sweden, where he is invited to give a number of conferences at the University of Stockholm. Also travels to Spain.

1984 *Arturo, la estrella más brillante* ("The Brightest Star") is published in Barcelona.

1985 Visiting Professor at Cornell University.

1986 *Necesidad de libertad* (The Need for Freedom) and *Persecución* (Persecution) are published.

1987 Diagnosed with AIDS. *La loma del ángel* (*Graveyard of the Angels*) is published.

1988 Is awarded a Woodrow Wilson fellowship and spends the year at the Woodrow Wilson Center in Washington D.C., where he works on the manuscripts of *Viaje a La Habana*, *El color del verano,* and *El asalto*.

1989 *El portero (The Doorman)*, *Voluntad de vivir manifestándose (The Will to Live Manifesting Itself)* appear.

1990 Publishes *Un plebiscito a Fidel Castro* (A Plebiscite to Fidel Castro) with Jorge Camacho. Completes *Antes que anochezca* in August and on 7 December commits suicide.

1991   *El color del verano* (The Color of Summer), *El asalto* (*The Assault*), and *Final de un cuento* (The End of a Story) are published.

1992   *Antes que anochezca* is published in Barcelona by Editorial Tusquets.

1995   *Adiós a mamá* (Goodbye Mother) is published in Barcelona by Ediciones Altera.

Chapter One

Arenas's Lifewriting:
Before Night Falls

On 7 December 1990, facing the last stages of his bout with AIDS, Reinaldo Arenas committed suicide. In a brief yet moving farewell letter sent to friends and various Spanish-language newspapers in the United States and abroad, Arenas made it quite clear that his suicide should not be interpreted as a sign of failure. "I do not want to convey . . . a message of defeat," he declared, "but of continued struggle and hope. Cuba will be free, I already am."[1] These, Arenas's final words, reveal the self-determination and indomitable spirit of one of Spanish America's most innovative literary voices of the twentieth century.

Like many Spanish American writers who have found it impossible to separate their literary careers from the sociopolitical realities of their countries, Arenas was an outspoken critic of his country's politics. As a young man who witnessed firsthand the monumental changes brought about by the Cuban revolution, Arenas was forthright in his criticisms of Fidel Castro's regime. Yet his criticism of the Cuban revolution was more than an attack on communism, or the Left for that matter; it was an angry cry against a system under which he, like many others, had been persecuted simply for being homosexual. At first a supporter of the Cuban revolution, Arenas turned away from the Castro regime in the mid-1960s when the government's open persecution of homosexuals began to escalate.[2]

Born on 16 July 1943 in the rural poverty of the Cuban countryside, Arenas experienced a childhood that can only be described as wretched. As a member of the poorest social stratum of society, one of his first memories was that of eating dirt because of a scarcity of food. Yet despite his impoverishment, Arenas saw his childhood as the most creative period of his life because of the freedom it afforded him: "I think the splendor of my childhood was unique because it was absolute poverty but also absolute freedom" (*BNF*, 5). As an escape from his desperate surroundings, the young Arenas would people the fields and groves near his house with mythical and supernatural characters, imaginary friends with whom he would spend his days. These flights of fancy were the genesis of his future literary aspirations: "What literary influence did I have in my childhood? Practically none: no books, no teaching. . . . But regarding the magical, the mysterious, which is so essential for the development of creativity, my childhood was perhaps the most literary time of my life" (*BNF,* 23).

As an idealistic teenager, Arenas joined Fidel Castro's rebel forces fighting against the dictatorial government of Fulgencio Batista. In his autobiography, Arenas claims that he never took part in any fighting or even witnessed a single battle during this time (*BNF,* 43); however, because he was on the winning side, following the triumph of the revolution he was awarded a scholarship to study agricultural accounting. After graduating and working for a short time on a state-run chicken farm near Manzanillo, in Cuba's Oriente province, Arenas moved to Havana and soon changed careers. In 1963 he started to work at the National Library, where he met writers and artists who influenced his literary development and introduced him to José Lezama Lima (1912–1976) and Virgilio Piñera (1912–1979), two very different and gifted writers who would become literary mentors for the young Arenas. It was at the library that Arenas wrote his first novel, *Celestino antes del alba* (*Singing from the Well*), the story of a child, persecuted by his family as well as by the impoverished conditions of his rural existence, who must rely on his imagination to survive. Shortly after its publication in 1967, this free-flowing narrative fell out of favor with the revolutionary cultural policy makers who at the time were demanding social realist literature that fostered the creation of a revolutionary consciousness.

Arenas was a writer in exile long before his actual escape from Cuba in 1980 through the Mariel boat lift that brought him to the United States. During the 1970s, for example, while his novels were being read and praised in Europe and Latin America, Arenas was censored in Cuba. Forced to live a somewhat picaresque life in Havana, he moved constantly and worked at odd jobs simply to survive. For a time he was imprisoned in El Morro, a Spanish colonial fortress converted by the revolution into a maximum-security prison, for charges of "lascivious abuses." In short, his life in Cuba from the mid-1960s on was reduced to silence, ostracism, censorship, and prison. Finally in 1980, as a result of a bureaucratic blunder, he escaped from the island through the Mariel exodus.

After his arrival in the United States, Arenas settled in New York City, where he reworked old manuscripts as well as wrote some new texts, such as *La loma del ángel* (*Graveyard of the Angels*) and *El portero* (*The Door-*

man). As always, writing was a refuge for Arenas, an act of self-expression in which he challenged and subverted all systems of power that are predicated on exclusion and closure and that attempt to silence variant forms of human expression. Yet although Arenas was finally able to express himself freely, he nonetheless felt out of place in the United States. Ostracized on the one hand by the Cuban exile community in Miami, whose reactionary politics and morality seemed hypocritical to him (Arenas's condemnation of repressive and life-destroying systems of power was never limited to the Left but was equally and symmetrically applied to the Right as well), Arenas also did not find a sense of community within the North American gay urban world, which he criticized for its pairing of same-type individuals and blind regimentation to conformity (*BNF*, 106–8). Finally, on 7 December 1990, so emotionally and physically deteriorated by AIDS that he could no longer write, no longer engaged in the act that had given his life the most meaning, he committed suicide.

Before Night Falls is the transcription of more than 20 cassettes Arenas dictated and then hurriedly corrected and edited in the last two years before his death. One of the most sexually uninhibited and liberating texts ever to come from Latin America, *Before Night Falls* marks an important milestone in the history of Latin American letters, because it is the first openly homosexual autobiography ever published in an area of the world traditionally known for its machismo and homophobia. Like a considerable portion of Arenas's previous work, the text first made its appearance in French as *Avant la nuit;*[3] the original Spanish version, *Antes que anochezca,*[4] was published a few months later.[5] In France and Spain the book immediately became both a critical and commercial success. In the United States, the English translation was chosen by the American Library Association, the New York Public Library, the *Village Voice,* and the *New York Times Book Review* as one of the best books of 1993. On 24 October 1993 the autobiography was reviewed in the *New York Times Book Review* by Latin American scholar Roberto González Echevarría. Prominently appearing on the front page accompanied by a large color photograph of Arenas, the review, titled "An Outcast of the Island," ends by stating that *Before Night Falls* is not only "crucial to understanding [Arenas's] works," but is also "a record of human cruelty and the toils of one individual to survive them."[6] González Echevarría's words underscore the universality of this inner history of one man's struggle to survive and maintain his dignity in the face of totalitarian oppression.

Before proceeding to a more thorough analysis of *Before Night Falls*— specifically its frank and uninhibited representation of homoerotic desire—it is necessary to address the question of classification (that is, is this an autobiography, memoir, reminiscence, self-portrait, or personal novel?) as well as to explore the even more thorny theoretical problems concerning the notion of translating or transforming a life into a text, a piece of writing.

Autobiographical Writing: The Construction of Self-Representation

It is the French theorist Philippe Lejeune who has worked most extensively on the literature of autobiography. His thorough and systematic approach to autobiography thus serves as a good point of departure for any discussion on the matter. Reduced to its bare essence, Lejeune defines autobiography as follows:

> Retrospective prose narrative written by a real person concerning his own existence, where the focus is his individual life, in particular the story of his personality.[7]

This definition delineates elements that belong to four distinct categories:

1. Form of language
   a. narrative
   b. in prose
2. Subject treated: individual life, story of a personality
3. Situation of the author: the author (whose name refers to a real person) and the narrator are identical
4. Position of the narrator
   a. the narrator and the principal character are identical
   b. retrospective point of view of the narrative

For Lejeune, any work that fulfills all the conditions designated in each of these categories would be identified as an autobiography. The absence of any of these elements separates autobiography from a number of related genres, for example, memoir (does not meet point 2); biography (point 4a); personal novel (point 3); autobiographical poem (point 1b); journal/diary (point 4b); self-portrait or essay (points 1a and 4b). Although these genres are related to autobiography, they nonetheless do not combine all the conditions clearly outlined in Lejeune's four categories. These distinctions and exclusions appear as rather extreme, but Lejeune does acknowledge that the different categories are not all equally restrictive and that certain conditions can be met, for the most part, without being satisfied completely. He indicates that the elements are not intended to be a straitjacket and that a certain degree of flexibility is permissible: "It is a question here of proportion, or rather of hierarchy: some transitions with other genres of personal literature work quite naturally (memoir, diary, essay), and a certain latitude is left to the classifier in the examination of particular cases" (Lejeune, 5). However, Lejeune stresses that categories 3 (the author [whose name refers to a real person] and the narrator are identical) and 4a (the narrator and the principal character are identical) allow neither transition or latitude; these elements, according to Lejeune, are a question of all or nothing.

Lejeune's four categories are indeed present in Arenas's text. *Before Night Falls* is a narrative of events (category 1a) in prose (1b) of the author's (Arenas's) individual life and the story of his personality (2). Moreover, the author (Reinaldo Arenas) and the narrator are one and the same (3); the narrator and the main character are also identical (4a). Finally, after an initial introductory chapter, *Before Night Falls* is recounted retrospectively (4b).

The following chart illustrates how *Before Night Falls* corresponds to each of Lejeune's four categories of autobiographical writing:

Philippe Lejeune, "The Autobiographical Pact"	Reinaldo Arenas, *Before Night Falls*
1. *Form of language*: (a) narrative, (b) in prose	*Form of language*: narrative prose
2. *Subject treated*: individual life, story of a personality	*Subject treated*: life and experiences of Arenas from childhood to shortly before his suicide in December 1990
3. *Situation of the author*: the author (whose name refers to a real person) and the narrator are identical	*Situation of the author*: the author is Reinaldo Arenas (a real person) who is at the same time narrator of his own work titled *Before Night Falls*
4. *Position of the narrator*: (a) the narrator and the principal character are identical (b) retrospective point of view	*Position of the narrator*: the narrator and the principal character are identical; after an initial narrative introductory chapter, the temporal structure is retrospective, from early childhood to shortly before death

The fact that *Before Night Falls* fits so comfortably within Lejeune's strict generic definition is ironic for a writer such as Arenas, who is generally recognized among literary critics for his spirit of subversion and literary nonconformity. Yet Arenas—whose writings violate neat boundaries between genres and (con)fuse the distinctions between fiction and reality—has written, with minor deviations, a rather conventional autobiography. As Robert Richmond Ellis asserts in his article "The Gay Lifewriting of Reinaldo Arenas: *Antes que anochezca*":

> In *Antes que anochezca* [*Before Night Falls*] Arenas ceases to engage in the textual experimentation of his earlier writings and assumes a conventional autobiographical discourse presupposing both the autonomy of the self and the referentiality of language. In his rush to finish "before night falls," he thus remains impervious to the deconstruction of autobiography undertaken by theoreticians of the genre usually far removed from either the AIDS ward or the homosexual concentration camps of his youth in Cuba.[8]

Ellis's assertion does not imply, however, that readers have not differed in their interpretations of *Before Night Falls* nor that *Before Night Falls* is without controversy. The controversies surrounding the text and the differences in terms of how it has been read are perhaps best illustrated by Roberto González Echevarría's prominent review of the autobiography in the *New York Times Book Review* and David Unger's letter to the editor of that same periodical, titled "The Archetypal Misfit," which challenges González Echevarría's assertions.[9]

González Echevarría's review recounts and underscores the sexual and political persecution Arenas fell victim to in revolutionary Cuba. Moreover, he highlights the absorbing, fresh, and profoundly original quality of the autobiography as well as Arenas's novels and short stories, which he describes as "difficult if not impossible to pigeonhole or even compare with [those of] other Latin American or Cuban authors, despite [their] very Cuban and Latin American themes" (González Echevarría, 33). González Echevarría suggests that Arenas's sexual and political marginality made it easy for Castro's government to "neutralize his enormous talent" (González Echevarría, 33). He ends his review by stating: "Anyone who feels the temptation to be lenient in judging Castro's Government should first read this passionate and beautifully written book" (González Echevarría, 33).

On 28 November 1993 the *New York Times Book Review* printed a short but well-designed letter to the editor by David Unger, who intended to cast doubt in the mind of any reader who had read González Echevarría's review. Directly confronting González Echevarría's assertion of Arenas's rebellious nature against authoritarianism, Unger maintained that Arenas was nothing more than an "archetypal misfit" whose literary penchant for hyperbole should make the reader skeptical of the political persecution he reportedly suffered in Cuba. In his letter, Unger objects to González Echevarría's statement that *Before Night Falls* holds "the fascination one finds in stories by survivors of death camps or in lives of the saints" because it repeats, according to Unger, "the often-heard analogy that Castro is to Cuban exiles what Hitler is to Holocaust survivors" (Unger, 35). After attacking Arenas's credibility, Unger moves on to attack González Echevarría's suggestion that Arenas's stories can be compared to those of Jorge Luis Borges, Julio Cortázar, and Juan Rulfo—the so-called Spanish American writers of the canon. Unger retaliates by stating: "[González Echeverría] seems to be affected by Arenas's hyperbole when he states that some of his short stories are 'among the best from Latin America' and that they rank alongside those of Jorge Luis Borges, Julio Cortázar and Juan Rulfo. This is total nonsense" (Unger, 35). (Postmodern criticism has shown that the concept of canon is a political and ideological construct created by those in power. Obviously, a writer like Arenas, who challenged and undermined all types of ideological dogmatism and who was not afraid of presenting a rebellious sexuality in his work, would have difficulty being accepted into the Latin American canon so bound to heterosexism.)

From this exchange, the reader senses the battle, if not the war, that can ensue from discussing *Before Night Falls,* the literary merits of Arenas's work, and Cuban politics. González Echevarría's review and Unger's letter are not isolated cases but rather are indicative of the two attitudes—one favorable, one discrediting—that have surfaced in other reviews and articles about *Before Night Falls.*[10] These positive and negative attitudes clearly indicate that the literary cannot be separated from the political when discussing Reinaldo Arenas. As both González Echeverría's review and Unger's letter illustrate, Arenas (subject, individual, writer, literary persona, fictionalized character, call him what you may) is indeed a site on which extrasubjective ideological forces clash with little hope of resolving differences. Reactions to *Before Night Falls* are directly correlated with whichever side of the political/ideological fence readers find themselves on. More than 39 years after the Cuban revolution, opinions and attitudes by those who have followed the developments in Cuba remain more polarized than ever. Thus, Fidel Castro is perceived as either a monster or a savior; the revolution as either having doomed or saved the Cuban people; the Cuban exile community as either a money-hungry conservative group of sore losers or the only hope of ever bringing democracy back to the island. Such either/or polarity, playing out now for almost four decades, clearly leaves scant room for dialogue or mediation. Perhaps even more telling, however, are the silence, misreadings, apologies, and overall nervous uncertainty that ensue when we turn our attention to the issue of the revolution's controversial policies toward homosexuals as well as how Cubans in general, both on and off the island, continue to struggle, for lack of a better word, with their own homophobia. I discuss the issue of homosexuality in Cuba and Latin America at greater length later in this chapter, but at this time I would like to indicate how it is treated in González Echevarría's review and Unger's letter.

Whereas González Echevarría makes constant references to Arenas's homosexuality and the revolution's persecution of homosexuals, Unger makes only a vague mention of what he calls Arenas's "generalizations about homosexual behavior in the United States" (Unger, 35). Granted, Unger's letter is limited by its very nature of being a letter to the editor; still, his silence on the revolution's poor track record in this regard speaks loudly, especially at a time when more and more supporters of the Cuban revolution are willing at least to acknowledge the antihomosexual crusade of the revolution over the years. Such is the case, for example, of the recent Cuban film *Fresa y chocolate* (Strawberry and Chocolate), which, although it presents ideological problems in its construction of a homosexual character, nonetheless admits the failures of the revolution over the years concerning homosexual rights.

In 1993, the late Cuban director Tomás Gutiérrez Alea was responsible for bringing fellow Cuban writer Senel Paz's 1990 *El lobo, el bosque y el hombre nuevo* (The wolf, the forest and the new man) to the big screen under the title *Fresa y chocolate* (Strawberry and chocolate). Paz's story, which was awarded the prestigious international Juan Rulfo Award the year in which it was published, describes the friendship between an openly homosexual man and a straight communist activist. Whereas many critics have interpreted *El lobo, el bosque y el hombre nuevo* as a sign of the regime's attempts at openness in relation to gays and lesbians, others think the book falls short in its treatment of the homosexual issue in Cuba. Despite their good intentions, however, both the novel and the film fail to address the homosexual issue in a significant way. By romanticizing the gay-straight friendship and desexualizing the homosexual,

El lobo, el bosque y el hombre nuevo/Fresa y chocolate makes the homosexual
fit comfortably within the revolutionary social structure, which supports
a value system grounded in uniformity. Throughout the story, the character Diego never oversteps the limits that have been imposed on him:
"Nuestra amistad ha sido correcta" (Our friendship has been proper); in
the end, Diego decides to leave the island. But before leaving, he advises
David that the revolution needs to soften its stance toward homosexuals, to stop punishing homosexuals for their sexual-object choices. Diego
hopes that David, an "hombre nuevo" (a direct reference to Che Guevara's idealized "new man"), will inspire others to be more accepting of
homosexuals. Although the representation of homosexuality in *El lobo, el
bosque y el hombre nuevo/Fresa y chocolate* appears at first glance to be a significant development in Cuban revolutionary art, Diego, in fact, is not
allowed to tell his own story in his own words through his own voice.
Diego's voice is mediated, rearticulated, filtered through David's
authoritative, that is, revolutionary discourse. In the end, Diego remains
the outsider while David reaffirms his heterosexuality. Their romanticized friendship, structured around a simplistic narrative device of sentimentality, does not challenge the revolutionary establishment's paradigm of power, nor does the story challenge ordinary readers/viewers
into confronting their attitudes toward homosexuals.

In his recent book, *Sexual Politics in Cuba*, Marvin Leiner, by his own
admission a long and ardent supporter of the Cuban revolution, will-
ingly highlights the weaknesses of the Cuban system when it comes to
the issue of homosexuality and the more recent quarantining of any
Cubans testing HIV-positive under the justification of the common
good. (This latter practice was abandoned in early 1994 because the revolution could no longer financially support it.) Leiner calls these weaknesses "the paradox of Cuba's revolution" that has turned many people
against the system: "In the United States, one of the most publicized
issues of postrevolutionary life in Cuba has been the treatment of homosexuals, and to it Americans have responded with a gamut of reactions,
from disappointment to rage. . . . [T]his issue alone has caused many on
the left to turn away from support of Cuba" (Leiner, 21). Cuban policies
toward homosexuality continue to be an embarrassment for Fidel Castro's government, which, "paradoxically," to use Leiner's word, has presented itself as the champion of the underdog and downtrodden. Hence,
read within the context of these general feelings of guilt and contrition
regarding the homosexual issue in Cuba, *Before Night Falls* serves as an
unpleasant reminder of governmental mistakes at a time when Cuba

needs more support than criticism. The so-called Special Period of economic austerity that Cubans have been facing for more than seven years
now is apparently indefinite. If Cuba hopes to survive its present dire
economic straits, it needs, now more than ever, the backing of those
who have defended the revolution. On the other hand, the Cuban exile
community's attitude toward homosexuality has not improved. "When
Reinaldo Arenas committed suicide in 1990," writes Cuban American
writer Achy Obejas in her review of *Before Night Falls,*

> Cuban-American writers across the country, but especially in Miami,
> wrote eloquent homages in the newspaper. . . . Only a few of these eulo-
> gies mentioned AIDS, and when they did, it was in passing. AIDS would
> tarnish Arenas's status as an exile hero, so the writers played it down. . . .
> I read a lot of these posthumous praises with sadness and frustration. My
> mother sent me envelopes stuffed with clippings from Miami's Spanish-
> language press. She held fast to the notion that the volume of paper ded-
> icated to him was proof enough of how much he had been loved. But I
> kept noticing that something even more important than AIDS was miss-
> ing: a direct mention of Arenas's homosexuality.[11]

Achy Obejas's observation reveals the extent to which homosexuality
continues to be considered taboo for Cuban Americans despite the fact
that they live in the United States, where homosexuality, although far
from being accepted, has at least entered the national debate.

   Autobiography is as much a way of reading as it is a way of writing.
It is this very idea that the Argentine critic Sylvia Molloy presents in her
book *At Face Value: Autobiographical Writing in Spanish America.*[12] Molloy
argues that it should come as no surprise that although there have been
many autobiographies written in Spanish America, "they have not
always been read autobiographically: filtered through the dominant discourse of the day, they have been hailed either as history or as fiction,
and rarely considered as occupying a space of their own" (Molloy, 2).
This binary opposition, history-fiction, highlights the attitude of many
readers who are suspicious of the autobiographical text's supposed neutrality of self-representation, that is, its claim to integrity, closure, and
totalization. One does not have to be a theoretician like Paul de Man to
understand that all autobiographers, regardless of their claims to truth
and accuracy, construct in prose attractive identities of themselves for
posterity. (Paul de Man, in his influential and landmark essay, "Autobiography as De-facement," deconstructs the traditional notion of autobi-

ography as a discourse of self-restoration. He suggests that autobiography is not a genre and that the autobiographical project is an impossibility given "the topological structure that underlines all cognitions, including knowledge of self.")[13] Clearly, the autobiographer is not a god-like chronicler exempt from the equivocations of language. Even the average lay reader, whose interests are not those of the theoretician or critic, intuits the struggle between what we might call the autobiographer-historian, who attempts to present the image of accuracy and exactitude, and the autobiographer-fabulist, whose interest is telling a compelling story. I would venture to say that the Spanish American readers (critical as well as lay) possess a greater suspicion of neutrality and that the Cuban readers' suspicions are perhaps even doubled, because their colonial legacy and their life under various forms of dictatorial governments has left them by nature suspicious of authority. Although the avowed principle of autobiography is to retrace the history of a life and to recall its deepest emotions, in practice, the autobiographer is engaged in a work of personal justification rather than an objective and disinterested pursuit. This very idea has led many postmodern critics to label the autobiographical project as an act of fiction, thus refusing to define and treat it as a unique literary genre in itself.

The idea that autobiography creates a fiction of a "self" has led some critics, like Michael Sprinker, to go so far as to speak of the end of autobiography in a postmodern era.[14] The traditional ideas of self-affirmation and creation and the postmodern ideas of representation and textual performance create internal contradictions and tensions in the autobiographical project. The thorny problem of establishing a clear boundary between factual and fictional modes of discourse in autobiographical writings appears far from being resolved by theoreticians in the field. According to Paul John Eakin, Philippe Lejeune's initial solution to this problem was his concept of "le pacte autobiographie" or autobiographical pact, "a form of contract between author and reader in which the autobiographer explicitly commits himself or herself not to some impossible historical exactitude but rather to the sincere effort to come to terms with and to understand his or her own life."[15] Lejeune's first version of the pact, which appeals to an essentially author-based criticism of autobiography, was replaced in later writing—as for example in Lejeune's *Moi aussi*[16]—by a reader-based poetics that considers notions such as "self" and "life story" to be culturally determined constructs. Eakin states that although critics such as de Man find themselves under the tutelage of a topological runaround precluding any cer-

tainty, Lejeune is at least willing "to concede the fictive status of the self
and then proceed with its functioning as experiential fact" (Lejeune,
xiv). Furthermore, according to Eakin:

> [For Lejeune] the documentary reference of popular autobiographical
> texts does not consist in the deliberate creation of a faithful copy of the
> real (as the correspondence theory informing the publicity of such texts
> proposes) but rather in the unwitting imitation of common narrative
> forms that constitute the lingua franca of verisimilitude at a given
> moment in the life of a culture. (Lejeune, xxi)

This "lingua franca" or sincere language that is part of a historical
moment best describes the autobiographical voice of *Before Night Falls,* a
voice that traces the development of homoerotic desire in a country
marked first by a religious and cultural legacy of prejudices and precon-
cepts in regard to homosexuality in general and more recently by a puri-
tanical revolutionary state that has considered homosexuality antitheti-
cal to the building of a socialist society.

Little disagreement exists among critics who work on the autobiographical genre today that the traditional perspective on autobiography
was blinded by the illusion of a pure and simple referentiality and representation. Still, the belief in "the self out of existence by deconstruction-
ists," to use Eakin's words, does not consider that autobiography, the
story of a particular culture written by an individual character from
within that culture, offers access to experiences that no other form of
writing can offer.

Reinaldo Arenas was a gifted writer, highly imaginative and compas-
sionate, reckless and idealistic, provocative, with a keen sense of humor
and with particular insights into life's contradictions. Any reader who
enters his worlds, fictitious and/or autobiographical, will not be disap-
pointed by his "lingua franca." After reading Arenas's oeuvre, contrary
to what David Unger suggests, the reader will see that Arenas is not an
archetypal misfit (a word that in itself implies a societal right or wrong
"fit"), but rather an archetypal rebel who ardently defended the individual's right to all forms of self-expression.

Before Night Falls: Fact or Fiction?

Arenas's unwavering allegiance to what we might call the truth of fiction and distrust of the historical makes it hard for the reader familiar

with his fiction to enter the more referential space of the autobiography. (In the introductory essay to *The Ill-Fated Peregrinations of Fray Servando,* Arenas states: "I have always distrusted the 'historical,' those 'minutiae,' the 'precise date' or 'fact.' ")[17] Yet, although *Before Night Falls* does deploy rhetorical tropes and figures, and does at times seem like a rewriting of Arenas's literary work, it is in fact a distinct discourse, albeit nurtured by the same rebellious spirit of nonconformity found in Arenas's fiction, poetry, and drama.

Arenas's literary universe is postmodern in its subversive undermining of the traditional belief that the literary text can be a guarantor of fixed meaning, a repository of irrefutable truths. As Eduardo C. Béjar successfully argues in his book *La textualidad de Reinaldo Arenas: Juegos de la escritura posmoderna* (Reinaldo Arenas's Textualism: Postmodern Writing Games), Arenas's "escritura nebulizante," or obscure and indeterminate writing, "abandons logical processes at the service of a single-minded causality and in their place the dynamics of the *récit* spread out to incorporate the paradoxes and ambivalence of human experience. . . . Uncertainty, decentralization and contradictions constitute the means by which [Arenas's] narrative fabrics are spun."[18] Contrary to Arenas's fiction, *Before Night Falls* adopts a referential method to give voice to past experiences. The autobiographical voice struggles with that slippery, socially constituted entity called the signifier in an attempt to anchor it to some type of signified meaning, at least temporarily. Very early in *Before Night Falls,* in articulating one of his first memories, that of eating dirt because of a scarcity of food in the Cuban countryside, Arenas states: "I should make it clear right away that to eat dirt is not a metaphor, or a sensational act. All the country kids did it. It has nothing to do with magic realism, or anything of the sort. One had to eat something, dirt was the only thing we had plenty of and perhaps that was why we ate it" (*BNF,* 11). Arenas's insistence that the statement "to eat dirt" should be read literally and not metaphorically illustrates his realization that the ambiguous, free-flowing, unrestrained flights of fantasy in his fiction will not serve him well in the autobiographical enterprise. However, just because Arenas seems to be more cautious in the words he picks, clarifying and explaining them, does not mean that "uncertainty, decentralization, and contradictions," to quote Béjar, are not present in *Before Night Falls.* Let us look at an example of how what is represented is not always what it first appears to be.

The chapter headings of *Before Night Falls,* "The Stones," "The Grove," "The River," and so on, used to describe Arenas's early child-

hood in rural Cuba, are not so innocent or childlike as they first appear.
In "The Stones," for example, the reader quickly realizes that the title is
used ironically. Instead of describing the wonders of this natural rural
life, Arenas points out that the stones are what his mother picks up from
the riverbank to throw at the husband who has abandoned her and her
child:

> One day my mother and I were on our way to visit one of my aunts. As
> we walked down to the river, a man came toward us; he was good-look-
> ing, tall and dark. My mother fell into a sudden rage; she began picking
> up stones from the riverbank and throwing them at his head, while the
> man, in spite of the shower of rocks, kept coming toward us. When he
> was close to me, he put his hand into his pocket, pulled out two pesos,
> and gave them to me. He then patted me on the head and ran away to
> avoid being hit by one of the stones. My mother cried all the way to my
> aunt's house, where I found out that the man was my father. I never saw
> him again, nor the two pesos; my aunt asked my mother to lend them to
> her and I do not know if she ever paid them back. (*BNF,* 2)

The reader familiar with Arenas's oeuvre will surely recognize in this
paragraph the playfulness and humor, as well as the violence, of the
childhood world of *Celestino antes del alba* (*Singing from the Well*), Arenas's
first novel. Like the novel, this passage avoids any psychological interpretation— readers have to draw their own conclusions—substituting
in its place suspense (i.e., the mysterious man walking toward mother
and child) and humor (the two pesos that the aunt never paid back).
This passage tips in favor of the autobiographer-fabulist who, unlike the
autobiographer-historian who is more interested in accuracy and details,
is more concerned with telling a compelling story. Still, this does not
imply by any means that the episode did not occur. Yet on the other
hand, and perhaps more importantly, it also does not mean that the
episode has sacrificed or undermined its authenticity by deploying a system of literary tropes and poetic allusions. Obviously it is impossible to
construct such a thing as pure history or pure fiction, although, as Sylvia
Molloy has pointed out, autobiography in Spanish America typically has
been read in this either/or fashion.

Arenas's reconstruction of the memory of the day he met his father in
Before Night Falls is not the first time that the writer attempted to recre-
ate this recollection. In his interview with Liliane Hasson and in Jana
Bokova's documentary film *Havana,* Arenas mentions that fateful
encounter.[19] Furthermore, the incident has also been fictionalized in

Arenas's novel, *El palacio de las blanquísimas mofetas* (*The Palace of the White Skunks*.[20] Near the end of the First Agony, printed in smaller type and set off to the left of the page,[21] we find the same account articulated with many more details. For example, the third-person heterodiegetic narrator identifies the child as being "about five years old," the aunt as the "Obnoxious One," and the river as the "Lirio River." In addition, we are informed that as she threw the stones, the mother screamed: "You asshole." The scene in *The Palace of the White Skunks* also offers, to a certain extent, a reflection by the child of the emotional impact the event had on his mother: "But what made the strongest impression on him was seeing his mother for the first time so furious that she cried. She never complained about anything, or showed her emotions at all" (*Palace,* 88). Curiously, the two pesos, which are crucial to both the suspense (i.e., the child Arenas and his mother, as well as the reader, are not sure what the man is pulling out of his pocket) and the humor of the autobiographical account, do not serve these functions in *The Palace of the White Skunks*: "[A] man appeared and gave him two pesos" is all that is said. What conclusions can be drawn from these two accounts? First, the autobiographical and the fictitious are intertwined in Arenas's work, which is true of all writers of fiction who draw from their own life experiences in the construction of their texts. Second, so-called realistic descriptions and details are not necessarily indicators of a more truthful discourse. The details that appear in *The Palace of the White Skunks* are all fabricated. Last and perhaps most important, despite the contradictions or variations that exist between the autobiographical and the fictitious versions, what is rescued from memory in the autobiographical account and narrated in the fictitious account are basically one and the same: a son's first memory of his father. For Arenas, whether in his fiction or his autobiography, it is never a question of fact versus fiction, but rather how fact and fiction nurture each other in the construction of their respective discourses.

The concept of reality is fluid in Arenas's oeuvre; personal biography (personal history) and imagination are fused. Literary characters are considered "real" because although they might not be made of flesh-and-blood, they nonetheless reflect life in all its vitality. In a 1988 interview with Nedda G. de Anhalt, Arenas makes clear the extent to which he felt that the characters he created in his novels were indeed real: "For me characters are very important in the construction of the work. I remember the time when I was writing *Singing from the Well,* I was with a friend of mine and suddenly Celestino appeared and I yelled out his name.

That is to say, I live with my characters, they are fundamental, they are a part of me; they are a reality that to a certain extent overpowers the other reality."[22] By not assigning privileged or hierarchical modes of being, Arenas's work proposes a nonrestrictive code of reality; so-called real experience, as manifested in the way most people attempt to secure an univocal meaning of experience and of themselves, is never opposed to other forms of personal experiences such as dreams, hallucinations, and fantasy. What most people call reality is never presented as one dimensional or strictly univalent in Arenas's writings, but rather is multifaceted and even magical. In an interview—later published in the limited edition of *La Vieja Rosa*—that Arenas gave shortly after falling into disfavor with the revolutionary regime, he reaffirmed his nonexclusive position concerning reality when he stated: "For me realism is not just saying: he got up, he took the bus. . . . For me that is real, but when a man goes to bed and begins to dream, that also, to a certain extent, is real. Is it real or isn't it real? Everything I imagine is real."[23] For the average lay reader, this attitude is quite acceptable in fiction, but autobiography becomes more complicated; readers expect secure, univocal representations of experience. But what exactly are secure, univocal representations of experience? And furthermore, can a reader not distinguish between a writer's fiction and an autobiographer's use of imaginative and metaphoric coloration to shape his or her personal experience into a meaningful narrative? Perhaps we should not underestimate the reader's ability to distinguish an authentic autobiography from fiction, despite the former's use of tropes and literary devices to present a more compelling account. As James Goodwin wisely proposes in *Autobiography: The Self Made Text*: "The uses in autobiography of resources commonly associated with the novel and the fusion of autobiography with fiction by some writers, while complicating matters, does not finally make it impossible to draw categorical distinctions between the two genres."[24] In the end, as most critics who reviewed the autobiography have stated, Arenas's literary virtuosity in *Before Night Falls* never blurs completely the line between fiction and autobiography; the reader senses the honesty behind the author's words and therefore trusts what is recorded.

In his article "Between Nightfall and Vengeance: Remembering Reinaldo Arenas," which appeared in the 1994 special issue of the *Michigan Quarterly Review* entitled "Bridges to Cuba/Puentes a Cuba," Abilio Estévez, a playwright, essayist, and poet who lives in Havana, reviews *Before Night Falls* in light of what he calls his own experiences with Arenas, *"the man* and *the myth."* Estévez begins his review/article by first informing the reader of how he met Arenas in Cuba toward the end of 1976, a time when younger Cuban writers were fascinated by the mystery and intrigue surrounding this writer who had been officially censored by the revolution. A number of paragraphs carefully develop the image of Arenas not as the "diabolical character" or "hedonist" that others had described to Estévez (by using these very descriptions Estévez already begins to plant a negative image of Arenas in the mind of his readers), but rather as a man who "lived *in* and *for* literature, [who] tried to live *from* literature, turning everything into words" (Estévez, 860, author's emphasis). When he finally turns his attention to *Before Night Falls,* Estévez suggests:

> There are those who deny that it is an autobiography and adduce that everything it narrates is pure fiction, that it is novelized, that Reinaldo exaggerates where he does not lie, that more than a book of reminiscences we face an act of vengeance, or as José Rodríguez Feo *brilliantly expressed it* when he loaned me a copy: "Here you go, a masterpiece of slander." (Estévez, 860, emphasis added)

When Estévez states that Rodríquez Feo's description of the autobiography as a masterpiece of slander is a "brilliant" characterization of the text, he reveals his own ideological position vis-à-vis *Before Night Falls.* As a writer trying to live and publish in Cuba, Estévez cannot afford to offend the powers that be, and thus he must discredit the book (and here I deliberately mean the traditional notion of the book rather than the text; the book *Before Night Falls* being that which physically stands for or in place of Arenas-writer-autobiographer in the world). Thinly veiling his disingenuous intention, Estévez states: "I do not doubt Arenas's sincerity—even though his pages at times fall short of the truth" (Estévez, 863). And to prove Arenas's alleged twisting of the truth, Estévez cites only one example, Arenas's account of Virgilio Piñera's burial. Estévez states that Arenas wrote that "a multitude of people and even boys, mounted on skates and bicycles, followed the corpse." Estévez, who says he was present at the burial, absolutely denies ever seeing such a multitude on bikes and skates and in a patronizing gesture adds: "But the *character* Piñera could be followed by a multitude of *characters* on skates and bikes, coming out of his own *Concilio y discurso.* There was no multitude: there should have been. The fact took place, in effect, thanks to literature" (Estévez, 863, author's emphasis). Obviously "the multitude on bikes and skates" is not a significant detail; more important is Arenas's grief over the loss of a very dear friend. Yet Estévez would rather have the reader believe that Arenas, a man who "lived *in, for,* and *from* literature," to quote Estévez's words, was a pure storyteller, a great one at that, whose words must all be taken with a grain of salt. It is clear that Estévez exploits Molloy's contention that Spanish American readers approach autobiography as either fact (history) or fiction to undermine Arenas's credibility in *Before Night Falls.* Yet it is significant that Estévez, whether consciously or unconsciously, chose this particular episode to discredit Arenas. Virgilio Piñera and Arenas were both persecuted in Cuba for being homosexual; while Piñera reacted to the oppression by living in constant fear and panic, and symbolically represented homosexual desire in obscure embedded images in his writings, Arenas chose a more bohemian and sexually active life in Havana and became progressively more audacious in representing homosexual desire in his writings. Piñera's initial support of the Cuban revolution quickly evaporated when on 11 October 1961 he was briefly incarcerated for being homosexual. From that point on Piñera, according to most accounts, was internally ostracized, living in fear and seldom publishing until his death in 1979. In his article "Fleshing out Virgilio Piñera from the Cuban Closet," José Quiroga examines what he calls Piñera's silence (read as fear and repression but also as the silence of the heroic) as "the theatrical embodiment of an impasse that many Cuban homosexuals felt and continue to feel within the repression of a masculinist order that condemns them to support either the capitalist or the socialist version of a nightmare."[25]

In *Before Night Falls,* Arenas declares on various occasions the importance of Virgilio Piñera as mentor and friend. In the opening pages of the autobiography, for instance, Arenas describes himself sick and desperate, addressing a photograph of Piñera hanging on a wall in his apartment: "Listen to what I have to tell you: I need three more years of life to finish my work, which is my vengeance against most of the human race" (*BNF,* xvii).[26] Arenas in fact did live almost three more years, which gave him the necessary time to complete his work. He ends the introduction by thanking Piñera ("Thank you, Virgilio") for the time given him. Regardless of the specific dynamics of their friendship and how both men reacted to the hate and intolerance that surrounded them, Arenas related to and saw a reflection of himself in Piñera.

As a final point of discussion about the fact versus fiction polarity as it pertains to *Before Night Falls,* I would like to address the extraliterary choice of book covers for the Spanish and English editions. Obviously Arenas had no control over this matter given the fact that the autobiography was published posthumously, yet the choice of book covers strikingly reveals how the book has been marketed for (that is, how it should be read by) Spanish and English speaking audiences.

The cover of the Spanish edition presents a vividly stylized colored painting of a white building located somewhere on a tropical beach; in the background we see the sand, the sea, palm trees. The white building has a window with thick metal bars, suggesting a jail, out of which two arms are seen typing on a floating typewriter suspended in midair outside the window; five pages that have already been written float off into the sky. The cover, whimsical and fantastic, is a metaphorical visual rendition of Arenas's struggles to continue writing under a political system that persecuted him. Yet, as if to offset the fantastic and whimsical nature of the cover, appearing clearly underneath the title is the subtitle "autobiografía," that is, the claim that the pages inside this cover are in fact "truthful." Furthermore, as if to compensate for the flight of fancy evoked by the cover, halfway through the Spanish edition are eight pages of photographs (as the adage goes, seeing is believing) of Arenas throughout different stages of his life. The last photo presents an ailing Arenas one month prior to his death. The choice of cover, the subtitle "autobiografía," and the inclusion of photographs from Arenas's life all represent, as Sylvia Molloy has pointed out, the dichotomy between fact and fiction that Hispanic readers face when reading autobiographies.

The English edition is altogether different. The cover dust jacket presents a large monochromatic close-up photograph of Arenas who looks directly at the reader; his expression is calm and appears to evoke trust. Over the photograph the writer's name clearly appears; under the photograph, in smaller letters, the words "a memoir" appear. Technically, a memoir focuses primarily on the individuals that a particular writer knew or on significant events that he or she witnessed. On the other hand, the subject matter of autobiographies is almost exclusively writers themselves. While Arenas indeed presents the reader with many anecdotes concerning the people he came in contact with and the events that affected his life, the focus of *Before Night Falls* remains Arenas himself and how certain individuals and events influenced him both negatively and positively. (Let us recall that Lejeune sees autobiography as a question of proportion or hierarchy and that transitions with other genres of personal literature, like memoirs, are quite natural.) Because the English speaking reader apparently does not suffer from the fact versus fiction dilemma, the eight pages of photographs present in the Spanish edition are not included. In sum, that the covers for both editions are so radically different is quite telling of how Anglo-American and South American cultures react to (read) autobiography.

Genesis, Structure, and Style of *Before Night Falls*

The introductory chapter to *Before Night Falls* is ironically titled "The End." In these few pages, Arenas informs us how the autobiography, originally begun in Cuba while he was a fugitive living in Lenin Park and titled even back then "Antes que anochezca" (Before Night Falls), was hurriedly written in a race against death. Commenting on this very issue, Robert Richmond Ellis writes:

> AIDS writing possesses a social commitment to the extent that it aims to reveal the human face of the disease and thereby generate a response to the crisis. Yet, unlike committed writing of previous generations, it is characterized by a tremendous urgency on the part of the writer not only to act but often merely to complete the writing project before dying. . . . AIDS writers . . . are in the midst of a battle and are also acutely aware from the outset of the outcome of their struggle. They nevertheless write in the hope that they might somehow affect the inevitable. For this reason their writing is both a political gesture and a means of survival. (Ellis, 126)

The manuscript of *Before Night Falls* is dated August of 1990, scarcely four months before Arenas committed suicide. Despite, or perhaps even because of, the fact that they were written in the face of death, these pages contain an authenticity and vitality that summarize the major passions that fueled Arenas's life: his "erotismo" or eroticism, a word the writer favored over the word "sex";[27] his dedication to literature and writing; his ability to create a liberating space in the most trying and precarious moments; his love for Cuba and his animosity toward Fidel Castro and the Cuban revolution; and his devotion to his friends (in these pages, Jorge and Margarita Camacho, Lázaro Gómez, Roberto Valero, María Badías, and Virgilio Piñera).

In an article titled "Los últimos tiempos de Reinaldo Arenas" (Reinaldo Arenas's Last Days), Roberto Valero recounts how he himself came up with the idea of recording Arenas's voice as a possible solution to help him complete his autobiography, a task that was becoming more and more difficult for the writer as a result of his failing health:

One day we talked about his memoirs and he said that he wouldn't be able to complete them, that his goal was to finish the *pentagonía* (his pentalogy, five Cuban agonies). It occurred to me to begin to tape him, I would ask him questions in an organized fashion in order for him to then continue on his own. He agreed to the idea and we taped around five cassettes, later he continued on his own, there are more than thirty tapes now. I would ask him to talk about his childhood, his grandparents (I would ask him if they were as scary as they appeared in his novels), the important writers with whom he had friendships, the Cuban exile community, his thoughts on Cuban history. *Before Night Falls* is the memoir that he completed whose title he took from the memoir he had started many years before when he was a fugitive in Lenin Park in Havana. Of course at that time he had to write before nightfall because he had no electricity, but now the title was much more suggestive.[28]

When one considers the structure of *Before Night Falls* in relation to other autobiographies, what immediately comes to mind is the curious division of the text into chapters, each titled and of varying length. Despite the fact that they are not all given the same attention by Arenas, the 71 chapters that make up *Before Night Falls* could be grouped into three overarching periods. The first would be Arenas's recollections of his poverty-stricken childhood and adolescence in rural Cuba (*BNF,* 1–47). Despite the hardships he had to endure, this era is recalled fondly and, in retrospect, is seen by the writer as the most creative period in his life. Also important in this period is Arenas's precocious sexual awakening; rural life is permeated with sexuality, and we see Arenas engaging in erotic encounters with everything imaginable: trees, animals, girl and boy cousins, an uncle. Arenas writes: "Those years, between the ages of seven and ten, were a time of great eroticism, of a sexual voracity that . . . was all-embracing" (*BNF,* 19).

The second period, the bulk of the autobiography and obviously the period that would mark his destiny, encompasses Arenas's arrival in Havana, the official beginning of his literary career, and his homosexual awakening that ultimately would be responsible for his persecution, imprisonment, and final escape through Mariel port in 1980 (*BNF,* 47–284).

The last 32 pages of the autobiography are devoted to Arenas's last decade of life in the United States. (To these 32 pages we might add the 9 pages of the introductory chapter, "The End." In the English edition, the introductory chapter uses roman numerals [ix–xvii], whereas the Spanish edition uses arabic numerals [9–16].) Reacting to this apparent disparity, Achy Obejas comments:

Before Night Falls takes place in Cuba. Of its 317 pages, only the last twenty-two [*sic*] are devoted to life in the United States. This would not be so odd if Arenas hadn't spent the last ten years of his life here; but it is, I think, important. Although Arenas finished his life's work in his tiny New York apartment, taught literature at universities in New York and Florida, founded the seminal *Mariel* magazine and continued many of his tempestuous relationships, in many ways he really stopped living when he left Cuba. (Obejas, 388)

Achy Obejas's observation is well taken and can be verified by simply looking at Arenas's literary production. Arenas's entire oeuvre treats the Cuban experience in one way or another. Even *El portero* (*The Doorman*), Arenas's only work set in the United States, is the story of Juan, a young exiled Cuban from the Mariel exodus who finds himself living in New York City and working as a doorman in an elegant building in Manhattan's upper West Side.[29] The novel recounts the tribulations of Juan's search for happiness in a world of absurdities, dehumanization, and excessive materialism. Yet this story of exile transcends the specific Cuban experience to represent how all individuals are spiritually exiled in one way or another, their lives driven by an insatiable search for plenitude and satisfaction in a world beset by disappointment, ignorance, and brutality. The same can be said of Arenas's other texts; that is, despite their concerns about the specific Cuban condition, they contain a universal argumentative center that persistently resurfaces: a staunch defense of the individual's imaginative capabilities and self-expression in a world beset by barbarity, intolerance, and persecution.

There is a clear unevenness in style and tone in *Before Night Falls*. On the one hand, this unevenness can be explained by the work's mode of production; Arenas dictating his experiences onto a cassette, followed by friends typing a written transcription of the tapes, then Arenas hurriedly correcting and editing the transcription, all the while not being certain whether he would have the strength to complete these, his final words. Exiled Cuban writer Guillermo Cabrera Infante has described *Before Night Falls* as "a book written in a race against death; crude, many times not only badly written, but hardly written at all: dictated, spoken, yelled out, this book is [Arenas's] masterpiece" (Cabrera Infante, 16, my translation). On the other hand, although I agree with Cabrera Infante, I would also underscore that what is at first perceived as the autobiography's uneven tone is at times a result of the subject matter that is treated. For example, during the childhood/adolescent period, which is romanticized from the vantage point of adult life, the prose is marked by a poetic quality. The chapters, in most cases not more than one or two pages in length, are like sketches, snapshots of particular moments, places, and events that impressed the young Arenas: the river, the morning fog, the harvest, Christmas Eve, the rain, the sea, and so on. Arenas purposefully provides little sense of time or space in this mystical and magical rural world. After his arrival in Havana after the revolution, the beginning of what I have designated the second period, the poetic tone is replaced by a more descriptive tone as Arenas presents for the reader his early years in Havana, initial support for the revolution, his education, jobs at the National Library and the Cuban Book Institute, and the two men who would be his literary mentors, José Lezama Lima and Virgilio Piñera. All this is followed by a short yet very important chapter titled "My Generation" (*BNF,* 88–91) that no longer describes but synthesizes and draws conclusions about the experiences faced by the generation of writers born in the 1940s who came of age under the revolution. In this chapter, Arenas attributes the trials and tribulations suffered by his generation to Cuba's "national history of betrayals, uprisings, desertions, conspiracies, riots, coups d'etat; all . . . provoked by infinite ambition, abuse, despair, false pride, and envy" (*BNF,* 90). And from this Cuban as well as Latin American tradition of having to answer to the dictator of the moment, Arenas describes two attitudes, or personalities, that consequently developed: the incurable rebels, lovers of freedom and therefore of creativity and experimentation; and the power-hungry opportunists and demagogues. After making this distinction, Arenas goes on to state how those who were young in the 1960s, like himself, managed to conspire not against the regime but in favor of life, and to achieve this they resorted to a clandestine erotic rebelliousness. Hence, it is not coincidental that from this moment on the autobiography takes on what could be called a carnivalesque tone as scenes of wild homosexual encounters are interspersed with scenes of persecution and webs of collusion and betrayal fostered by a totalitarian state hunting down dissidents in an attempt to silence them. In addition, the chapters now become significantly longer and anecdote after anecdote is recounted specifically as an adventure (for example: "I remember another adventure" *BNF,* 95). The frivolity and exaggerated quality of these daring adventures, or misadventures, reach the level of camp. Contrary to Susan Sontag's original suggestion that camp is disengaged and apolitical,[30] these chapters demonstrate a clear camp sensibility that attempts to confront and undermine the rigidity and dominant heterosexist revolutionary codes of behavior that had made homosexuality a crime: "I think that in Cuba there was never more fucking going on than in those years, the decade of the sixties, which was precisely when all the new laws against homosexuals came into being, when the persecutions started and concentration camps were opened, when the sexual act became taboo while the 'new man' was being proclaimed and masculinity exalted" (*BNF*, 105).

The last 32 pages of *Before Night Falls,* the last decade of Arenas's life in the United States, combine both descriptive and poetic tones. Arenas describes succinctly his arrival in Key West, his move to New York City, and his travels through Europe. The last chapter, titled "Dreams" (*BNF,* 311–16), again because of its subject matter, a recounting of particular dreams and nightmares, is marked by a poetic tone. The chapter ends with the figure of the moon, a maternal leitmotiv in Arenas's work, who during life had guarded his survival but who now heralds the arrival of the final night, death:

> O Moon! You have always been at my side, offering your light in my most dreadful moments; since I was a child you were the mystery that watched over my terrors, you were the comfort of my most desperate nights, you were my very own mother, bathing me in a warmth that perhaps she never knew how to give me. In the midst of the forest, in the darkest places, in the sea, you were there with me, you were my comfort, you have always guided me in my most difficult moments. My great goddess, my true goddess, you who have protected me through so many calamities; I used to look up toward you and behold you; up to you rising above the sea, toward you at the shore, toward you among the rocks of my desolate Island, I would lift my gaze and behold you, always the same; in your face I saw an expression of pain, of suffering, of compassion for me, your son. And now, Moon, you suddenly burst into pieces right next to my bed. I am alone. It is night. (*BNF,* 316)

This scene is in fact the last in the autobiography because the next chapter, titled "Farewell," which is Arenas's suicide letter, was added to the text after his death. That Arenas ended his autobiography, the story of his remembered life, on such a poetic note tells of the importance that literature had in his life. The moon can be read metonymically as a symbol of literature while the language of this last paragraph reads like that of a prayer. Arenas prays to the goddess Moon, to the literature that has provided him with the only solace he has known in an otherwise hellish existence. But now, too sick to continue writing, the Moon abandons him and he is left alone.

Literature, Politics, and Homosexuality

In his review of the Spanish edition of *Before Night Falls,* Guillermo Cabrera Infante sums up Arenas's life and career as follows: "Three passions ruled Reinaldo Arenas's life and death: literature, not as a game, but as a consuming fire, passive sex, and active politics. Of the three, the dominant passion was, obviously, sex. Not only in his life, but also in his work. He was the chronicler of a country ruled not by the already impotent Fidel Castro, but by sex" (Cabrera Infante, 15–16, my translation). At the same time that Cabrera Infante attempts to mark a distinction between literature, sex, and politics, he interlinks and overlaps all three, illustrating how virtually impossible it is to discuss one in isolation from the others when it comes to Arenas's work. In Cuba, which has spent more than 39 years constructing a socialist society in which the rights of the individual are secondary to the rights of the masses, the personal (sex), the literary (literature), and the public (political) are intrinsically tied together. Private spaces (sexual and literary; although the literary can become public through publication, it indeed begins as a solitary and private act of creation) are scrutinized and judged in the public (political) arena.

Before Night Falls can be read as the construction of one man's homoerotic identity in opposition to the hegemonic and patriarchal definitions of the chastely virile image of the "new man" promoted by the revolution. One only needs to hear the words of Fidel Castro in the early 1960s to understand the homophobia that the Cuban revolutionary government systematically deployed when it came to power: "[W]e would never come to believe that a homosexual could embody the conditions and requirements of conduct that would enable us to consider him a true revolutionary, a true Communist militant."[31] It was out of this hypermasculine and homophobic Marxist-Leninist ideology that the now infamous UMAP concentration camps organized by the army and the Yellow Brigades instituted in the school system were developed.

As early as 1965 forced labor camps under the name of UMAP (an acronym for *Unidades Militares de Ayuda a la Producción,* or Military Units for Aid to Production) were constructed in the province of Camagüey with the purpose of correcting so-called antisocial behaviors that, according to the government, threatened the creation of a true revolutionary consciousness. (As Ian Lumsden states in his book, "In Cuba, *antisocial* has been a code word for allegedly ostentatious homosexuality" [Lumsden, 83].) This period of repression has been documented by Néstor Almendros and Orlando Jiménez-Leal in their 1984 film *Conducta impropia* (Improper Conduct). *Conducta impropia* is constructed from individual testimonies that document what it was like to be homosexual in early revolutionary Cuba. In the film, Arenas recounts his own experiences with homosexual discrimination while living on the island. During the height of the homosexual purges, Arenas states that any individual who was identified as homosexual or "extravagant" was carted off to an UMAP camp for not adapting to the revolutionary model. Allen Young's account of homophobia in Cuba supports Arenas's accusations of the regime's intolerance toward any manifestation of so-called extravagant behavior. Young writes: "The people carted off to UMAP camps included youths who showed 'too much' concern with their personal appearance (long hair, colorful clothing, etc.); they were said to be victims of *la enfermedad* (the disease) or of 'cultural imperialism' " (Young, 22).

The Yellow Brigades, organized during the same period of the UMAP concentration camps, were a systematic attempt to toughen up effeminate boys. Marvin Leiner reports that in the 1960s, special national schools were created in Cuba to address the needs of children with behavior problems:

> Children at such schools were divided into groups according to five categories of behavior problems: hyperactive and aggressive children, anxious and withdrawn children, boys with effeminate tendencies, bed wetters, and children with eating problems. Each group or "brigade" was then identified with a color. The effeminate boys were in the Yellow Brigade. The brigade's purpose was to instill in these boys, who were "encountering difficulties in accepting their masculine role," an enjoyment of masculine games so they would give up "feminine games." (Leiner, 34)

Although homophobia in Cuba is clearly tied to its Spanish and Catholic cultural heritage, there is no denying that after 1959 homophobia became politically institutionalized on the island. The idea of a national campaign aimed at "toughening up" effeminate boys reveals the extent to which the revolution, despite its attempts to radically transform other areas of life such as education and health care for the average Cuban, continued to reinforce the traditional heterosexist paradigm prevalent in Latin America in which behaviors are clearly identified as either masculine or feminine. To understand both male and female homosexuality in Latin America, one must first understand traditional gender-identity constructs.

It is quite difficult, if not perhaps impossible, to provide general comments about gay and lesbian sensibilities when referring to such an enormously diverse region of the world as Latin America. Even though the countries of this region share a common language—Brazil of course is an exception—social and cultural experiences are nonetheless quite diverse. Some Hispanic scholars and gay activists have proposed that importing U.S. and European queer theory to explain Latin American experiences reiterates the margin/center polarity by placing Latin America in a compromising and subordinate position. Still, to begin to get a sense of how homosexuality is understood in Latin America, one must first look at the specific ways in which the concepts of masculine and feminine are constructed in Hispanic societies.

In her informative introductory essay to *Latin America Writers on Gay and Lesbian Themes,* Lillian Manzor-Coats provides a detailed account of homosexuality in Latin America and clearly presents the dichotomy of gender constructs in the region.[32] Manzor-Coats begins her essay by summarizing the codes of the marianismo/machismo dichotomy on which Latin America's traditional gender constructs are based and from which homosexuality is read. Stated simply, the construction of woman in terms of marianismo (from the name Mary) is based on the Virgin Mary as symbol of maternity and chastity. For Manzor-Coats, "the image of Mary as virgin and chaste obliterates woman's sexuality as pleasure and casts her solely into a reproductive role" (Manzor-Coats, xix). On the other hand, masculinity within the codes of machismo is equated with male dominance, "an exaggerated aggressiveness and stubbornness in male-to-male relations, and arrogance and sexual aggression in male-to-female relations" (Manzor-Coats, xix). (As we can see, the medieval hierarchy of the sexes that prevailed in Europe, that is, man as lord and master, woman as servant and reproductive machine, serves as paradigm.) Traditionally, the marianismo/machismo dichotomy has been articulated socially in the clearly differentiated "active" and "passive" roles, both culturally and sexually, assigned to masculinity and femininity. Male and female homosexuality in Hispanic societies must be understood or read within these performative gender constructs. Thus, for instance, an individual identified as homosexual in the Hispanic world is *not* necessarily one who is involved in same-sex erotic practices, but rather one who deviates from the gender constructs. In

other words, a man, for example, who engages in homosexual activity
with other men is only considered to be a *marica* or *maricón,* a fag or
queer, when he does not play the macho role—that is, when he assumes
the sexual and social role of the passive, the open, the weak; when he
assumes the position and plays the role of woman. In his entry on "Latin
American Literature" for *The Gay and Lesbian Literary Heritage,* David
William Foster uses the terms "insertor/insertee" to convey the same
idea: "Some of the most diverse societies in Latin America offer examples of the macho who make it with both men and women without ever
yielding an iota of his masculine persona. The figure of the maricón is
reserved exclusively for the insertee."[33]

In the field of Spanish and Latin American literary criticism, the
study of gay and lesbian themes in writing is a very recent phenomenon.
David William Foster's book *Gay and Lesbian Themes in Latin American
Writing,* for example, was the first book-length study to explore gay and
lesbian literary themes originating from an area of the world traditionally known for its machismo and homophobia. However, since its publication, there has been a gradual increase in the number of articles and
books exploring gay and lesbian topics in Hispanic literatures. Among
the most prominent books are: *¿Entiendes?* (literally, Do you understand? but also a euphemism for Are you gay?), a collection of essays
that analyze both Spanish and Latin American texts exploring lesbian,
gay, and bisexual identities; Elena M. Martínez's *Lesbian Voices from Latin
America: Breaking Ground,* a significant contribution in its study of the
works of five contemporary Latin American women writers (Magaly
Alabau, Nancy Cárdenas, Sylvia Molloy, Rosamaría Roffiel, and Luz
María Umpierre) who clearly present lesbian themes and issues in their
writings; and David William Foster's *Sexual Textualities: Essays on
Queer/ing Latin American Writing,* an examination of homosexuality in
twentieth-century Latin American and Chicano writings as well as other
cultural manifestations.[34]

To return to the Yellow Brigades that were set up in Cuba to toughen
up so-called effeminate boys, we can see that within the marianismo/
machismo model, acting effeminate is equivalent to acting like a woman,
that is, a person without power in the social Imaginary. Clearly, the Cuban
leadership has fostered and celebrated the deeds of so-called powerful men
in its efforts to support the revolution; masculine virility has been become
emblematic of the nation's strength and moral rectitude. In Cuba, the
prototype of this powerful hombre nuevo, or new man, has traditionally
been the guerilla and revolutionary ideologue Ernesto (Che) Guevara, who

sacrificed everything for the revolution and who coined the term "new man" in his writings. It was Che Guevara, a man who wanted to develop to its maximum the new man's revolutionary consciousness, who in 1964 at the Cuban Embassy at Algiers went into a frenzy fit when he discovered a copy of Virgilio Piñera's *Teatro completo* in the embassy library. Guillermo Cabrera Infante, in his introduction to the English translation of Piñera's *Cold Tales,* tells us that the Spanish writer Juan Goytisolo was a witness to Che Guevara's fury. According to Goytisolo, Che Guevara threw the book against a wall shouting: "How dare you have in our embassy a book by this foul faggot!"[35] Che Guevara's homophobic comment well illustrates that in the early revolutionary years homosexual desire was considered subversive to Cuba's national strength.

Arenas's representation of homosexuality in *Before Night Falls* cannot be considered positive in the way that contemporary North American and European egalitarian gay models strive to celebrate homosexual identity and represent ideal same-sex relationships based on mutual respect and equality. Moreover, Arenas never clearly explains in his auto-biography the psychological motivations, anxiety, or pain behind his coming out—a fairly common theme in English speaking gay and les-bian writings. Instead, the author's voracious sexual appetite is presented with piercing frankness, disregarding any attempt at what is presently labeled political correctness. Rejecting all efforts to attach himself to any particular sexual or political gay identity or agenda, Arenas presents his sexual orientation as fluid. Thus, the Cuban writer has no reservations about affirming his sexual preference for macho heterosexual men (*BNF,* 107) nor about claiming that monogamy, as far as he is concerned, is an impossibility in the homosexual world (*BNF,* 64). Arenas, who spent 10 years getting to know the urban gay world in the United States, is in fact rather critical of it in *Before Night Falls:* "[I]n exile, I found that sexual relations can be tedious and unrewarding. There are categories or divi-sions in the homosexual world. The queer gets together with the queer and everybody does everything. . . . How can that bring any satisfaction? What we are looking for is our opposite. The beauty of our relationships then was that we met our opposites" (*BNF,* 106). Arenas's rejection of North American gay conformity and assimilation is not based on cate-gories or divisions, which he never identifies. Nevertheless, in *Before Night Falls,* Arenas does create his own categories of male homosexuality in Cuba (pp. 77–78): the *dog collar gay,* boisterous and flamboyant, whom the government provides with a permanent "collar" around his neck with which he can easily be hooked and hauled to jail; the *common gay,* who generally has relations with other gays and "never gets to know a real man"; the *closet gay*, who is married but nonetheless has sex with men; the *royal gay*, unique to communist countries, who provides important functions for the party, thus permitting his homosexuality to be overlooked. It seems that what Arenas most objected to in homoerotic relations in the United States is the pairing of same-type individuals, specifically "common gays" whose relations demonstrate no play of difference, difference being essential for the beauty of eroticism to exist. Any type of regimentation or blind conformity is rejected by Arenas. *Before Night Falls* presents a candid account of a legion of diverse sexual adventures and misadventures on the part of Arenas and his friends that collapse any attempt to establish sexual or gender norms. Thus, for example, despite his preference for so-called active macho men, Arenas sometimes plays the active role (*BNF,* 102–3, 152); Miguel Figueroa finds passive gay men for his wife, Olga, who prefers them as sexual partners (*BNF,* 113); Arenas refuses to engage in any sexual activity while in prison out of the belief that in prison, sex is an act of submission and subjugation (*BNF,* 179); Hiram Prado enjoys incestuous relations with his 80-year-old grandfather (*BNF,* 234). In addition, throughout *Before Night Falls* Arenas and his male friends, individuals identified as "passive," are in fact not passive at all, but rather quite active in their powers of seduction and in their constant outsmarting and outmaneuvering of so-called real macho men. In *Before Night Falls* Arenas challenges such simplistic binary oppositions as normal/perverse, active/passive, homo/hetero because they do not take into account the diversity and complicated dynamics of erotic roles and performances.

The U.S. post-Stonewall gay and lesbian liberation movement's emphasis on equality, sexual reciprocity, and the building of lasting relationships by same-sex couples was an alien notion to Arenas, a man born into a society marked by clear-cut gender differences. By this I do not mean to suggest, however, that Arenas was not militant or not in favor of homosexual rights, nor that he supported the repression of women. On the contrary, throughout *Before Night Falls* Arenas criticizes the sociopolitical and erotic roles assigned to women within Cuban society. At one point he even unites the homosexual and woman issue when he writes that the "Castro regime . . . regarded women, along with homosexuals, as inferior beings" (*BNF,* 151).

Arenas's interest in pursuing sexual relations with "hombres de verdad" or "real macho men" (*BNF,* 108) could be interpreted negatively by some readers. Achy Obejas, for example, falls into the trap of reaf-

firming terms of value to discuss such a fluid and variegated affair as
Arenas's homoerotic desire. She ends her review of *Before Night Falls* by
calling Arenas "a sexual anachronism" (Obejas, 389) for scoffing at the
notion of sexual reciprocity in relationships. For her part, Manzor-Coats
also cast doubts on the idea of men whose sexual object of desire is
macho-type men. In her essay she fails to challenge the value-ridden
term "archaic" to describe homosexuality in recent sociological writings:

> Modernization in the sexual realm . . . has resulted in the coexistence of
> two classificatory models for male homosexuality, one traditional and one
> "modern." The traditional or "archaic" model is the popular and hierar-
> chical one. As previously described, this model is based on the relation-
> ship between the macho, who is not identified as homosexual, and the
> *marica,* the effeminate homosexual. The violence at the core of this para-
> digm, the same violence that is constitutive of the conventional model of
> masculinity, connects this archaic model with patriarchal and authoritar-
> ian forms of "micro-fascism." In contrast to and coexisting with the
> above model, is the more recent, egalitarian "modern" model of homo-
> sexuality. In this model, typical of the more urban middle class, a subject
> who identifies himself as homosexual relates as an equal to another sub-
> ject who also assumes a homosexual identity. . . . These modern homo-
> sexuals who assume a gay identity are generally considered to base their
> sexual practices on foreign scripts. (Manzor-Coats, xxiv)

Throughout *Before Night Falls* Arenas does not limit himself to simply
declaring his homosexuality, but rather he graphically presents his erotic
obsessions and sexual escapades, going beyond what many Hispanic
readers would consider good taste. As Robert Richmond Ellis states in his
article, Arenas's unabashed "in your face attitude" (Ellis, 126) has
received negative criticism by some Hispanic reviewers. Miguel Riera, for
example, in a 1992 review for the Spanish publication *Quimera,* wrote:

> When in *Before Night Falls* Arenas declares himself homosexual, he does
> not limit himself to discretely narrating his amorous experiences or the
> repression that his condition brought to him in Cuba. Reinaldo goes
> much further, and he rubs his homosexuality in our faces (Riera, 59, my
> translation).

Arenas was quite aware of the homophobia of his Hispanic audience;
but rather than making concessions, allowing himself to be closeted by
bigotry disguised as good taste, he expressed his experiences honestly, to

the point of alienating certain readers. In 1992 in his review of the autobiography, Mario Vargas Llosa observed: "This is one of the most moving testimonies that has ever been written in our language about
oppression and rebellion, but few will dare to acknowledge this fact
since the book, although one reads it with an uncontrollable appetite,
has the perverse power of leaving its readers uncomfortable" (Vargas
Llosa, 15, my translation).

Arenas's militancy was in support of individual freedom. If one thing
is constantly repeated throughout his work it is the challenging and
undermining of all systems of power that attempt to establish themselves as absolute authority, discourses of the highest truth that infringe
on individual rights to free expression. Arenas's undermining of dogmatism and authoritative rules was not just an instance of pure anarchy.
His rebelliousness and subversion were creative and directed toward
positive and life-affirming actions: the right of individuals to express
themselves freely. This profound sense of individual freedom and human
dignity is present in all his texts. Arenas's purposely exaggerated subversion, what might also be called his carnival sense of the world—
much like what the Russian critic Mikhail Bakhtin proposed in *Rabelais
and His World*[36]—was a direct challenge to the authoritative rhetoric
and centralized discourse of power that the Cuban writer witnessed
around him while living in Cuba. Like Rabelais, who confronted the
medieval world's asceticism with excess and grotesque laughter, Arenas's subversion, or carnival sense of the world, was a result of having to
confront a similarly powerful foe, the Cuban revolutionary state.
Although one might be inclined to see Arenas as an anarchist who proclaimed pure and total relativity in his works, such a judgment would
significantly limit the resonance of Arenas's writings, which in fact
achieve creativity and authentic artistic representation.

If anyone should have benefited from the Cuban revolution, surely it
would have been a poor country boy who was forced to eat dirt because of
a scarcity of food and who came of age with a revolution intent on right-
ing social wrongs. Ironically, however, Arenas did not grow up to become
an ardent defender of Castro's regime, but rather one of its most outspoken critics. *Before Night Falls* is marked by Arenas's vitality, love for life,
and capacity for resistance. On a universal level this remarkable autobiography serves as a powerful testimony of one individual's struggles to survive and maintain his dignity in the face of repeated horrors. On another,
more specific level, this text reveals one homosexual man's gift for turning
his condition of "otherness" into a dynamic position of difference.

Chapter Two

A Homosexual Bildungsroman: The Novels of the *Pentagonía*

Arenas's oeuvre is quite prolific, incredibly so if one considers the persecution and censorship he suffered in Cuba and the fact that he died at the age of 47. Throughout his life Arenas explored all the major literary genres: novel, short story, poetry, theater, and essay. Moreover, he was an insightful critic, illuminating the works of such important Spanish American writers as José Martí, José Lezama Lima, Juan Rulfo, Gabriel García Márquez, and others. Still, it is the novel that Arenas most consistently cultivated and that was responsible for his critical success and recognition both in Latin America and abroad. Arenas took advantage of the novel's open-endedness, its inexhaustible ability to accommodate and incorporate different discourses, its world of play and hypotheses, its metaphysical questioning, to give free rein to his imagination and existential inquiries. The fact that he consistently went back to writing novels after exploring other literary forms indicates his predilection for this broadly encompassing, highly flexible, and ever changing genre.

At the time of his death, Arenas had written eight novels, five that had been published and two that had not. (*El color del verano* [The Color of Summer] and *El asalto* [*The Assault*] were finally published in December of 1991 by Ediciones Universal, Miami.) Within this prolific novelistic production, *Celestino antes del alba* (retitled *Cantando en el pozo* in 1982)[1] (*Singing from the Well*), *El palacio de las blanquísimas mofetas* (*The Palace of the White Skunks*), *Otra vez el mar* (*Farewell to the Sea*), *El color del verano* (The Color of Summer), and *El asalto* (*The Assault*) form a five-book sequence—described by Arenas as both a writer's autobiography and a metaphor of Cuban history—that constitutes a unique intradependent unit.

Arenas once stated that he first began to write at an early age out of necessity: "When I was ten years old I was already writing . . . and now I realize I needed to write; otherwise I wouldn't have wasted my time."[2] This exigency to write is evident in *Celestino antes del alba* (*Singing from the Well*), Arenas's first novel, published in 1967 in Cuba when he was only 22 years old. This first work, awarded an honorable mention in the *Con-*

curso Nacional de Novela Cirilo Villaverde (Cirilo Villaverde National Novel Competition) in 1965, heralded the arrival of this innovative and unconventional young writer. However, because only a limited number of copies (2,000) were issued, Arenas's literary reputation was restricted to a small number of Cubans on the island.

In 1968, after having fallen from favor with the revolutionary government, Arenas secretly sent the manuscript of his second novel abroad, and the French editorial house Editions du Seuil published it as *Le monde hallucinant*. One year later the novel appeared in Spanish as *El mundo alucinante* (*The Ill-Fated Peregrinations of Fray Servando*). Arenas's international literary reputation took off as a result of the success of this novel. Among his texts, *The Ill-Fated Peregrinations of Fray Servando* has received the most critical acclaim both in Latin America and abroad.

In 1975 the publication of *Le palais des très blanches moufettes* marked the second time that one of Arenas's novels appeared first in French. In this novel—later to be published in 1980 in Spanish as *El palacio de las blanquísimas mofetas* (*The Palace of the White Skunks*)—the writer continues the family saga that he had started in *Singing from the Well*. In addition, he conceives of these two works as part of a *pentagonía* (pentagony)—a neologism for the Spanish *pentalogía* (pentalogy)—a word that underscores the *agonía* suffered by the characters in this quintet, who find themselves pressured and persecuted by abusive authoritarian systems and discourses of power. Whereas *Singing from the Well* focuses on the experiences of an unidentified child-narrator persecuted by his family as well as by the impoverished conditions of the prerevolutionary Cuban countryside, *The Palace of the White Skunks* explores the world of the adolescent Fortunato, a chaotic world of torment and spiritual hardship played out against a backdrop of revolutionary upheaval.

Otra vez el mar (*Farewell to the Sea*), rewritten three times over a period of 16 years, was finally published in 1982 by the publisher Argos Vergara in Barcelona.[3] Arenas considered this third and central novel of the five-book sequence to be the most important of his then-published works. In 1983 Severo Sarduy wrote, "*Otra vez el mar* is, with [José Lezama Lima's] *Paradiso*, one of the best novels that our country has produced, as well as one of the most critical and most Cuban."[4] With an entire history behind him (childhood and adolescence), the adult Hector of *Farewell to the Sea*, conscious of his homosexuality and now living under an institutionalized revolution that systematically persecutes homosexuals, continues questioning his alienation and tortured existence.

Arenas completed *El color del verano* (The Color of Summer)[5] and *El asalto* (*The Assault*) shortly before his death in December 1990. The novels appeared one year later, published by Ediciones Universal, Miami. Hector is reborn in *El color del verano* as Gabriel, who is also identified in the text as Reinaldo and the Tétrica Mofeta (the Gloomy Skunk). With their extravagance and festive laughter, the trinity—Gabriel/Reinaldo/ the Tétrica Mofeta—move within a homosexual subculture that challenges the bureaucracy, hostility, and persecution of the dictator Fifo's tyrannical society. In *The Assault,* Gabriel/Reinaldo/the Tétrica Mofeta are metamorphosed into the nameless narrator, who lives in an abominable future society in which individual rights are sacrificed for the good of the state. Ironically, however, this final novel of the pentalogy leaves the reader with a glimmer of hope. The decrepit tyrant, El Reprimerísimo Reprimero (the Represident),[6] is destroyed, and the protagonist, who has suffered countless persecutions throughout the five-book cycle, can finally stretch out on the beach and rest.

Singing from the Well, The Palace of the White Skunks, Farewell to the Sea, El color del verano (The Color of Summer), and *The Assault* rely predominantly on the use of a first-person narrative voice (the child-narrator/ Celestino, Fortunato, Hector, Gabriel/Reinaldo/the Tétrica Mofeta, and the nameless narrator of *The Assault*) to recount the situations and events in the story. Yet at the same time, these novels break open the homogeneity of traditional one-sided or dogmatic singular points of view by denying exclusive authority to any one voice. In Arenas's novels no single character's words are granted more importance or authority than are the words of any other character, and often the statements made by one character are contradicted or challenged by another. Moreover, as a result of their constant mutations, splittings, transformations, and metamorphoses, the characters of the pentalogy are never presented as whole and autonomous. For this reason the five novels are ideally read together, for each is progressively developed from traces of the previous text. (This suggestion, of course, does not invalidate the reading of each novel for its own singularity.) The interrelationship or intratextuality of the works gives rise to a reconceptualization of the traditionally closed vehicle of the realistic novel, for the ending of one novel is but a new beginning. In this way the child-narrator/Celestino, Fortunato, Hector, Gabriel/Reinaldo/the Tétrica Mofeta, and the nameless protagonist of *The Assault* are presented as a protean consciousness that can never be fully defined or exhausted.

In his autobiography, *Before Night Falls,* Arenas recounts his determination, despite his hospitalization from AIDS-related complications, to complete the last two novels of the pentalogy:

> I really had to finish my *pentagonía*. While in the hospital I had started working on the fourth, and for me essential, novel in the series, *El color del verano* [The Color of Summer]. I still had some IVs stuck in my hands, making writing somewhat difficult, but I was committed to continue. . . . [A]fter leaving the hospital . . . [I] continued working on "The Color of Summer." At the same time, with the help of Roberto Valero and María Badías, I was also revising *The Assault,* the fifth novel of the *pentagonía.* The manuscript had been written in Cuba in great haste so it could be smuggled out of the country. Roberto and María had to transcribe it from my almost unintelligible scribblings into readable Spanish. (*BNF,* xiii–xiv)

The completion of the *pentagonía,* a project that he had worked on intermittently since he was 18 years old, was of paramount importance for the dying writer. Arenas furiously labored to complete it once he sensed his death was imminent.[7] The intradependent narratives of the *pentagonía* not only provide for the reader a significant insight into the literary concerns and creative processes of the writer—perhaps more so than any single text in Arenas's entire literary production—but also, by presenting the struggles and persecutions of a protean character whose life spans from childhood to adulthood during different moments of Cuban history, address the Cuban experience just prior to and after the Cuban revolution. Still, among the many possible critical readings that exist of this quintet (i.e., historical, postmodern, and carnivalesque, among others), it is significant that scholars have overlooked reading the *pentagonía* as a homosexual bildungsroman that traces the development of the ever-changing main character from childhood into adolescence, then into adulthood, through a troubled quest for a sexual identity.[8] (The *pentagonía* also describes the protagonist's formation as a writer, thus overlapping with the *Künstlerroman,* the German term meaning "artist-novel.") Throughout the rest of this chapter I analyze the novels of the *pentagonía,* paying particular attention to the development of a homoerotic discourse.

Singing from the Well

Although Arenas's first novel contains no explicit mention of homosexuality, it does contain sufficient passing references, innuendoes, and codification to warrant such a reading. Recent queer theory has shown us that sexual orientation, once seen as the essence of personal identity, is nothing more than a cultural or historical category created by the medical and legal discourses of the late nineteenth century. Thus, in recent years, there has been a shift in the way that homosexuality has been read; a shift from homosexuality as essence or identity to homoerotic desire presented as construct, performance, or activity that cannot be pigeonholed into specific or concrete categories. As I established in chapter 1, Arenas in his autobiography is critical and skeptical of North American "gayness" in which same-type individuals, whose relations demonstrate no play of difference—difference being essential, in Arenas's estimation, for the beauty of eroticism to exist—pair themselves off. According to Arenas, this type of regimentation or blind conformity does not take into consideration the diversity, fluidity, and complicated dynamics of erotic roles and performances. With Arenas's attitude in mind, readers should not be surprised to find in the novels of the *pentagonía* a clear resistance to the representation of a fixed, stabled identity.

Singing from the Well[9] displays an intentional undermining of the representation of a stable and closed monologic consciousness unfolding within itself. The construction of subjectivity is deprived of any power to define or finalize characters as indisputably individualistic. Not pinning down or reducing characters to the relative or the limited requires the reader to take a more active role, to establish meaning on a poetic-symbolic-allegorical level rather than on a referential level. This rejection of a fixed subjectivity has enormous implications because it opens the door for the representation of nonheterosexual sexualities traditionally vilified and demonized by societies. The novel's use of splitting characters, imagined doubles, and metamorphoses—techniques that will be reintroduced in the subsequent novels of the *pentagonía*—decenters the notion of a fixed continuous and integral identity. In the novels of the *pentagonía,* as we shall see, homoerotic desire is never the basis for a character's identity, but rather is a libidinal flow of desire that vehemently resists all authoritarian attempts to be repressed or controlled. Thus, in *Singing from the Well,* for example, the main character, the child-narrator/Celestino, battles against forces intent on destroying expressions of difference, difference being intentionally left open to accommodate all marginalized discourses not accepted by a traditional heterosexist hegemony. At one point in the novel, Celestino, the magical cousin imagined or created by the child-narrator, is suspected of being homosexual simply because he writes poetry: "That's what girls do," said my mother,

when she found out Celestino had got it into his head to start writing"
(*Singing*, 4). Later in the novel we read:

> "He cries like a girl!"
> "The lizard's kid is crying like a girl!"
> "Cut from the same cloth as Celestino—pants outside, but petticoats underneath!" . . .
> "Celestino the crazy kid's cousin! He's Celestino's cousin, the one that writes poetry on the trunks of the trees!"
> "They're both queers!"
> "Queers!" (*Singing*, 25)

In the socially closed and normatively gender-minded world of rural prerevolutionary Cuba, dichotomies such as masculinity/femininity, heterosexual/homosexual, male/female are clearly distinguished. The poetic act, already foreign to the practical sensibilities of the Cuban *guajiros* (peasants), when performed by a male is seen as a double mark of difference or "queerness." Although the theme of homosexuality will be articulated more openly in Arenas's subsequent novels, in *Singing from the Well* homosexuality is already presented as a creative rebelliousness transgressing and confronting the intolerance of difference.

Singing from the Well possesses no traditional plot; temporal sequences related to cause and effect, a before and after, are undermined. Story time (the period in which the situations and events occur, that is, the late 1940s and the early 1950s) is clouded and obscured by a magical and lyrical discourse time (the time of the enunciation, or actual narrating act). From its onset *Singing from the Well* is set in a concrete locality: the impoverished reality of the prerevolution Cuban countryside. From this spatial marker the fantastic and explosive imagination of the child-narrator is allowed to unfold. Yet beyond the presentation of this initial locality, steeped in historical time, it is impossible to distinguish among days, months, years, or any type of precise sequence of events. The most flagrant dismissal of chronology is seen in the use of three endings: "The End," "The Second End," and "The Last End" (*Singing*, 101, 135, 206).[10] The use of three separate endings supports the novel's devaluation of chronology and its emphasis on simultaneity. The text creates a literary tension as it repeatedly strives to escape from its condition of finitude, to stretch out from the limitations and confinement of a final determinacy.

From the very first sentence of *Singing from the Well*, the narrative discourse is focalized through the voice of a child-narrator who remains nameless throughout the entire story and whose unrestrained and whimsical imagination subjugates any respect for accuracy or objectivity. This choice of focalization is best suited in presenting the character's world of imagination and limitless possibilities. The child-narrator's narrative voice, unable to cope with the desolate conditions of the prerevolutionary Cuban countryside as well as with the ignorance and conventionalism of his family, splits itself in order to create an alter ego, a more pure being, an imaginary cousin (Celestino) who is also a poet. In this way the child-narrator—"el buen creador" (the good creator), as the Cuban poet Eliseo Diego referred to him—duplicates the creative capacity of the extraliterary writer (Arenas).[11] In *Singing from the Well,* the boundaries between writer, narrator, and character are blurred. This blurring will continue in Arenas's subsequent novels, in which characters create other characters, doubles that complement them or show other aspects of their personality. This mirroring, or doubling, of the creative process within the texts makes Arenas's characters, on a literary level, extremely rich and complex.

In his study of the menippean satire tradition—a form of intellectually humorous work characterized by comical discussions on philosophical topics, dating back to antiquity—the Russian critic Mikhail Bakhtin observed that the use of a split personality in the menippea was a common device to proliferate the subject, thus making it cease to coincide with itself. In this fashion, doubles continually reflect aspects of one another rather then existing as isolated, self-enclosed psyches: "[The] destruction of the wholeness and finalized quality of a man is facilitated by the appearance, in the menippea, of a dialogic relationship to one's own self (fraught with the possibility of split personality)."[12] This decentering or dismantling of a unified subject, embryonic in the menippea, creates a psychic interweaving in *Singing from the Well,* making it difficult to clearly differentiate the various fragments and furthermore challenging the reader's notion of the representability of individual wholeness through language. In *Singing from the Well,* the reader is required to participate actively in the child-narrator's act of creation. The dialogic relationship proposed by Bakhtin, inherent in the split personality of the menippea, is an important aspect of the relationship between the child-narrator and Celestino.

What I have taken as obvious, that Celestino is the creation of the child-narrator, has not always been fully seen by the critics who have studied the novel.[13] The mistaken view that both subjects are separate characters can be attributed to the fact that not only the child-narrator but also all the other characters in the text react to Celestino's presence. Celestino is introduced as the son of Carmelina, who after being abandoned by her husband hanged herself and set herself afire. (Present in the death of Carmelina is a foreshadowing synthesis of both Fortunato and Adolfina of *The Palace of the White Skunks*; Fortunato is supposedly hanged by the Batista police and Adolfina sets herself afire. This metamorphosis or permutating of the character [Carmelina into Fortunato and Adolfina] further illustrates the pentalogy's dismantling of the notion of a concrete and stable subjectivity. In Arenas's novels characterization is not closed or finalized, but proceeds like a continuous permutation. In various interviews that Arenas gave during his life he always made it quite clear that the child-narrator was the creator of Celestino. Even if Arenas had not revealed this, their fusion is suggested in the text. I offer one of the more revealing episodes as an example. Near the end of the novel Celestino, who has metamorphosed into a bird, is revealed to be dying. The use of a bird, *un pájaro* in Spanish, is quite telling. Within Cuban slang *pájaro* (bird) is a pejorative term used to refer to homosexuals. Throughout the novel Celestino is accused of being *loco* (crazy), *pervertido* (perverted), *maricón* (faggot) simply because he writes poetry. The poet Celestino, like the homosexual, is ostracized and becomes the victim of scorn simply because he is different. In the following passage the child-narrator, identified as "YOU," speaks to his grandfather about the fragile bird:

YOU:	Show me the bird! Show me the bird!
GRANDFATHER (*very cheerfully*):	Here it is! Look at it!
YOU:	Celestino!
GRANDFATHER:	Yes, you! (*Singing,* 166)

This passage shows us how individual subjectivity is decentered by the use of a technical device that turns the other ("You") into a reflection of the "I." This devaluing of the defining properties of personal pronouns will reappear in Arenas's second novel, *The Ill-Fated Peregrinations of Fray Servando,* in which a juxtaposition of first, second, and third-person points of view will be utilized to undermine and parody the notion of a reliable speaking subject.

Near the end of *Singing from the Well* the child-narrator finds himself talking with a goblin who reproaches him for not believing in his existence:

> You never paid any mind to me, and every time I got close to you, you
> tried to imagine you were dreaming. It was so incredible to you that some-
> body could just for no reason try to give you a helping hand! Is it that you
> don't trust anything you can't put your hands on?—and your hands, I'll
> tell you, are a lot less real than any of my legends. (*Singing,* 205)

Soon after, as the goblin begins to disappear, the child-narrator asks him
his name; the answer, "My name is Celestino." The novel has come full
cycle: the creation (Celestino) has usurped the child-narrator's position
of dominance thereby calling into question his very existence. Much the
same as in Jorge Luis Borges's masterful piece "Borges y yo" ("Borges
and I"), the creator/child-narrator's identity is fragmented and finally
usurped by his very creation. Ironically, however, at the same time the
character's stability is undermined, the power of the human imagination
as a defense against life's brutality is underscored.

   This defense of a rebellious creative spirit present throughout *Singing
from the Well* is first suggested in the text, or rather pre-text, in the three
epigraphs at the beginning of the book: quotes from Oscar Wilde, Jorge
Luis Borges, and Federico García Lorca. The source of each epigraph
proposes an intertextual game that highlights the value of the creative
power of the imagination, an impulse that challenges and undermines
all normative discourses intent on reducing or pigeonholing the infinite
possibilities of human expression. Moreover, the epigraphs, carefully
chosen by Arenas, encode a link between homosexuality and writing. By
choosing writers known for their marginal sexuality (as is the case with
Wilde, Lorca, and Borges—although not explicitly out of the closet during his lifetime, Borges was certainly ambiguous as to his own as well as
some of his characters' sexual orientation),[14] Arenas purposefully joins
and associates a rebellious poetic act with the expression of a socially
transgressive homosexual performance.

   The first epigraph is a Spanish translation of a quote from Oscar
Wilde's story "The Young King": "But no man dared look upon his face,
for it was like the face of an angel." Central to this tale is the notion that
dreams can indeed contain states of consciousness that are more worthy
than the hypocrisies that humans are capable of committing in life. The
story is about a country lad who recoups the inheritance that is right-
fully his as legitimate heir to his kingdom's throne. The night prior to
his coronation the young prince, who demonstrates a poetic sensibility
to his surroundings from the time of his arrival at the palace, has three
dreams in which he sees represented the injustices of those who labor to

finish his royal robe, crown, and scepter. Awakening on the day of the coronation and affected by what he has dreamt, the lad instead of dressing in his regal attire decides to wear the leathern tunic in which he had come to claim the throne. When the courtiers discover that the lad refuses to wear the royal raiment simply because of the dreams he has had, they suspect that he has gone mad. When the young man arrives at the cathedral dressed like a pauper, the attacks and criticism begin; no one wishes to see the king dressed like a humble shepherd. The protest quickly becomes menacing with the arrival of nobles prepared to assassinate the man who has brought disgrace to the kingdom. However, at that precise moment, the young man is transfigured by a celestial light that comes accompanied by a divine music; in the end, "no man dared look upon his face, for it was like the face of an angel."

In this story, Wilde fuses the referential space of the kingdom with an oneiric or imaginative space (the protagonist's three dreams) in order to question human motives. The oneiric space, typically considered inverisimilar, contains elements from the referential space that are transformed to display a phantasmagorical reality. In Wilde's story, like in *Singing from the Well,* what is imagined or dreamt is valued as much as what is normally considered "real." Furthermore, the authenticity of presenting yourself as who you truly are, as is the case with the young lad undaunted by the criticism around him to succumb to an expected behavior, symbolically underscores the homosexual's need to be true to himself or herself.

The second epigraph to *Singing from the Well* is the last line of the poem "Insomnia," the first poem of the collection *El otro, el mismo* (The Other, Myself) by Jorge Luis Borges:[15] "Coarse clouds the color of wine sediment will disgrace the heavens; dawn will break on my tight-squeezed eyelids." The problem of insomnia appears in many Borgesian texts as an abominable lucidity that does not allow the individual to escape the banalities of everyday existence. In "Insomnia" the poet, "the abhorrent sentinel" of universal history, cannot relieve himself of the vigilance of reason, that is, his anguished present. The poet's reasonable mind does not allow him to separate from his body and for that he suffers, condemned to "a frightful wakefulness." The poem ends with the arrival of the new day and the poet still yearning for the forgetfulness of the dream of imagination.

In Borges's poem, the valorization of the wakeful state, traditionally seen as the only reality (like heterosexuality has traditionally been seen as the "normal" sexuality) is subverted by the oneiric activity. In Borges's literary universe dreams are equivalent to creation, the possibility to achieve new realities in art; hence, insomnia is the state of no creation. Thus for Borges, as for Arenas, the capability of dreaming is equivalent to the poetic expression. The creative impulse is like a dream, a directed dream, that grants the individual endless possibilities of expression. In the world of the child-narrator/Celestino the boundary between what is real and what is dreamed or imagined is erased. Any reader wishing for clear limits is met by a multiplicity of realities that bifurcate and extend throughout the text.

The last epigraph is a section of the poem "Rhythm of Autumn" from Federico García Lorca's first collection of poetry, *Libro de poemas*.[16] In this poem, the dream of the imagination is presented as the orchestrated dream of the poetic act. The "lyrical cry" of the poet is presented as his only comfort against the frustrations of not being able to reach "the blue infinite," a metaphor for all that is denied to humanity. The poem suggests that when oppression becomes intolerable, the most absolute expression of freedom is the human imagination.

In *Singing from the Well,* the child-narrator idealizes a pure being, a poet (Celestino), who cannot be destroyed by the violence of his surroundings. Celestino is a liberating force, an indomitable spirit that uncovers oppression and struggles against it. Celestino, who is always the same—"mad, sad, happy, and everything at the same time," (*Singing,* 59)—does not permit the violence that surrounds him to stop him from completing his literary work. The paradoxical nature of this statement underscores the child-narrator's need to harmoniously integrate the full gamut of human emotions in an ideal image of himself. Thus Celestino transcends, like the Lorquian poet, his surrounding brutality with an insatiable need for self-expression that compels him to write even on the trunks of trees. Through his incessant writing on tree trunks and branches in the countryside, the child-narrator/Celestino attempts to express his desires. This rebellious act underscores the need to articulate intimate feelings and emotions through the written form, despite obstacles and intimidation. Persecuted by the grandfather's hatchet (the grandfather, symbol of repression within the text, is personified in the word "hatchets," a word that is visually repeated 113 times on a single page of the text), Celestino passionately writes a mysterious poetry that separates him and makes him different from the rest. Within the novel, in a moment of absolute rage, the young narrator defends the poetic activities of his cousin: "They're a bunch of savages! If they don't understand something, they automatically hate it. They say it's ugly or it's dirty. Animals!" (*Singing,* 159). The child-narrator's cry reaffirms the infinite possibilities of expression in a world with rigid social codes. It is a cry of defense for all those whose unorthodox conduct, considered by the "superficial ones" as improper, represents the infinite game of difference that is life. The "superficial ones," as Arenas calls them, are those who wish to domesticate plurality, those individuals who are bothered by any act—literary as well as personal—that is considered to be at variance with so-called normal social behavior:

> Ah, but when we try to express the different realities that are buried and hidden under an apparent reality, those superficial individuals, who swarm in an alarming fashion and demand that everything that is presented to them be ground up and chewed for them beforehand, complain loudly.[17]

For Arenas, characters in a literary work, just like human beings in life, are not logical and coherent beings anchored in an objective empirical reality but are complex and contradictory souls ceaselessly transforming themselves.

Finally, I would like to closely examine the novel's dedication, which reads: "For Maricela Cordovez, the prettiest girl in the world." This dedication might be read as an encoded message of solidarity with Federico García Lorca—in Spanish, "Maric(*el*)a Cordovez"; the faggot from Córdoba, Spain—who, for being a poet and a homosexual, was assassinated by the oppression of a regime that would also not tolerate difference. (One of Lorca's better known poems is his "Canción de jinete" [Rider's Song] with its famous opening lines, "Córdoba / Lejana y sola" [Córdoba / Far away and alone]. This and other poems about this Andalusian town written by Lorca might explain Arenas's reference to him as the "cordobés" [Cordovan]. In addition, it was Lorca and others from the generation of 1927 that were responsible for resurrecting the work of "el cisne de Córdoba" [the Cordovan Swan], the baroque poet Luis de Góngora y Argote [1561–1627].)

In his book, *La textualidad de Reinaldo Arenas: Juegos de la escritura posmoderna* (Reinaldo Arenas's Textualism: Postmodern Writing Games), Eduardo C. Béjar makes the following suggestion in regard to the dedication in *Singing from the Well*:

> The proper name MARICELA can be considered as the construction of three morphemes, each one the result of a transformation of the lexemes 'mar'

(sea), 'cielo' (sky), and 'marica' (faggot). In them, the isotypes of rebellion against the fixed are subsumed . . . On another issue, the intertextual relationship that the nickname CORDOVEZ establishes with the poetic world of Federico García Lorca is also apparent." (Béjar, 158–59, my translation)

Lorca's assassination can only be explained by a militant fascist mentality hostile to the fame and recognition that the liberal homosexual poet from Granada was receiving nationally and internationally. In his well documented biography of Lorca, Ian Gibson writes: "Among the assassins . . . was Juan Luis Trescastro . . . who boasted later that morning in Granada that he had just helped to shoot Lorca, firing, for good measure, two bullets into his arse for being a queer."[18] Although many reasons have been cited for Lorca's assassination (among them, his liberalism, his rebellion against traditional values, his communist leanings), it is evident that his homosexuality was not absent from the motives of those who tortured and killed him. Spain's traditional inquisitorial Catholicism refused to permit the expression of a sexuality that challenged the dominant Christian morality. This intolerant environment—reminiscent of Arenas's own situation in revolutionary Cuba—well explains Lorca's fears and deliberate concealment of his homosexuality both in his personal life and in his work.[19]

The Palace of the White Skunks

Like the phoenix ensured its progeny, the child-narrator/Celestino is destroyed in Arenas's first novel to reincarnate as the adolescent Fortunato in *The Palace of the White Skunks*. This novel covers the adolescent stage of the protean main character of the quintet. Fortunato, a sensitive and restless young man living through a turbulent political period in Cuban history (the insurrectional struggle against the Batista regime), is desperate to escape the cruelties of his family—he refers to them as "beasts"—as well as to escape from Holguín, a conservative, small rural town "of symmetrical streets and townfolks inalterably practical" (*Palace,* 36). The rigidity and conservatism of Holguín suffocate the young Fortunato, who is beginning to show signs of homoerotic interests. Like the child-narrator/Celestino, Fortunato is considered crazy by his family for not adapting to the heterosexual hypermasculine model. Again, as in *Singing from the Well,* this second novel of the *pentagonía* contains no explicit mention of homosexuality. Still, Fortunato's attraction to men is made evident in the novel. In one scene, for example, that takes place in the town's brothel, Eufrasia's Rub Pub, Fortunato, who has come to the whorehouse with his buddies Aby and Cipriano, is unable to achieve an erection with a prostitute who is servicing him. (Arenas dedicates a chapter of his autobiography to Eufrasia's Rub Pub, a site that actually existed in his hometown of Holguín. That chapter begins with the following sentence that underscores the traditional heterosexist atmosphere of Holguín, which aggravated life for any young man beginning to address his homoerotic desires: "Holguín had a totally macho atmosphere which my family shared and in which they raised me" [*BNF,* 35]. The chapter goes on to chronicle Arenas's early homosexual attractions as well as the many girlfriends he had in order to keep up appearances in town.) Later during one of Fortunato's private sessions of masturbation, he is only able to achieve an erection by evoking the image of his friend Aby:

> Only when Aby appeared—tall, thin, in his tight pants—to usurp the others' places, laughing, walking through strange vegetation, did the rhythm of his stroking increase—and in a whirl of fragmented, desperate faces and strange falling leaves, Fortunato at last achieved his tranquilizing goal . . . (*Palace,* 261)

In the end, Fortunato's decision to *alzarse* (join the rebel forces) is motivated more because he will do it with Aby than out of any fervent political commitment. The following romanticized fantasy of male camaraderie contains homoerotic and phallic images. Here we see Fortunato, with "machine gun in hand," defending and protecting his friend Aby, who after being wounded is carried off to a remote and intimate area of the forest where he is nurtured back to health by Fortunato:

> Go off with Aby to join the rebels. Go off to the Sierra to fight together. He would defend him. Shots—and he, machine gun in hand, would keep him from being killed. He'd kill every steel pot there was, and then he would carry his wounded friend's body into the depths of the forest and there he would make him well again. He would fight, shoot, defend his friend. (*Palace,* 260)

The other characters in *The Palace of the White Skunks,* all members of the same family, live brutally agonizing lives expecting to find solace only in death. But death brings no relief, as is evident in the sections entitled "The Life of the Dead." The story of *The Palace of the White Skunks* is not just the story of Fortunato, it is also the story of Fortunato's eccentrically cruel and obsessive family: Polo, the grandfather who considers himself cursed for having engendered only daughters; the superstitious and blasphemous grandmother, Jacinta, who spends her days compulsively going to the bathroom; Aunt Celia, who is driven to madness after her only daughter, Esther, commits suicide; Aunt Digna, abandoned by her husband, Moisés, and left to raise the mischievous Tico and Anisia; Aunt Adolfina, a spinster desperate to lose her virginity; and Onerica, Fortunato's mother, who abandons him and goes to the United States in search of her own "fortune." These characters, or rather voices (for the text is constructed as a cacophony of voices), are given the opportunity to recount their own obsessive stories of despair. In this Tower of Babel in which no one understands anyone else, personal agonies are fated to echo within the chambers of the novel. That the characters, prisoners of their own suffering, yearn in desperation to find a receptive listener only underscores their alienation.

The Palace of the White Skunks challenges the notion of a single reliable voice that can faithfully telegraph reality to the reader, for the audibility of Fortunato's testimony, a testimony that wishes to see itself as the authentic voice of the family, is incessantly drowned out by the multiplicity of voices of the other family members eager to tell their own sides of the story. Although the first-, second-, and third-person narrative voices are all utilized in *The Palace of the White Skunks,* the first person predominates. This narrative "I" is shared by all the family members, who speak in the first person. The proliferation of a first-person focalization produces a cacophony of voices in which each individual—at times unrecognizable—struggles in vain to be heard. Multiple narrative "Is" contradict each other, in this way not granting referential stability to any speaking subject. Thus, the text is reduced to a crisscrossing of affirmations and contradictions that totally refuse the concentration of veracity into a single authoritative voice.

The Palace of the White Skunks is divided into three parts: "Prologue and Epilogue," "The Creatures Utter Their Complaints," and "The Play." In the first part, "Prologue and Epilogue," the crisscrossing of voices is so entangled that it is extremely difficult for the reader to decipher the narrative during a first reading. (These fragments of voices will be contextualized and expanded in the second and third parts of the novel). With the (con)fusion of what is traditionally the first word (prologue) and last word (epilogue) of the traditional novel, the suggestion is made that there is no first or final word on any given matter; rather, discourse is open-ended, without a finalizing period. In the end, the supremacy of any narrative continuity is undermined as words appear to be but muffled echoes reverberating within the pages of the text.

The second part of the novel, "The Creatures Utter Their Complaints," constitutes the major portion of the text. This part is subdivided into "agonies" instead of chapters. Each family member attempts in monologue to present his or her most intimate suffering. These spoken accounts are presented as a rambling hodgepodge of voices that often conceal the identity of the speaking subject. The gallery of voices is reminiscent of the divided spoken sections by different characters in Guillermo Cabrera Infantes's *Tres tristes tigres* (*Three Trapped Tigers*), a work in which it is similarly difficult to delineate the individual voices that present themselves in the first person. Although the characters of Cabrera Infante's novel do engage in dialogues (for example, in the section "Bachata," Silvestre and Cué converse as they drive around Havana in a convertible), the characters of *The Palace of the White Skunks,* in contrast, are reduced to mere diatribe. At times the typography of a single page is literally adjusted to accommodate two or more voices whose speech crisscrosses, but never intersects. In 1981 Arenas stated:

> [*The Palace of the White Skunks*] is structured around completely isolated monologues; even when it appears at certain moments that the characters are talking, they are only concerned with telling their own tragic story. They are so alienated by their own pain that all possibility of dialogue is out of the question.[20]

Fortunato wishes for his words to represent the others' (his family's) experiences. However, Fortunato must pay a price for his identification with other individuals who are equally oppressed. The following excerpt, presented in the third person, begins to reveal the young man in the role of victim and martyr. The adolescent wishes to bear the cross for his family's pain, a cross that will lead to the destruction and fragmentation of his vision of *self*:

> And that was when he started to look at, and try to understand, his family, and he began to suffer for their tragedies even more than they themselves did. . . . That was when he set himself afire, when he went voluntarily into exile, when he became a grouchy old coot, when he went mad, when, transformed into an old maid, he ran out into the streets to try to find a man. (*Palace,* 104)

Previous to this passage the reader learns that Fortunato begins to steal reams of paper from his grandfather's store and begins to write "incessantly" his constant "sensation(s)"—a word that is repeated throughout the text to express the ineffable in regard to the boy's feelings. Fortunato's sensibility and capacity for empathy is in total contradiction to the egoism of his family, in which each member is only concerned with his or her suffering. This desire to bear his family's suffering, to understand (to feel) their intimate pain and frustrations, places Fortunato on the path to *self*-destruction. The adolescent-poet, whose existence is already marked by total isolation and hopelessness, begins to fragment under the weight of all this misfortune. Indeed, his name, Fortunato, is ironic. In the following passage we see the final outcome of this direct identification with his family:

> Many times he had been Adolfina—he had suffered as she had (or perhaps more) the urgent need to be embraced, penetrated, to have his throat cut, to be strangled and asphyxiated, to be annihilated in the name of love. Many times he had been Celia. . . . Many times he was Digna. . . . Many times he had been Polo and Jacinta. . . . Many times he had been Tico and Anisia. . . . Many times he had been Esther. . . . Many times—all the time, really—he had been all of them, and he had suffered for them, and perhaps when he had been them (for he had more imagination than they did, he could go beyond the mere here-and-now) he had even suffered more than they, deep within himself, deep within his own, invariable terror. And he had given them a voice, a way of expressing the stupor, the dull horror, the fear, the blind terror which they, surely, would never be fully able to know or to suffer. (*Palace,* 234)

Fortunato's desire to become the authentic interpreter of his family's pain erases the boundaries between *self* and *other,* leaving the adolescent overwhelmed by the frustration and destitute existence of his family. Fortunato wishes to give voice to his family's agonies, but this close identification with the *other* produces a loss of *self* that results in confusion and ambiguity, as the following passage demonstrates: "Those are just 'those ideas' of yours. Those are just 'those ideas' of mine. Those are just 'those ideas' of myours" (*Palace,* 183).

In *The Palace of the White Skunks,* the use of the doubling pair Fortunato/Adolfina or Adolfina/Fortunato goes further than the use of the split personality in *Singing from the Well.* Adolfina is as much the feminine double of Fortunato as he is her masculine counterpart; neither character's story or emotional struggles is presented as more important or consequential than the other's. Let us recall that although Fortunato is the adolescent reincarnate of the child-narrator of *Singing from the Well,* who furthermore wishes to see himself as the authentic voice within the family, his voice is never granted a position of supremacy over the other characters. The presentation of the doubling pair Fortunato/Adolfina or Adolfina/Fortunato problematizes the rigid gender paradigms and masculinist philosophies of Western notions of subjectivity built on the integrity of the sex and gender of the subject.[21] By erasing the boundaries of gender that have so easily defined characters in the realistic literary tradition, Arenas reveals the intricate complexities of the human subject that will not allow itself to be pinned down to a singular identity. This very notion will be reintroduced and further explored in *Farewell to the Sea,* in which the subject of the enunciation of the first part (the nameless wife) at the end of the novel is revealed to be the feminine side of Hector's personality.

In *Palace of the White Skunks* Fortunato and Adolfina share similar sensibilities. Both experience feelings of extreme loneliness, dissatisfaction, and helplessness due to their respective situations: Fortunato's spiritual isolation as he develops homoerotic attractions in a small repressive town with a macho atmosphere, and Adolfina's emotional isolation in not having found a man. In the following passage Adolfina identifies herself directly with Fortunato:

> Sometimes I stop being Adolfina and turn into Fortunato. And I *am* Fortunato. I sit up on the ridgepole of the house and I have long conversations with the pigeons and I pick up two or three scorpions and pop them in my mouth and swallow them just like *that,* or maybe I let them sting me in the eyes. Sometimes I am Fortunato. (*Palace,* 203)

Adolfina identifies with Fortunato's liberating spirit, his ability to express himself freely. She finds in the dreaming and sensitive Fortunato, who spends his hours having "long conversations with the pigeons," a spiritual kinship. Yet, whereas Fortunato expresses himself openly, Adolfina, by contrast, must bury her emotions. As the oldest daughter and sister in a traditional Hispanic family, Adolfina takes on the role of the responsible caretaker who must abandon her dreams and hopes and sacrifice herself for her family.

In the following passage we see how Fortunato finds in Adolfina's deep frustration and emotional pain an equally reciprocal counterpart:

> It was at those times that he began to celebrate his first private sessions of weeping. It was at those times that he would hide behind the corn-

press and imitate Adolfina. . . . One day he picked up a withe of dried palm and put it up his ass just, perhaps, to feel a new kind of pain. That time he cried like Adolfina . . . (*Palace,* 38–39)

Like Adolfina, Fortunato is unfulfilled and desperate for emotional and physical contact with another individual. This is represented in the above passage by the (homo)sexual act of inserting the "withe of dried palm" into himself. This sexual stimulation establishes a special identification with Adolfina.

Throughout the novel Fortunato is seen in the bathroom, "his only refuge since they had moved to town" (*Palace,* 100), masturbating. The bathroom is likewise presented in the novel as Adolfina's only refuge. It is here, in private, where she can express her anger and dissatisfaction in long monologues of bitter resentment:

What *I'd* give good money to see is God showing His face around here. Let Him be a man and come in here, I'd show Him. I'd bust His face for Him. Listen, you old faggot, I'd say to Him—Why? Why? . . . I'd first say to Him and then I'd jump all over Him and then I'd kill Him again. Why don't you just come down here, You son of the biggest bitch that ever lived. (*Palace,* 131)

The grandmother's pleading "Adolfina! How long are you going to stay in the bathroom!" (*Palace,* 76) becomes a constant refrain throughout the entire text. In the end, both Fortunato and Adolfina reach such a state of frustration that even these momentary self-gratifying fantasies (Fortunato's masturbation and Adolfina's monologues of anger) are no longer sufficient. Action (or rather *interaction*) must be taken. Hence, Fortunato decides to join the rebel army and Adolfina makes one last attempt to find a man. In the following passage Fortunato, who has just finished masturbating, is overcome by a sense of futility; the "sensations" of this act, of his fantasies (also note how the "magic cousin" [Celestino] is mentioned), of his dreams, are no longer satisfying to him:

Sensation, sensation. Once again the awesome sensations . . . the voyage to dreamed-of places, . . . the fantasy of an encounter with that dreamed-of ideal person. . . . The place where all the slugs came out, the dog-rose bush, the magic cousin. . . . Pure invention. . . . But life is not to be borne when it is filled with only made-up people and unreal things. Life needs adventure, change, diversity— . . . the collisions of bodies, the running through real, and different, places. . . . It was futile to mastur-

bate again, futile to dance, . . . futile to gesture, cry like Adolfina . . .
(*Palace*, 101–3)

In a similar yet more delirious tone, Adolfina is moved to action. She
must do something, she must stop complaining and act. Thus, she
decides to go out on the town and lose her virginity:

> This very day I'm going to leave this house and go out and go to bed
> with the first man I find. Or a horse, for all I care, or a lizard, or a dog.
> Anything. . . . Do anything you feel like doing. Go to bed with any man
> that comes along. But do something. Do something. Do something. Ay,
> I want to do something. (*Palace*, 225)

Both Fortunato and Adolfina are moved to action by their isolation and
frustration. In the "fifth agony," characterized by a tremendous amount
of crisscrossing of voices, there appears on the same page Fortunato's
decision, "I think the best thing I can do now is go off and join the
rebels" (*Palace*, 248), as well as Adolfina's, "I'm going out this very night"
(*Palace*, 248). According to Jorge Olivares, the fifth agony "consists of the
pendular narration of these characters' respective quests; and, although
aware that Fortunato left home some days before Adolfina's special
evening, the reader is deceived by this narrative strategy and senses a
feeling of simultaneity."[22] The drawing together of Fortunato and Adolfina's attempts to change their existing situations is of interest because
one method of change or "revolution" (from the Old French *révolution*: a
sudden radical, fundamental, change) is not favored or valorized over the
other. Fortunato's political engagement is not presented as a superior or
nobler act than Adolfina's quest for physical and emotional contact. Still,
in the end both quests fail; Fortunato's flight for freedom tragically ends
when he is arrested, tortured, and executed by the Batista police, and
Adolfina returns home defeated, still a virgin, and sets herself afire.

In *The Palace of the White Skunks* Arenas provides the reader with a
disturbing portrait of the poverty and misery that were present in rural
Cuba shortly before the triumph of the revolution. Ironically, however,
while many Cuban novelists during the 1970s were writing documentary works idealistically presenting the revolution as the decisive
moment that radically transformed Cuban society for the better, Arenas,
undermining this rather utopian vision of history, portrays the revolution as the catalyst responsible for the death of his protagonist and the
emotional destruction of a family.

Farewell to the Sea

Fortunato dies in *The Palace of the White Skunks* only to reappear in *Farewell to the Sea* as the adult Hector.[23] With an entire history behind him (childhood and adolescence) Hector, now living under an institutionalized revolution, continues questioning his tortured existence and marginality. Structurally, *Farewell to the Sea* is an interplay of two monologues of personal frustration that work as a duo. Part I (the wife's discourse) and Part II (Hector's discourse) present the histories, dreams, memories, and hallucinations of this Cuban couple as they drive home to Havana after a six-day vacation at the beach. Part I is a straightforward narration that divides itself into six chapters, each corresponding to the six days spent at the beach. Part II, narrated by the poet Hector, is a dramatic meshing of poetry and prose divided into six cantos, each likewise corresponding to the six days of vacation. Furthermore, there exists an intertextual web that links both parts. Situations that occur in Part I are continued or resolved in Part II.

The story of *Farewell to the Sea* commences precisely when the six-day vacation has ended and the couple abandons the beach and begins their return trip home by car. At this moment both characters—first the wife, then Hector—begin to speak, to remember, to imagine, to dream, to sing of their personal frustrations and disenchantment. Although the wife relates the entire first part of the novel, she remains nameless throughout the text. The dominance of her discourse within the textual linearity of the novel (Part I) sets up the reader to rely on the authenticity of her voice. However, her discourse, and very existence, is challenged in the last sentences of the novel, when it is revealed that she is only an invention, a ghost or obsession of Hector's imagination: "There I go alone—like always—in the car. To the last second equanimity and rhythm—fantasy" (*Farewell,* 412). The traditional separation between creator and creation and the instance of narrating the fictional account are called into question. Like the child-narrator of *Singing from the Well,* Hector has created a double, an alter ego, in order to survive in a repressive environment that, in his particular case, excludes and condemns him on two counts: for being a political dissident and for being a homosexual. In *Farewell to the Sea* the autonomy and integrity of the character of the wife is totally discredited when it is revealed that she does not exist. Yet it is precisely through the negation of this developed and complex character, who narrates her memories, dreams, hallucinations, and fears over 193 pages of the text, that attention is called to Hector's need to invent, create, compose as a way to defend himself from a rigid and intolerant society that is extremely hostile toward transgressions from the norm and that believes that order is to be found in the preservation of an exemplary revolutionary social consciousness.

In my analysis of *The Palace of the White Skunks,* I established how Adolfina is presented as the feminine double of the adolescent Fortunato. This doubling pair reemerges not only in Hector/the nameless wife, but also in the figure of Tedevoro from canto 6 of *Farewell to the Sea,* a character who will also reappear in *El color del verano.*[24] (I use the original Spanish name "Tedevoro" instead of the English translation, Eachurbod.) Tedevoro serves as a symbolic synthesis of the three main pairing doubles we have examined so far: child-narrator/Celestino, Fortunato/Adolfina, and Hector/the nameless wife. Tedevoro's "constant yearning, . . . his perpetual need (never sated or appeased)" (*Farewell,* 357) is present in all three pairs. Furthermore, Tedevoro's sexual inversion echoes the masculine/feminine doubles of Fortunato/Adolfina and Hector/the nameless wife. In the text both masculine and feminine pronouns and past participles are used to refer to Tedevoro. When Tedevoro reappears in *El color del verano,* he (she) is described as carrying around a pistol and a little bottle of gasoline to kill himself (herself) just in case "estaba condenada a la virginidad" (*El color,* 70) (*she* was condemned to remaining a virgin). This passage is fraught with meaning because the pistol and gasoline are the objects responsible for Fortunato and Adolfina's deaths in *The Palace of the White Skunks.*

The Tedevoro story, as I call it, occurs immediately after the frustrated meeting between the adolescent young man and Hector at the beach. Therefore, it is composed by the poet-Hector in the aftermath of unfulfilled homoerotic desire. Tedevoro's inability to turn a trick is a reiteration of Adolfina's similar failure and of Hector's refusal to consummate his desire with the young man for fear that he is an agent of the secret police. Tedevoro's name—literally translated as "I devour you"—although meant as a pun, exposes the yearning and unsatisfied desire of Arenas's characters. The Tedevoro story is the final anecdote encountered by the reader before the text literally breaks open into a bifurcation of nervous anxiety. (The Tedevoro story concludes with a parody of Hamlet's famous soliloquy in which the poet-Hector questions his attempt even to continue speaking at all):

> Go on?
> Not go on?
> That is the question. (*Farewell,* 375)

The Tedevoro story injects the cantos, which at times are marked by the seriousness of Hector's tortured psyche, with a playfulness of camp laughter. Like other characters in Arenas's texts, Tedevoro creates an imaginary world populated by cartoon heroes and homosexual fantasies that allow him to escape from his own cruel environment. In the end, the reader discovers that Tedevoro, alias José Martínez Mattos, is found dead one morning, killed by the members of his very own community, the other homosexuals that frequented the beach urinals. It is important to recognize that the death of Tedevoro is not blamed on the political system but on human cruelty. In *Arturo, la estrella más brillante* ("The Brightest Star"), written around the same time as *Farewell to the Sea* but not published until 1984, Arenas again avoids simplistic political propaganda by suggesting that oppression is not solely the result of a repressive political system but of human cruelty. As we see in chapter 3, in "The Brightest Star" oppression not only is the result of a repressive government but is also evident in the behavior of the homosexual prisoners of the UMAP camp, who create their own hierarchy of power, a *sistership,* as they call it, that does not tolerate homosexuals who do not assimilate.

El color del verano (The Color of Summer)

In his autobiography, *Before Night Falls,* Arenas informs us that although *El color del verano* is the fourth novel of the *pentagonía,* it was in fact the last novel he wrote (*BNF,* xiii). He also tells of his determination, despite his precarious health, to complete the novel. In this respect *El color del verano* is a significant text, for with it Arenas was finally able to bring to a close a cycle of novels he began writing three decades earlier. The prologue to *El color del verano*—which playfully appears halfway through the text (pp. 246–50) and purposely erases the lines between fiction and metafiction—underscores that this fourth novel of the quintet documents through fiction the homosexual experience in Cuba during the 1960s and 1970s:

> De alguna forma esta obra pretende reflejar, sin zalamerías ni altisonantes principios, la vida entre picaresca y desgarrada de gran parte de la juventud cubana, sus deseos de ser jóvenes, de existir como tales. Predomina aquí la visión subterránea de un mundo homosexual que seguramente nunca aparecerá en ningún periódico del mundo y mucho menos en Cuba. Esta novela está intrínsecamente arraigada a una de las épocas

más vitales de mi vida y de la mayoría de los que fuimos jóvenes durante las décadas del sesenta y del setenta. *El color del verano* es un mundo que si no lo escribo se perderá fragmentado en la memoria de los que lo conocieron. (*El color,* 249)

To a certain extent this work pretends to reflect, without flattery or high-sounding principles, the life of a great portion of Cuban youths—somewhere between the picaresque and dissolute—their desires to be young and to exist as such. The underground vision of a homosexual world, which surely will never appear anywhere in newspapers, and much less in Cuba, predominates here in these pages. This novel is intrinsically tied to one of the most vital eras of my life and that of a great majority of us who were young during the sixties and seventies. If I don't write about it, *El color del verano* is a world that will be lost and fragmented in the memory of those that knew and lived it.

Who writes this prologue? The willfully ambiguous but provocative answer lies in the fact that both Reinaldo Arenas (the flesh-and-blood writer) and Gabriel/Reinaldo/the Tétrica Mofeta (the fictitious writer) are the writers of a novel entitled *El color del verano*. This *mise-en-abyme* undermines the authority of traditional authorship in which the writer presumes that he or she controls the work and can convey precisely what he or she wishes. Yet, the writer(s) of the prologue to *El color del verano* carefully underscore(s) the importance of recording this particular era in Cuban history that would be lost forever if not preserved in writing.

The prologue also reveals how the novel, originally conceived and started in Cuba, fell victim to revolutionary censorship on the island. In *El color del verano,* the Tétrica Mofeta, Arenas's fictitious alter ego, is forever rewriting his novel because it has been either confiscated, stolen, lost, or destroyed (for example, see pages 66, 108–9, 122, 202, 441); while Arenas, the extraliterary writer, recounts that he had to memorize certain chapters of *El color del verano*—for example, "El hueco de Clara" (Clara's hole) and the 30 tongue twisters—in order to guarantee the survival of these portions of the manuscript. (In fact, it was the manuscript of *Farewell to the Sea* that was confiscated and destroyed twice by the Cuban security police while Arenas was in Cuba. The author recounts his protracted struggles to rewrite and hide the manuscript to this novel in *Before Night Falls* [pp. 114, 119, 227].)

The prologue also underscores both the importance of the *pentagonía* in the writer's life as well as the societal significance of metaphorically representing twentieth-century Cuban history. Still, the writer confesses his contradictory feelings of grief and tenderness over what he refers to as the malady of Cuban history:

> Siento una desolación sin término, una pena inalcanzable por todo ese mal y hasta una furiosa ternura ante mi pasado y mi presente. Esa desolación y ese amor de alguna forma me han conminado a escribir esta pentagonía que además de ser la historia de mi furia y de mi amor es una metáfora de mi país. (*El color,* 248–49)

> I feel an interminable anguish, an unreachable pain as a result of all that wrong. Yet, I also feel a raging tenderness for my past and present life. In some way, that anguish and that love have driven me to write this pentagony, which in addition to being the story of my fury and my love is also a metaphor for my country.

The driving force behind the writer's desire to write this cycle of novels is revealed as a complicated combination of love and pain, a fusion of conflicting emotions that requires a metaphorical (literary) language to articulate and suggest. Thus, the novels of the *pentagonía* do not presume to be anything but what they are, fiction. And as fiction, they delight in the deployment of a poetic and metaphorical language that alludes, suggests, and evokes, touching the reader and drawing him or her into a dazzling and provocative literary space of multiple possibilities.

At one point in *El color del verano* we read:

> En aquella isla todo el mundo vivía por lo menos una doble vida: públicamente no dejaban ni un instante de alabar al tirano, secretamente lo aborrecían y ansiaban desesperadamente que reventase. (*El color,* 123)

> On that island everyone led at least a double life: in public they would unceasingly praise the tyrant while secretly hating him and desperately hoping he would kick the bucket.

The island on which the story of *El color del verano* is played out is explicitly identified as Cuba (p. 124). It is the summer of 1999 and the dictator Fifo is celebrating "fifty" years in power: "cincuenta años que en realidad son cuarenta, aumentados por él en diez más, pues él ama . . . los números redondos y la publicidad" (*El color,* 64) (fifty years which in fact are only forty, but he increased them because he loved . . . round numbers and publicity). Under Fifo's tyrannical rule the people on the island must shield their true feelings for fear of recrimination; they are forced to live double, even triple, lives in order to survive. In addition to creating an internal dialogue that enriches the resonances of characterization, the splitting of characters underscores the dishonesty and fear present within this totalitarian state in which individuals must fragment themselves into a multiplicity of selves, each fulfilling and meeting different social functions.

In *El color del verano* the first-person narrative voice is shared by Gabriel/Reinaldo/the Tétrica Mofeta. This trinity, like the poet Hector in part two of *Farewell to the Sea,* is responsible for writing the anecdotes, letters, tongue twisters, stories, and so forth that make up the novel and in turn give voice to Cuba's excluded and marginal homosexual subculture of the 1960s and 1970s. The splitting of the protagonist in three is explained early in the text. Gabriel, returning from the United States to visit his mother in the small Cuban town of Holguín, imagines himself confessing to her of his true self, or selves:

> No soy una persona, sino dos y tres a la vez. Para ti sigo siendo Gabriel, para aquéllos que leen lo que escribo y que casi nunca puedo publicar soy Reinaldo, para el resto de mis amigos con los cuales de vez en cuando me escapo para ser yo totalmente, soy la Tétrica Mofeta. (*El color,* 101)

> I'm not one person, but two or three at the same time. For you I am Gabriel, for those who read what I write, which I'm rarely able to publish, I'm Reinaldo, for the rest of my friends with whom from time to time I can escape and be totally myself, I'm the Tétrica Mofeta [the Gloomy Skunk].

In addition to underscoring how society's rejection of homosexuality forces the homosexual to hide behind a mask to avoid suspicion, Arenas's poetic trinity is also a parodic, sullen, and blasphemous (sub)version of the Catholic Trinity (Father, Son, and Holy Spirit in one divine Godhead) that reflects and gives voice to the very complex and contradictory human facets of the protagonist's personality. Reinaldo is the writer-creator (God the Father) who gives life to his characters. The nostalgic recollections of Gabriel (a biblical name of one of the archangels who appears as a divine messenger) must be sacrificed, like the son Jesus Christ, in order for the Tétrica Mofeta (the protagonist's vital homosexual spirit) to exist. In one of the last interviews he granted shortly before his death Arenas declared:

The Gloomy Skunk [the Tétrica Mofeta] undergoes a metamorphosis so he can extend his existence through that of various characters. He is a homosexual who lives in Cuba, the victim of all sorts of persecution. In spite of it all, he's trying to write a novel which the government is trying to find and destroy. He's got a double in the United States, Gabriel, . . . [who] has a series of complexes he can't overcome . . . because he didn't fulfill his mother's dream.[25]

The splitting of the protagonist in three is also alluded to in the novel's subtitle, "El nuevo jardín de las delicias" (The New Garden of Delights). Hieronymus Bosch's famous and provocative triptych, *The Garden of Delights*—a portion of which, incidentally, is reproduced on the cover of Arenas's 1989 collection of poems *Voluntad de vivir mani-festándose* (The Will to Live Manifesting Itself)—is a combination of three panels that represent the Garden of Eden and the creation of Adam and Eve (left panel), the joy of the senses of the world of the flesh (center panel), and the anguish of hell (right panel). Each character of the trinity Gabriel/Reinaldo/the Tétrica Mofeta corresponds to one of the panels: Gabriel who reminisces about his childhood in Holguín, his beginning (right panel, the creation); the homosexual extravagance and carnal exploits of the Tétrica Mofeta (center panel, the carnal desires and sensual appeal of the world of the flesh); and Reinaldo, who as he writes is dying from AIDS (left panel, the nightmarish and pestilential scenes of hell).

El color del verano contains one final allusion to a triad. The notion of trinity is also evoked in the divine Parcaes, or Three Fates, "Clotos, Láquesis y Atropos," who have condemned "Arenas (alias Gabriel, alias la Tétrica Mofeta)" (p. 235) for not trusting them with the fate of his novel. The three Parcae, or *Tria Fata,* who in Roman mythology were represented as spinners who presided over birth, marriage, and death, were identified by the Romans with the severe Greek Moirae. Originally a single divinity, the Moirae were three sisters: Cloto, whose turning distaff symbolized the course of existence; Lachesis, who distributed the lots received for each man; and Atropos, who without remorse cut the thread of life. As we can see, the sequence of birth (Gabriel), life (the Tétrica Mofeta), and death (Reinaldo) is again alluded to through the divine Parcaes.

El color del verano is an ambitious novel that synthesizes many of Arenas's major themes: among others, the quest for freedom, the love/hate relationship with the mother, the writer's need for expression. The story contains hundreds of characters engaging in wildly transgressive adventures as they prepare to celebrate the dictator's official fiftieth anniversary in power. The celebration ends in a homoerotic carnival that precipitates the fall of the state. The celebration within the novel is reflected in the carnivalesque images and structure of the actual text. *El color del verano* delights in what Mikhail Bakhtin saw as carnivalesque literature's mingling of the sacred with the profane, the high with the low, the sublime with the ridiculous and its attack on dogmatism, established authority, narrow-minded seriousness, and, we might add to this list, heterosexism. In his seminal study *Rabelais and His World* Bakhtin explored the roots of carnivalesque folk humor and observed: "No dogma, no authoritarianism, no narrow-minded seriousness can coexist with Rabelaisian images; these images are opposed to all that is finished and polished, to all pomposity, to ever ready-made solutions in the sphere of thought and world outlook" (Bakhtin, 3).

During the sixteenth century the world of the carnival was an opportunity to liberate individuals from all one-sided official seriousness through the inversion of hierarchy, of all so-called high culture. The topsy-turvy world view of the carnival revealed that established official authority was something relative that only led to dogmatism, a concept quite hostile to all progressive ideas of change and evolution. What Bakhtin saw in the Rabelaisian text—a rebellion against dogma, authoritarianism, and all type of seriousness—is likewise present in Arenas's texts. Like Rabelais, who subverted with excess and grotesque laughter the medieval world's ascetic worldview, the carnivalesque transgressions in *El color del verano* propose a festive and parodic critique of "Fifoism" (read Castroism) with its insistence on Marxist thought (historical materialism) taken to its limits. Arenas undermines the Marxist systematic view of history (that is, the idea of continuous progress, perpetual evolution) with the assertion that *El color del verano* is circular in structure, with no clearly distinguishable beginning or end. In the prologue Arenas (Gabriel/Reinaldo/the Tétrica Mofeta) proposes:

> Dejo a la sagacidad de los críticos las posibilidades de descifrar la estructura de esta novela. Solamente quisiera apuntar que no se trata de una obra lineal, sino circular y por lo mismo ciclónica, con un vértice o centro que es el carnaval, hacia donde parten todas las flechas. De modo que, dado su carácter de circunferencia, la obra en realidad no empieza ni termina en un punto específico y puede comenzar a leerse por cualquier parte hasta terminar la ronda. Sí, está usted, tal vez, ante la primera nov-

ela redonda hasta ahora conocida. Pero, por favor, no considere esto ni un
mérito ni un defecto, es una necesidad intrínseca a la armazón de la obra.
(*El color,* 249)

> I leave for the sagacity of the critics the possibilities of deciphering the
> structure of this novel. I would only like to point out that one is not deal-
> ing with a linear, but rather a circular work and for that very reason
> cyclonic, with a vertex or center that is the carnival, toward which all the
> coordinates radiate. And so, given its circumferential nature, the work
> really doesn't begin or end at a specific point and one can start to read it
> at any part going once around. Yes, you are perhaps holding the first
> known round novel. But please don't take this to be a sign of virtue or
> defect, but simply an intrinsic necessity in the framework of the work.

The insistence that the novel is circular challenges the idealistic
(utopian) notion of historical materialism by underscoring the simultaneity of events and not their serialization. This simultaneity is evi-
denced by the coexistence of famous Cuban historical and literary figures from different ages. In the end what is suggested is that the
corruption, banishment, political foul play, and injustices that have
plagued the Cuban people throughout their history have not been sur-
mounted but have been senselessly repeated.

Although the story of *El color del verano* takes place in the summer of
1999, the entire novel is but a carnivalesque document of what it was
like to be young and homosexual in Cuba during the 1960s and 1970s.
As we have seen, this setting is made evident in the prologue (pp.
246–50). When Arenas (Gabriel/Reinaldo/the Tétrica Mofeta) writes:
"*El color del verano* es un mundo que si no lo escribo se perderá fragmentado en la memoria de los que lo conocieron" (*El color,* 249) (If I don't
write about it, *El color del verano* is a world that will be lost and fragmented in the memory of those that knew and lived it), he emphasizes
his concern for preserving in fiction this particular era in Cuban history.

In his autobiography Arenas informs the reader of how he invented
tongue twisters while living in Cuba as literary weapons against those
individuals who betrayed him in one way or another (*BNF,* 238–39).
(Among others, Arenas mentions Miguel Barnet, Nicolás Guillén, and
Roberto Fernández Retamar.) Taken as a whole, the tongue twisters
lampoon the diabolical and backstabbing literary scene in revolutionary
Havana as well as that of the international literary establishment.
According to Arenas the tongue twisters became quite famous in

Havana in 1977. Roberto Valero confirms this in *El desamparado humor de Reinaldo Arenas* (The Forlorn Humor of Reinaldo Arenas) when he writes: "The majority of the tongue twisters circulated extensively throughout Havana. Writers knew them by heart, and a kind of oral and satirical samizdat was achieved" (Valero, 327, my translation). Valero's description of the tongue twisters as oral and satirical samizdats (from the Russian *samo,* or self, + *izdat* (*elstvo*), or publishing house) underscores their nature as subversive counter-texts to the established official publications of the revolutionary regime that were sanctioned and freely distributed on the island. In *El color del verano,* 30 of these tongue twisters are interspersed throughout the pages of the novel. Printed for the first time in this novel, these "oral" documents are finally free to express what was once prohibited and censored in Cuba. Through their publication the tongue twisters become powerful literary "documents" of Arenas's turbulent years in Havana after falling into disfavor with the Castro regime. For the most part, each tongue twister is a scathing attack directed at a given writer for his or her literary ego, sexual inclinations, or hypocrisy in supporting the Castro regime. In typical fashion, Arenas does not spare himself in these attacks; in one of the tongue twisters he deprecates himself for his own conceit and homosexual exploits:

> Ara, are, IRA, oro, uri . . .
> Con un aro y dos cadenas ara Arenas entre las hienas, horadando los eriales en aras de más aromas y orando a Ares por más oro porque todo su tesoro (incluyendo los aretes que usaba en sus areítos) los heredó un buga moro luego de hacerle maromas en el área de un urinario de Roma. Más no es Ares sino Hera quien con ira oye sus lloros. Y Arenas, arañando lomas, con su aro y sus cadenas, en el infierno carena teniendo por toda era (¡ella que era la que era!) un gran orinal de harina oriado con sus orinas. (*El color,* 107)

> Ara, are, IRA, oro, uri . . .
> With his hoop and two chains Arenas ploughs among the hyenas, tunneling into uncultivated lands for the sake of more aromas and praying to Ares for more gold, because he lost all his treasures (including the earrings that he used for his dances) to a Moorish bugger after fooling around with him in a urinal in Rome. But it isn't Ares but rather Hera who with ire hears his sobs. And Arenas, scraping hills, with his hoop and chains, careens into hell, having for all time (she who was who she was!) a great chamber pot of flour laced with his urine.

In *El color del verano* the inclusion of four letters written to and from the alter egos (Reinaldo/Gabriel/the Tétrica Mofeta) is another example of subversive literary documentation that, while it ignores any pretense to the reproduction of precise facts and figures, poignantly captures through its poetic liberties the emotional weight, the trials and tribulations, of living first under a revolution and then in exile. The first three letters (*El color,* 84, 166, 288) are marked by a tone of despair, sadness, and disillusionment in having to live in exile (Paris, New York, and Miami). Although the individual enjoys free expression in these cities, Reinaldo/Gabriel/the Tétrica Mofeta feels alienated and out of place. For example, the grey and coldness of Paris is contrasted to the tropical climate of Cuba; the dirty beaches of Long Island, New York, are quite different from the warm and blue waters of the Caribbean; and despite its tropical climate Miami is presented as a plastic imitation, a mere shadow of Cuba. The three letters written from exile also document the horrors of AIDS. In the fourth letter (p. 344) the Tétrica Mofeta, who finds himself in Cuba, writes to Reinaldo, Gabriel, and the Tétrica Mofeta, who are living in exile. In this final letter the Tétrica Mofeta sympathizes with the sorrows and afflictions of his alter egos, but feels that their pain cannot compare to the horrors of living under a tyrannical system in which citizens must cooperate with the laws and whims of a dictator. In addition, living with AIDS under a system that persecutes homosexuals, and that furthermore cannot provide needed medical attention, is far more horrifying. But instead of concentrating on the negative, the Tétrica Mofeta goes on to talk about his (their) writings, all of which make up "una sola obra totalizadora [cuyo] espíritu burlón y desesperado [sea tal vez] el de nuestro país" (*El color,* 344–45) (a single complete work [whose] mocking and desperate spirit [is perhaps] that of our own country). In *El color del verano,* just as in the other novels of the *pentagonía,* the precision of historical facts and figures is sacrificed for the vital and dynamic "documentation" that only fiction can provide. The four letters of *El color del verano* poetically and intuitively capture the complex feelings of fragmentation, dissatisfaction, and confusion that the protagonist (Reinaldo/Gabriel/the Tétrica Mofeta) experiences living both in and outside Cuba.

The Assault

The Assault presents a futuristic vision of Cuban society that Arenas allowed himself to imagine and completely create.[26] The text functions

as a literary forewarning of totalitarianism left unchecked, at its fright-
ening extreme. *The Assault* can be read as a Spanish American (Cuban)
version of the dystopian novel tradition as defined by such writers as
Aldous Huxley (*Brave New World*) and George Orwell (*Nineteen Eighty-
Four*). In fact, in one of Arenas's last interviews he stated that among the
novels that affected him most when he was young were *Animal Farm*
and *Nineteen Eighty-Four*: "I remember . . . that when I finished reading
Animal Farm and *Nineteen Eighty-Four* I was crying."[27]

The theme of a utopian new world has persisted in Latin American
literature, from Columbus's first description of a new earthly paradise in
his navigation diaries, through the accounts of Latin America's struggle
for independence in the early nineteenth century and its hope to build a
new polity (the most obvious literary example being Domingo Faustino
Sarmiento's famous essay *Facundo,* which denied the validity of the colonial past and projected all goals toward a utopian future), to Cuban revolutionary literature with its notion of a historical dialectic that progresses from darkness to a future enlightenment. *The Assault,* a cynical,
misanthropic, and dark novel, derides the notion of establishing an
American Utopia, much less a sane and caring world. Whereas many
Cuban novelists have written and continue to write realistic documentary works that idealize the revolution as radically transforming Cuban
society for the better, Arenas refused to subscribe to this idealistic vision
of history and portrayed the revolution as the catalyst responsible for the
persecution of certain members of Cuban society who simply failed, for
whatever reason, to fit the revolutionary model. In *The Assault,* the revolutionary misfits are once again homosexuals who become targets of the
nameless narrator, one of the great heroes of the nation, intent on eradi-
cating these "disgusting perverts" (*Assault,* 104).

The nameless narrator of *The Assault* is quite different from the
child-narrator/Celestino, Fortunato, Hector, Gabriel/Reinaldo/the Tétrica
Mofeta. Unlike these characters, who are victims of persecution, the
protagonist of the last novel of the *pentagonía* is the ruthless persecutor:
first and foremost of his mother, but also of homosexuals. Both persecutions, that is, hunting the mother down with the aim of destroying
her (introduced immediately on the first page of the novel) and the per-
secution/extermination of homosexuals (introduced with sarcastically
humorous overtones in chapter 32), are coupled together in the novel.
In fact, it is precisely when the nameless narrator is having no luck in
finding his mother that he decides to tackle the "homosexual problem,"
a situation that reaches ridiculously hyperhomophobic proportions and

serves to mitigate his rage toward his mother. (As the head of the "Army of Moral Reconquest of the Nation," the nameless narrator mercilessly carries out orders to annihilate any male who lets his gaze, even for a split second, fall on the area bounded between the knees and the waist of another male. As it turns out, some of the special agents assigned to rounding up "perverts" request that they be allowed to wear special blinders to keep them from accidentally looking down on the prohibited area. This request so enrages the nameless narrator, for in it he sees an implicit admission of criminal tendency, that he annihilates "all the agents that wrote it [the request], touched it, carried it, caught sight of it, etc." [*Assault,* 98].) In *The Assault,* the protagonist's repressed homosexual desire and Oedipus complex is literally played out for the reader, who is challenged to confront his or her own anxieties and panic concerning these issues.

The nameless narrator's misanthropy is the result of having lived all his life under a tyrannical and abominable society that degrades and debases human beings. In the world of *The Assault* individuals have no names; they are referred to as "vermins," "wild beasts," "filthy rodents." With their claws, grunting and snorting noises, and fetid smells, they are more like animals, sometimes walking on four legs and coupling, or "grappling" (as it is also called), for purposes of procreation. The nameless narrator is repulsed by all physical contact. At one point in the novel, when a female creature makes advances toward him, his physical as well as emotional repugnance is evident: "*She touched me, the filthy creature touched me, I have been pawed by that disgusting rodent.* I shiver in disgust, and I go on beating myself. *She touched me, she squeezed me.* As I run, I vomit. My flesh crawls" (*Assault,* 73).

The nameless narrator's hate for his mother is the result of a castration fear/Oedipal desire. Believing that he resembles her more and more each day and that the moment will arrive when he will finally turn into her, he decides to destroy her: "My face was more and more my mother's face. I was coming to look more like her every day . . . . I ran outside . . . touching my face with my claws and saying to myself *I'm her, I'm her, and if I don't kill her soon I'll be exactly like her*" (*Assault,* 2). *The Assault* transgressively challenges one of the most revered images of Cuban society, the mother as symbol of goodness, selflessness, and virtue.[28] (In the first four novels of the pentalogy the presentation of the figure of the mother fluctuates between two diametrically opposed images: the loving, caring, affectionate, and nurturing mother and the brutal, diabolical, chastising witch. *Farewell to the Sea* contains a foreshadowing of the last novel of the pentalogy in the allegory of the tyrannical Great Big Mama of the second canto, a type of tropical female Big Brother. This diabolical mother, malevolent, forever vigilant, described as cupping her imaginary testicles, attempts to procreate an ideal society of the future. The allegory is centered around her pursuit of a heterosexual couple whose only crime is that they wish to escape to a place where dreaming is permitted. But their refusal to adhere to her orders drives Great Big Mama into a frenzy, for she is not accustomed to disobedience by her faithful subjects who, always submissive, have modeled themselves after the dog: "The dog! The dog! LET US ALL BE LIKE HIM!" [*Farewell*, 215]. Thus begins an interplanetary search for the fugitives; it ends in their death, but at the cost of an apocalyptic destruction of the universe.)

In *The Assault,* the mother is presented as an uncompromising malevolent authoritarian force who ties down and makes demands on the nameless narrator. If the nameless narrator wishes to be (sexually) free, his only choice is to rebel against, that is, destroy, the mother force that circumscribes him. But to kill the mother, he must go across the nation looking for her, and in order to do this, he first has to obtain special permission from the government, which no longer allows its citizens to move around freely. As an agent of the Bureau of Counterwhispering (because the citizens are forced to say what the government tells them to say, they sometimes rebel by whispering other words, something that is prohibited) the protagonist can freely go across the country looking for his mother. One day when the Represident, the absolute dictator, is about to speak, the protagonist, who as a national hero finds himself on the platform with the dictator, suddenly realizes that the dictator is in fact his mother in disguise. He advances toward her in order to kill her, but as he advances he begins to get an erection. His member grows to excessive proportions as he advances toward his mother. The mother, recognizing her son, fears for her life. The battle between them then commences; the protagonist penetrates his mother with his erect member and the mother cries out and explodes. What remains are some nuts and bolts, oil and mechanical gears. The novel is precisely titled *The Assault* because the protagonist overtakes his mother's power and control. In the end, the people who had been enslaved start to whisper louder and louder as they advance toward the platform. The final moment of the novel has the protagonist retreating to the sea while the people destroy everything and finally take control.

This aberrant and unorthodox final scene, with its graphic taboo image of incest, challenges the reader. With this, the last novel of the pentalogy, Arenas has written perhaps one of the most dark and inhuman novels in Spanish American literature. Yet, through the excessive negativity and malevolence of the protagonist and his dystopian vision of society, the reader is given access to the sinister and pervasive brutality of totalitarianism run amok.

Unlike the other novels of the *pentagonía,* in which the first person narrative voice is contradictory, unreliable, split and permutated, the narrative voice in *The Assault* appears at first glance to be quite reliable. Yet, as the reader begins to sense the extreme anger and hostility of the nameless protagonist, the question no longer becomes whether the reader can rely on his voice but rather what reader would take sides or identify with such a vile and repulsive individual whose verbal onslaughts and vilifications directly assault him or her. The narrator's tirades, outspoken hatred for his mother, misanthropic nature, and relentless persecution of homosexual activity do little to help establish an immediate and trusting relationship with the reader.

The Assault relies more heavily on the use of chronology than do the other novels of the *pentagonía* as a result of the thriller-detective format that it utilizes.[29] The detective story supports the idea that history can be reinterpreted and rescued from distorted accounts. The belief in causality, the complicity between the subject and his or her consciousness of a past, is very much the product of a belief that clues and vestiges of the past can be used to reveal the so-called truth about the present.

Arenas's cultivation of the thriller-detective genre in no way follows the Cuban revolutionary model for the genre. In the latter the detective-protagonist is an ordinary member of society who works with an efficient revolutionary police force that is assisted by concerned and responsible Cuban citizens. In *The Assault* the thriller-detective structure describes a very specific milieu with unique characters and events: a vile and abominable Orwellian society in which individuals have been so persecuted and browbeaten by the state that they have virtually lost their humanity.

Tzvetan Todorov dedicates a chapter of *The Poetics of Prose* to the detective fiction genre.[30] He begins his essay by making a distinction between two subgenres of detective fiction: the whodunit and the thriller. I would like to focus on the two characteristics of the thriller subgenre as Todorov discusses them. First, in the thriller (unlike in the whodunit, in which the story of the crime ends before the [second] story of the investigation begins) there is no story told about a crime anterior to the moment of the narrative. The act or process of saying coincides and is simultaneous with the (chronological) action; the reader's interest is sustained by suspense, the expectation of what will happen. Second, according to Todorov, is the thriller's tendency to description. Todorov quotes Marcel Duhamel, the thriller's most active promoter in France, as saying that in the thriller the reader finds "violence—in all its forms, and especially the most shameful—, beatings, killings. . . . Immorality is as much at home here as noble feelings . . . There [are] also . . . violent passions, implacable hatred" (Todorov, 48). Todorov summarizes Duhamel's thoughts when he adds: "Indeed it is around these constants that the thriller is constituted: violence, generally sordid crimes, the amorality of the characters" (Todorov, 48).

The thriller's two main characteristics are present in the last novel of the pentalogy. First, the narrative world of *The Assault* is indeed filled with sordid images and scenes of extreme violence, beatings, and general depravity. Second, chronology is respected and utilized to build suspense, also a necessary element of the thriller subgenre. Nonetheless, Arenas's thriller is anything but traditional in its subject matter, descriptions, or themes. The nameless narrator, fearing he is turning into his mother, spends the entire novel in search of her so that he can destroy her. This frantic search, creating suspense, intensifies throughout the novel until the moment when the nameless narrator is invited to the Gran Tribune where he finally spots his mother, who in the end turns out to be the dictator. Perla Rozencvaig, in her last interview with Arenas, comments on the mounting suspense present in *The Assault*: "The tension really mounts when we find out who the hunted man is." Arenas's reply: "Sure, but that's like all my novels: masks and carnival, where the object of the chase reveals its double identity when captured. That's how the pentagony was supposed to end" (Rosencvaig, 80). Arenas's remark underscores the deliberate ambivalence of his novels, their duplicity (masks) and carnivalesque qualities. The denouement of *The Assault,* which the writer professes is the way the cycle "was supposed to end," can be read as a carnivalesque scene that indulges in the excess of the material body (grotesquerie) as a way of coming to terms with the (homo)sexual body-image of the protean narrator of the pentalogy who has struggled with his sexual feelings since the first novel of the five-book series.

Bakhtin saw in Rabelais's work a predominant role assigned to all corporeal bodily functions. Inherited from the culture of folk humor, these bodily functions created what Bakhtin termed a "grotesque realism." Grotesque realism uses material bodily functions, despite their vulgarity, as images of fertility and growth. According to Bakhtin, images of the human body as bulging and over-sized are common in carnivalesque literature. The image of the carnival body is one of impure corporeal bulk, with its lower regions (buttocks and genitals) given priority over the upper ones (head, spirit, reason). All these grotesque qualities are seen as positive and cosmic forces in Bakhtin's analysis. In the final scene of *The Assault* the nameless narrator penetrates his mother with his enlarged penis and finally destroys her. This passage recreates a scene of grotesque realism in which the protagonist finally defeats the mother (authoritarian symbol of power who repressed her son's sexual orientation) by sexually possessing her. Through this act the protagonist accepts his own body-image and is finally able to stretch out on the sand and rest. (The German tradition of the bildungsroman [e.g., J. W. von Goethe's *Wilhelm Meister's Apprenticeship,* 1795 – 1796] ends on a positive note. If the dreams of the hero's youth are perhaps over, so too are the many painful disappointments of life.) Clearly, the copulation with the mother, a societal taboo, can be read as a transcoding or displacement of the narrator's reaffirmation of his own homosexuality.

To enter the fictive universe of the novels of the *pentagonía* is to enter a precarious space that (re)asserts its freedom from the rigidness and the banal set of narrative responses of orthodox Cuban socialist realism. Arenas's novels belong to contemporary postmodern literature's unmasking of the inherent naivete in the realistic novel's claim to veracity, to the belief that the literary text can indeed be a guarantor of fixed meaning, a repository of irrefutable truth. *Singing from the Well, The Palace of the White Skunks, Farewell to the Sea, El color del verano,* and *The Assault* are self-conscious texts that present a plurality of voices that dismantle all hierarchical discourses. The *pentagonía* shatters all expected generic boundaries and limitations in an attempt to provide the reader with a literary space of multiple possibilities. For Arenas, writing as a literary creative act was a necessity, a liberating act of self-expression, an emotional act of fury in which he challenged, undermined, and subverted all types of ideological dogmatism, all forms of absolute truths. This liberating energy, which takes on its own singular meaning and particular artistic goal in each text in the writer's oeuvre, is the single most salient feature of Arenas's writing.

In *The Art of the Novel* the Czechoslovakian writer Milan Kundera has suggested that perhaps all writers write a kind of single theme in their first work, and variations thereafter.[31] I believe that this observation is valid in speaking of Arenas's work. If one carefully examines his entire literary production one finds an argumentative center that persistently resurfaces: a staunch defense of the individual's imaginative capabilities and self-expression in a world beset by barbarity, intolerance, and persecution.

Arenas's declaration that the *pentagonía* can be read as both a secret history of Cuba and a writer's autobiography underscores the polysemous and intentionally paradoxical nature of these texts, which are part history, part autobiography, and part lyrical cry against the malevolent forces of society that impede the individual's (and most specifically the homosexual's) search for happiness. Despite, or perhaps as a result of, their fictitious, magical, and lyrical qualities, these novels succeed in presenting a vital and critical attitude of twentieth-century Cuban politics, economy, and society, and on a more universal level, of humankind's propensity for discrimination, bigotry, and intolerance. In the end, the novels of the *pentagonía* speak not only to the Cuban community in and outside of Cuba, but to all individuals who cherish and respect the individual's right to choose and express him- or herself freely.

Chapter Three

Two Tales of Oppression: "Old Rosa" and "The Brightest Star"

"La Vieja Rosa" ("Old Rosa") was first published in the short story collection *Con los ojos cerrados* (With My Eyes Closed),[1] which Arenas managed to smuggle out of Cuba with the help of the distinguished Uruguayan critic Angel Rama. As Roberto Valero documents in his book *El desamparado humor de Reinaldo Arenas* (The Forlorn Humor of Reinaldo Arenas), Arenas gave the manuscript of *Con los ojos cerrados* to Angel Rama during a visit the critic made to Havana. At the time, Arenas had fallen out of favor with the revolutionary regime and was considered a marginalized writer. It was only after arriving in the United States in 1980 that Arenas found out that *Con los ojos cerrados* had indeed been published by Editorial Arca in Uruguay. According to Valero, Arenas received not a single copy of the book or any royalties for the Arca edition. As a result, a deep hostility developed between Arenas and Angel Rama (Valero, 287).[2]

In 1981 the stories of *Con los ojos cerrados* were republished under a new title, *Termina el desfile* (The Parade Ends).[3] In addition to the eight stories of *Con los ojos cerrados,* this collection contained a new story, "Termina el desfile," serving as counterpoint to the first story of the previously published collection, "Comienza el desfile" (The Parade Begins).[4] "Comienza el desfile" and "Termina el desfile," the first and last stories of the text, fictionalize two poles of the Cuban historical process: the triumph of the revolution in 1959 and the 1980 Peruvian Embassy incident in which more than 10,000 Cubans, dissatisfied with the regime, sought refuge. This last incident ultimately led to the Mariel exodus in which 125,000 Cubans, Arenas among them, left the island via the port of Mariel.[5] With the exception of "Termina el desfile," written in Miami in 1980, and thus making it Arenas's first piece of fiction written in the United States, all the stories in *Termina el desfile* were written between the years 1964 and 1968. Before proceeding with an analysis of "Old Rosa" and "The

Brightest Star," let me briefly comment on the homosexual undercurrents already present in these earlier stories of *Termina el desfile*.[6]

Termina el desfile

Out of the eight stories of *Termina el desfile* that are dated between 1964 and 1968, six stories contain subtle yet clear homosexual allusions. Only "Con los ojos cerrados" (With My Eyes Closed) and "Bestial entre las flores" (Bestial Among the Flowers) do not contain homosexual references. Because of the presence of a young child-narrator, these two stories are closely tied to Arenas's first novel, *Singing from the Well*. Although there are no homosexual allusions in "Con los ojos cerrados," "Bestial entre las flores" in fact does contain one brief passing mention of homoerotic activity at the beginning of the story when Bestial tells the child-narrator, " 'Get down on all fours and I'll show you what feels good,' (I ran away)" (*Termina*, 113; my translation). The years 1964 to 1968 coincide precisely with the most dramatic persecution of homosexuals in Cuba, which led to the creation of the now infamous UMAP concentration camps active from 1965 to 1969. Hence, Arenas's caution in the treatment of the theme of homosexuality in these stories is well warranted. Still, Arenas did inscribe, albeit in a veiled fashion, homoerotic desire into many of these earlier tales.

In the first story, "Comienza el desfile" (The Parade Begins, 1965), the narrator's friendship with and admiration for a rebel soldier is marked by homosexual undertones. Throughout their triumphal march back to Holguín, the young adolescent narrator literally cannot take his eyes off the rebel soldier, who he has befriended. Admiration becomes mixed with homoerotic desire as is evident in the following comment by the adolescent narrator: "Tú, con el uniforme que de mojado se te pega a las nalgas" (*Termina*, 10) (You, with your wet uniform sticking tightly to your ass).

In "La sombra de la mata de almendras" (In the Shade of the Almond Tree, 1967) the narrator attempts to seduce a young woman but suffers from sexual impotence, a condition metaphorically associated with the threat of cutting down a beloved almond tree in the young man's backyard. Apparently, the beloved tree is where "todos los pájaros del barrio se refugian" (*Termina*, 76) (all the birds [let us recall that *pájaros* in Cuban slang refers to homosexuals] in the neighborhood seek refuge).

"Los heridos" (The Wounded, 1967) presents the theme of the double so common in Arenas's work. Here the main character, suggestively named Reinaldo, hides and secretly nurtures a wounded young man, his alter ego, also named Reinaldo, who is on the run from the police. (The scene is reminiscent of a moment in *The Palace of the White Skunks* in which Fortunato fantasizes nurturing back to health his wounded friend, Aby.) The entire incident occurs against the backdrop of the watchful eye of an authoritarian mother on the lookout for deviant behavior.

In the enigmatic tale "El reino de Alipio" (Alipio's Kingdom, 1968), the character Alipio is presented as an avid observer of the heavenly stars. Early in the story it is noted that the only career Alipio would have been interested in had he studied would have been uranography, a branch of astronomy concerned with the description and mapping of the heavens. Yet the term also evokes the word "Uranian," derived from Plato's *Symposium* and used by the leaders of the English homosexual emancipation movement in the late nineteenth century to designate male love for adolescent boys. In "El reino de Alipio" Alipio has an allegorical dream in which he is persecuted by a menacing light that "lanza chispazos que fulminan a los pájaros de la noche" (*Termina,* 102) (hurls down sparks that fulminate the birds of the night). (Note: In Spanish, when the noun object of a verb is a definite person or personified thing, it is preceded by the preposition *a*. Arenas's choice to use the personal *a* before the direct object noun "pájaros" [birds] reveals that these birds symbolize individuals.) After his dream, Alipio awakes to find himself in a pool of semen. Terrified, he abandons his habit of looking at the stars.

In "El hijo y la madre" (The Mother and Son, 1967) a son, whose room is described as "una pajarera gigante" (a large bird cage), awaits the arrival of a male friend. Yet the son is quite afraid of telling his mother about the visit given the mother and son's unspoken pact in which no one should come between them. The son's fear and guilt so overpower him that he does not answer the door when the friend finally arrives. In a clever ending, the reader discovers that the son, now an old man and his mother long dead, is living alone in the house. This rather pathetic ending reveals the experiences of homosexuals who sacrifice their sexual desire for the sake of traditional social expectations.

As we can see from these brief descriptions, these stories represent subtle homosexual moments that when read retrospectively take on greater signification. Even the story "Termina el desfile" (The Parade Ends), written in the safety of the United States in 1980, only dares to hint at the special friendship that the main character, depicted as living "al margen" or on the margins, has with another young man, a man who he describes as "su triunfo, su tabla de salvación, su consuelo" (*Ter-*

mina, 151) (his triumph, his last resource, his consolation). Even when the special friend turns out to be a government informer—a theme that will subsequently reappear in such texts as *Farewell to the Sea* and "Viaje a La Habana" (Journey to Havana)—at least the protagonist, unlike the son/old man in "El hijo y la madre", allows himself to engage in an intimate relationship with another man.

"Old Rosa" and "The Brightest Star"

Dated 1966, "Old Rosa" was originally intended for publication in Cuba, but after the controversial censorship of Arenas's well-known novel *The Ill-Fated Peregrinations of Fray Servando,* the Cuban revolutionary government never permitted its release. As previously noted, "La Vieja Rosa" was first published in the short story collection *Con los ojos cerrados* (1972). Later it appeared by itself in a limited edition of three thousand copies published by Editorial Arte in Caracas in 1980.[7] One year later, the novella once again appeared in the new collection, *Termina el desfile.* When it was finally translated into English, "Old Rosa" appeared together with *Arturo, la estrella más brillante* ("The Brightest Star")—a story completed in 1971 but not published until 1984— under one title, *Old Rosa, A Novel in Two Stories;* "Old Rosa" was translated by Ann Tashi Slater and "The Brightest Star" by Andrew Hurley.[8] Although "Old Rosa" and "The Brightest Star" together tell the stories of Old Rosa and her youngest son, Arturo, the 1989 English edition was in fact the first time that both texts had been presented together in one volume. In Spanish, both works have always been published and rereleased in separate editions.

"Old Rosa" and "The Brightest Star" have been identified by different critics on various occasions as either long stories or short novels, that is, novellas or novelettes. In English there exists both "novella" and "novelette" as terms to describe a short novel or extended short story that concentrates on a single event or chain of events that often has a surprising turning point or conclusion. (In the United States novelette is synonymous with novella, whereas in England novelette has the connotation of being a trivial or sensationalistic novel.) The actual term "novella" comes from the Italian word *novella,* meaning "novelty," which was first applied to the short stories found in Boccaccio's *Decameron.* At the end of the eighteenth century, German writers, among them Johann Wolfgang von Goethe, adopted the Italian term to German. In German, *novelle* describes a fictional prose tale that conforms more or less in meaning and length to the English sense of novella. In Spanish, *novella* is rendered either as *novela corta* (short novel) or *noveleta*.

In Arenas's correspondence (dated 1980–1983), housed at the Princeton University Firestone Library, are a number of letters that were written and exchanged between the author and the prominent Cuban film director Néstor Almendros. In one letter Arenas writes to Almendros about "The Brightest Star," a text he refers to as "un cuento" (a story). In his reply, Almendros corrects Arenas by calling "The Brightest Star" "una narración larga" (a long narration) of political strength. The debate over whether "The Brightest Star" and "Old Rosa" are indeed long stories, short novels, novellas, or novelettes is futile, especially in light of Arenas's designation of both texts as two instances, two narrative moments, that together constitute a novel—that elastic, inherently anarchical, ill-defined, and inexhaustible genre that critics have spent centuries trying, unsuccessfully, to pin down. Throughout this chapter, I will use both the terms "story" and "novella" to refer to "Old Rosa" and "The Brightest Star." (Later, in chapter 4 where I analyze the collection *Viaje a La Habana* [Journey to Havana], I will also use both "story" and "novella" to refer to the three stories/novellas that make up that collection, a collection that Arenas significantly subtitled "Novela en tres viajes" [A Novel in Three Journeys]).

The 1980 edition of *La Vieja Rosa,* published by Editorial Arte in Caracas, contains an appendix that reproduces an interview with Arenas conducted by Cristina Guzmán while Arenas still was living in Cuba. In a brief introduction, Ms. Guzmán first describes her odyssey in trying to find Arenas, who she describes as living a secret and clandestine life: "Nadie en La Habana parece poder o querer recordar su nombre. Menos aún su dirección" (*Vieja Rosa,* 103) (Nobody in Havana appears to be able or even wants to remember his name, much less his address). Yet Ms. Guzmán eventually does find Arenas living in a tiny apartment in Old Havana; this dwelling of course is the run-down Monserrate Hotel that Arenas describes in detail in his autobiography, *Before Night Falls* (239–73). Given the fact that the interview was conducted with the intention of being included in the Editorial Arte limited edition of *La Vieja Rosa,* Ms. Guzmán specifically asks Arenas to explain his particular use of the *noveleta* form. With his usual propensity for not allowing himself to be pinned down, Arenas responds:

> Perhaps the novella or novelette allows one to write something that is not either the short story or a large scale novel; the novella or novelette does

not take all the time and energy that a novel with so many characters and such a large scale world takes . . . Perhaps one can also say that it is a large scale novel, but written as a novella or novelette. Later the characters can be connected and one can make a novel. (*Vieja Rosa*, 107–8, my translation)

The idea of connecting or joining characters is precisely what Arenas did when he agreed to publish "Old Rosa" and "The Brightest Star" in the same English edition, an edition he rechristened "A Novel in Two Stories." Together, "Old Rosa" and "The Brightest Star," originally written five years apart and independently published in Spanish for the first time in 1972 and 1982 respectively, tell the stories of Old Rosa—a powerful landowner whose desire for absolute control is undermined by the social changes of the Cuban revolution—and her youngest son, Arturo—an individual imprisoned and persecuted both emotionally, by the memories of his domineering mother, as well as physically, by a new revolutionary system that locks him up in a forced labor camp simply for being homosexual.

If one carefully examines Arenas's oeuvre—for example, such works as *Singing from the Well, The Ill-Fated Peregrinations of Fray Servando, Farewell to the Sea, Persecución, The Doorman,* among others—one finds an argumentative center that persistently resurfaces: a staunch defense of the individual's imaginative capabilities and freedom of expression in a world beset by brutality and persecution. Although this preoccupation with freedom of expression and the struggles that unavoidably arise whenever human beings find themselves oppressed by authoritarian systems of power is articulated in many texts by the Cuban writer, the development of the oppressor/oppressed theme in "Old Rosa," and then the continuation of the story and the further consideration of other aspects of the same theme in a subsequent companion text, "The Brightest Star," calls for special critical attention. Whereas each novella deals with its own particular issues of oppression, manifested during two distinct eras (prerevolutionary and revolutionary Cuba), a reading of both texts interconnects, transforms, and rewrites these issues, thus providing a more penetrating look at the broader questions of domination and submission. Although the intertextual relation between oppressor and oppressed that links these two stories, a relation based on violence and repression, is played out in the specific context of Cuban history, the author's observations concerning these issues have timeless and universal resonance.[9]

"Old Rosa"

Set in rural Cuba shortly before the outbreak of the revolution, "Old Rosa" is the story of a strong-willed woman whose unrelenting pride and desire for absolute control demand that things be done her way. This inflexible, authoritarian, and domineering female figure is not new within the Hispanic literary tradition. In Spanish literature, for instance, we have the examples of Benito Pérez Galdós's doña Perfecta (*Doña Perfecta,* 1876) as well as Federico García Lorca's Bernarda Alba (*The House of Bernarda Alba,* 1936).[10] Similarly, in Spanish American letters Rómulo Gallegos has provided us with the figure of doña Bárbara (*Doña Bárbara,* 1929), "la devoradora de hombres" (the man-eating woman), and Gabriel García Márquez has also presented all-powerful matrons in his work: the tyrannical Big Mama of "Big Mama's Funeral" (1962) and the heartless grandmother in "The Incredible and Sad Tale of Innocent Eréndira and Her Heartless Grandmother" (1972).

It is not my intention here to enter into a discussion of the possible misogyny behind certain portrayals of women in Hispanic letters. Let me establish, however, that Arenas's character of Old Rosa is not a misogynous portrait, as perhaps some might erroneously conclude, but rather is a deconstruction of the figure of the oppressor (by that I mean an individual, regardless of gender, who considers him- or herself to be the only source of authority and who subsequently utilizes a tyranny of "Truth" to control, dominate, and exploit others). Furthermore, the figure of the domineering mother also allows Arenas to explore the mother-son love-hate relationship at the heart of the Oedipus complex, which in traditional Freudian analysis has been used to explain male homosexuality. In short, "Old Rosa" deals with the broader question of domination and authority figures who abuse their power and position to dominate others capriciously. In Arenas's texts, repressive figures of authority are not delineated by gender but rather by their abuse and hostility. The representation of abusive masculine figures as well as oppressive institutions created and supported by a dominant masculine ideology abound in Arenas's writing, for example, the grandfather in *Singing from the Well* and *The Palace of the White Skunks* who persecutes the protean character of the first two novels of the *pentagonía* for his unorthodox writings. On the other hand, the civil and ecclesiastical persecutions suffered by Fray Servando in *The Ill-Fated Peregrinations of Fray Servando* as well as the excessive capitalism that oppresses Juan in *The Doorman* are examples of patriarchal institutions that likewise favor the masculine. Finally, Old Rosa can also be seen as a precursor of the tyrannical Great Big Mama of the second canto of Arenas's *Farewell to the Sea* (210–26).[11]

In *Old Rosa,* Rosa's dictating nature, modeled after a patriarchal logic that utilizes religion and traditional family values to maintain power, are underscored in the very first pages of the novella, when the reader immediately sees how she behaves with her fiancé, Pablo, during a typical Sunday visit:

> [Pablo] grasped her hands in his and asked her to let him sit on the sofa, next to her, for the wedding would be very soon. But she, as always, not only forbade him to sit at her side, she also withdrew her hand and recited the words *honor,* and *family,* and *respect.* And Pablo moved uneasily in his chair, and when it came time to leave he stood up very solemnly, with his hands in his pockets. ("Old Rosa," 4)

Even after marrying Pablo, Rosa's obsessive need to exercise control over every aspect of her life is made evident in her refusal to have sexual relations with her husband on their wedding night. Submitting to her husband's sexual desires bring a whole new set of problems for Rosa, who finds it difficult to lose herself, give up her control, in such a carnal act. Sex becomes a power issue for Rosa, who must now decide where it fits, or even whether it should fit, into her new life. But in spite of her doubts and misgivings concerning sex, Rosa, a woman bound by the traditional social mores of her era, does have children. First Armando, then Rosa María are born. A few years later, although two months premature, Arturo is born. One year after Arturo's birth Rosa has another son, but this time the baby immediately dies. In bed, her body racked by convulsions, Rosa swears to herself never again to become pregnant. And to ensure this, she refuses ever again to have sexual relations with Pablo. Through her negation, her forced chastity, Rosa regains the power and control she felt she had lost. Meanwhile, Pablo begins to lose his position as husband and man of the house. Rosa's stubborn refusal to have sexual relations with him, coupled with his heavy drinking, ultimately drives Pablo to commit suicide on Christmas Eve. Far from feeling grief or sorrow, Rosa interprets her husband's suicide as a personal assault intended to spoil and ruin the Christmas Eve festivities that she had carefully organized to impress the neighbors of their growing wealth:

> At midnight, when the laughter of the guests was at its noisiest, [Rosa's] mother called her to the yard and led her to the trees that grew near the

well. Look, she said, gesturing toward the topmost branches of the cus-
tard apple tree. Rosa crossed herself, as she was saying, My God, she was
thinking: he did it to spoil my Christmas Eve. That's why he did it. She
had organized this celebration (in spite of the fact that the waste of
money and food vexed her soul) to show the neighbors and her family her
position. And also, she said, because this is the one celebration of the year
you can't miss. Such were her thoughts. ("Old Rosa," 12)

After Pablo's death Rosa, little by little, by buying land from her
neighbors and assuming mortgages, manages to become a great
landowner who rules over her workers, as well as her children, with dictatorial severity. No one dares to question Rosa's autocratic authority, a
position of absolute power that pleases her greatly. Rosa becomes a
wealthy and despotic landowner whose word must be taken as law.

Even though Rosa works hard to acquire her wealth, the reader is
never mistaken in seeing her as a woman who simply wishes to be
accepted as an equal within a male-dominated society. Much more than
that, Rosa formulates her self-identity by adopting a phallocentric order
that works within the dominating discourse of a patriarchal logic.
("Phallocentrism," or the primacy of the phallus, posits that men are the
origin of meaning and value. It has been used by feminist theorists to
describe the structuring of man in society as the central reference point
of thought.) Rosa empowers herself within a masculine economy that
takes on (mimes) the exploitative discourses of patriarchy.

By classifying Rosa as a patriarchal figure, I am utilizing patriarchy as
it has been defined by feminist criticism, that is, an abusive authoritarian
system that privileges the masculine and marginalizes the feminine.
Nelle Morton states: "[Patriarchy] has been described as a way of
structuring reality in terms of good/evil, authority/obedience, power/
powerless, . . . master/slave. The first in each opposite was assigned to
the patriarchal father, or the patriarch's Father God, frequently indistin-
guishable from one another. The second, to women as "the other" and in
time to all "others" who could be exploited."[12] In "Old Rosa," Rosa sees
herself as a feared figure of authority. She bosses everyone around and
considers those who surround her as mere figures of servitude who must
obey her unconditionally. In his study, "Treinta años de soledad: La Vieja
Rosa" (Thirty Years of Solitude: Old Rosa),[13] William L. Siemens presents
Rosa as a matriarchal figure without ever defining or explaining matriarchy, a term that, as Lisa Tuttle has well pointed out, must be carefully
explained as a result of its many definitions: "[Matriarchy] has sometimes

been depicted as the mirror-image of patriarchy, a system under which women dominate men, but this is not how the term is most often used by feminists. . . . Feminists who do define matriarchy as a system in which women rather than men have the power conceive of female power as something very different from the manipulative, domineering and aggressive power of males. The rule of women is seen as being in harmony with nature, non-coercive, non-violent, valuing wholeness and the sense of connection between people."[14] Hence, conforming to the definition accepted by the majority of feminist criticism, Rosa in no way could be considered a matriarchal figure. Moreover, even if one accepted the ethnological definition of matriarchy, Rosa would not be considered a matriarch given the fact that one of the basic characteristics of matriarchy as studied by ethnology is little or no valuation of virginity. Virginity is indeed important for Rosa, as Siemens himself points out in his article: "Rosa . . . is one of those religious fanatics who attributes much value to women's virginity" (Siemens, 51, my translation).

In short, although Rosa is indeed a woman, she embodies the abusive characteristics of patriarchy: aggression, a rigorous delineation of social roles for men and women (for example, Rosa supports Armando's promiscuity, calling it natural in men, while criticizing the Pupos daughters for being "miserable whores"), the importance granted to family and matrimony, defining men in terms of their power and control over others, the valuation of a rational, practical and persuasive discourse, the intolerance toward all marginal discourses. The image that the reader has of Old Rosa is of an intolerant, quick-tempered individual who dictates orders with an authoritarian voice while refusing to show emotions. Even in her prayers, kneeling before the altar in her bedroom, the proud Rosa refuses to place herself in a position of submission or supplication:

> [Rosa's] words did not well up in a long supplication, invested with an unmistakable note of submission; her intonation did not seem that of a prayer but of an order. There was too much assurance in her voice. And sometimes, as she addressed the images that now had multiplied, anyone who happened to hear her from the living room might well have thought she was addressing one of her laborers in the fields. Her children grew up listening to this authoritarian voice that spurred the men of the farm to action, that could order the hut under the ceiba tree torn down and made into charcoal ("Old Rosa," 13).[15]

The image of Rosa that the text evokes, that of the rural landowning patriarch whose word must be taken as law, was a familiar one within the Cuban Republic. Even today the image is not anachronistic in many areas of Latin America in which landowning patriarchs continue to rule. With this story, Arenas presents a criticism of an unjust social system.

In his texts, Arenas repeatedly presents at least one rebellious character who undermines and subverts the abusive system of power (represented either by an individual, the Church, politics, or traditional moral values) that attempts to limit or reduce individuals to a fixed identity or norm. In "Old Rosa," Rosa's patriarchal vision and obsessive need for power are undermined by those closest to her, her three children, who do not agree with and ultimately go on to challenge her authoritarian and materialistic life. Rosa's unyielding strictness alienates her children, who rebel, each in his or her own way, against their mother's tyrannical domination. Armando, the oldest son, goes off one day without warning and joins the revolutionary forces. As a revolutionary he becomes an atheist who challenges the patriarchal logic of traditional Catholicism and who calls for land reform on the island. Rosa first dismisses Armando's actions as foolish, but later, after the revolution triumphs, she is alarmed to discover that Armando is responsible for carrying out the very laws for agrarian reform that threaten to confiscate her lands. Rosa María, the daughter, rebels against her mother by leaving home and secretly marrying a black man. When Rosa finally discovers what her daughter has done she is unable to forgive her. For Rosa, a woman whose values and attitudes reflect the prejudices of Cuba's prerevolutionary privileged white class, the new regime's openness to interracial marriages is unacceptable, as is evident when she states: "The day I'm equal to a Negro, I'll hang myself" ("Old Rosa," 25). And finally, one day, Rosa discovers her youngest, Arturo, her brightest star, her favorite child, in his room embracing and kissing another boy. With this, the ultimate disloyalty, Rosa drives Arturo out of the house by symbolically shooting at him and his companion with the very gun Armando had used to fight in the revolution. Finally, in her anger and need for control, Rosa sets her house and lands on fire.

In "Old Rosa" the *énonciation* (the narrative process) works concurrently with the *énoncé* (the story).[16] Much like Rosa's own strong-headed determination to get things done quickly and efficiently her way, "Old Rosa" utilizes a retrospective technique that articulates chronologically—at a brisk pace, without delay for long descriptions or interruptions—the narrated events. The structure of the novella is circular, commencing and ending with the blazing fire that destroys the very property and lands the iron-handed Rosa struggled to obtain. The story's beginning passage is reproduced at the end of the text with only minor vocabulary changes. Hence, the entire story is a flashback, a remembering by Rosa, who is condemned to a useless reiteration of the incidents that led to her downfall, a downfall she cannot bring herself to accept. In "Old Rosa," fire is not a symbol of rebirth or change as sometimes occurs in other literary works, but rather a symbol of a futile and endless repetition.

Throughout the novella the superstitious Rosa is haunted by the resplendent figure of an angel who appears at her back during what she considers to be the most terrible moments of her life, that is, when she feels out of control. Near the end of the story, when she finally feels that all is lost, Rosa angrily confronts the angel, her "worst enemy," and attempts to destroy it. But as she approaches the angel, Rosa sees the radiant figure raise one of its delicate hands "to the region of the body where men [flaunt] their virility . . . and she [sees] it laughing, its hands placed over *that accursed region*" ("Old Rosa," 42). As the fire begins to spread, it consumes the two figures, Rosa and the angel, who no longer appear distinguishable. The woman and the angel (an obvious patriarchal religious symbol embodying the phallocentric identity that Rosa had adopted) are simultaneously commingled and consumed by the fire, a symbolic act that puts an end to Rosa's abusive authoritarianism.

Old Rosa is an oppressor, a victimizer, yet, unlike the old dictator in Gabriel García Márquez's well-known *The Autumn of the Patriarch* (1975), for example, her character is not sentimentalized for the reader. Although Rosa's inner frustrations are displayed in the text, these appear as rather trivial and foolish. The reader experiences little sympathy for this unyielding character who is racist, mistrustful of others, and keeps her emotions tightly in check. Rosa's need for absolute power blinds her to anyone else's wishes or needs, thus making it difficult for the reader to empathize when her world begins to crumble.

The ending of the story, that is, the downfall and ultimate destruction of an abusive patriarchal figure struggling to hold on to conservative values in the light of monumental revolutionary changes, can be read not just as an example of literary poetic justice, but also, and at the time more importantly, as an example of social justice, the very motive for which the revolution was fought. With this view in mind, it is significant that Arenas, in addition to presenting in "Old Rosa" the issues of religious domination, racism, and gross inequality in land distribution— all challenged and vigorously denounced by the Cuban revolution—also chose to include homophobia, an issue, as we have seen, not challenged but actually supported by the nascent revolutionary government. It is ironic that while vigorously championing such ideas as agrarian reform, improved interracial relations, and the debunking of traditional religious values, the Cuban revolution was actually in the process of spearheading a campaign to hunt down and imprison homosexuals with the aim of purging the new society of this so-called social perversion. In a symbolic touch, Arenas has Rosa drive Arturo out of the house with the very gun that Armando had used to fight in the mountains against the abusive authority of the old regime. By including homophobia in a text that also presented a number of key issues for the revolution, Arenas was challenging the new government to reexamine Cuba's traditional reactionary mentality when it came to same-sex relations. Unfortunately, however, we know that homophobia, which up to that time ("Old Rosa" was completed in and dated 1966) was still predominantly a social issue, was becoming a political concern for revolutionary leaders who were in the very process of drafting specific laws and measures attempting to regulate sexual practices that would "solve" the homosexual problem.

"The Brightest Star"

The rather simplistic ending of "Old Rosa," in which the figure of the oppressor meets a tragic end, is reopened and reexamined in "The Brightest Star," the story of Rosa's youngest son, Arturo. Arenas's "The Brightest Star," finished in Havana in 1971 but not published until 1984 in Barcelona, is the work of a writer who witnessed firsthand the abusive persecution of individuals as a result of their homosexual orientation and, in response, began to treat more subtly and discerningly the theme of oppression. During 1980, the same year Arenas escaped from Cuba through the Mariel exodus, he granted the *Nouvel Observateur* an interview (this interview was later translated into English in *Encounter,* January 1982)[17] in which he spoke out against the hostility of the Cuban revolutionary regime toward noncommitted writers as well as homosexuals. In his interview, Arenas maintains that while he lived in Cuba the exteriorization of any form of difference, be that verbal, written, or even physical, was considered as an outright counterrevolutionary attack because it went against the model archetype of the so-called disciplined revolutionary, "el hombre nuevo" or new revolutionary man. In response to the question "What is it like to be a homosexual in Cuba today?" Arenas answered:

An outsider in danger. Because Castroism is really a very *macho* system, and it has taken over the most reactionary prejudices of old Spanish morality. . . . Castroist legislation is thoroughly repressive in its morality. Homosexuals are supposed to be "reeducated," which means that they can sometimes be sent far away from the towns, on forced labour. They can't go to university; artistic careers in the cinema or the theatre are closed to them. Castro himself put it very clearly: "It is not permissible that homosexuals, in spite of their artistic qualities or reputation, should have influence over the cultural upbringing of the young." (*Encounter,* 62)

As previously noted, as early as 1965 forced labor camps under the name of UMAP were constructed in the province of Camagüey, Cuba, with the purpose of specifically "correcting" homosexual behavior, which, in the revolutionary policy makers' eyes, threatened the creation of a true revolutionary consciousness among the Cuban people. In his study, *Fidel Castro y la revolución cubana* (Fidel Castro and the Cuban Revolution),[18] Carlos Alberto Montaner reechoes Arenas's response cited in the *Nouvel Observateur* (*Encounter*) interview by giving testimony of how hundreds of Cuban students were thrown out of the University of Havana in the 1960s simply for being accused of being homosexual. Montaner writes:

The accusations were incredible: "He writes strange poems," "He wears his hair too long," "They are always seen together" . . . As a result of the macho paranoia, all this was considered to be counterrevolutionary and, therefore, punishable. In this way the guilty figure known as "the social scum" was immediately born, and in order to "correct" these deviations forced labor camps were built: the now sad and notoriously well-known UMAP camps. (Montaner, 132; my translation)

The story of "The Brightest Star" is a fictitious account of one man's experiences in one of the many UMAP work camps that existed in Cuba in the late 1960s. Although Arenas focuses on the conditions of the UMAP camps from a literary perspective, his text, presented as pure fiction, was nonetheless born out of a desire to remember his friend Nelson Rodríguez Leyva, a writer of children's books who was imprisoned in one of Cuba's homosexual prison camps from 1965 to 1967. Rodríguez Leyva himself wrote a book of stories about his own experiences at the UMAP camp, but it was confiscated and destroyed by the Cuban authorities. In 1971, desperate to escape from Cuba, Rodríguez Leyva tried to use a hand grenade to hijack a Cuban National Airlines plane to

Florida. As Arenas informs us in his note to "The Brightest Star": "Overpowered, in fear of being assassinated by the military guards on the plane, [Nelson] threw the grenade, and it exploded. The aircraft, however, managed to land at José Martí International Airport in Havana. Nelson and his friend and traveling companion, the poet Angel López Rabí, age sixteen, were shot by a firing squad" ("Brightest Star," 105).[19] As we can see from Arenas's words, Nelson Rodríguez Leyva's tragic experiences and defiant stance to flee the island at whatever cost served as a very real foundation for the writing of "The Brightest Star." In 1981 Arenas wrote a poem ("Si te llamaras Nelson" [If You Were Called Nelson]) in which he again paid homage to Nelson Rodríguez Leyva, this time by contrasting the persecution and humiliations suffered by young homosexuals such as Nelson in Cuba to the lives of their North American counterparts, who were oblivious to the nightmare that Cuban homosexuals were enduring.[20] The poem begins with a telling epigraph from Cuba's renowned liberator José Martí that reads: "Los que te tienen, oh libertad, no te conocen" (Those that have you, Oh Liberty, do not know you).

"The Brightest Star" is perversely faithful to Cuban testimonial, or documentary writings, which in Cuba reached its crowning point in what has come to be called the documentary novel. The Cuban documentary novel is a genre that when it first appeared was immediately sanctioned and promoted by the cultural policy makers of the revolution, who defined the function of literature as a political task of immediate practical utility. Roberto González Echevarría attests in his essay *"Biografía de un cimarrón* and the Novel of the Cuban Revolution" that the Cuban documentary novel is "one of the most popular forms of narrative to emerge in Cuba since the triumph of the Revolution."[21] According to Miguel Barnet, the genre's most recognized proponent in Cuba and the author of such celebrated documentary novels as *Biografía de un cimmarón* (1966; *The Autobiography of a Runaway Slave*) and *Canción de Rachel* (1969; *Rachel's Song*), the documentary novel gives voice to "la gente sin historia" (people without history), who would otherwise not have a voice within society.[22] This avowed principle, however, has not always applied to all marginal members of Cuban society, as has been the case with homosexuals, who have not been the subject of any documentary novel. In *Cuba: The Shaping of Revolutionary Consciousness,* Tzvi Medin proposes that documentary literature, in its desire to give testimony of revolutionary reality, has been actively promoted by the revolutionary authorities since 1959. When the Batista regime collapsed in

January of 1959 the revolutionary leaders that took power were not interested in merely reinstating a democratic regime conforming to the Cuban constitution of 1940. The intention rather was to reshape the Cubans' conceptual world through a revolutionary consciousness that would completely break with twentieth-century Cuban history. This break called for an immediate revision of history that would legitimate the new social order in light of the first independence movements of the previous century. To this end, the documentary genre, which uses both historiographic discourse and literary realism to reflect Cuban revolutionary reality, has been vigorously supported by the state because it provides a revision of Cuban history from an official revolutionary perspective.

Through Arenas's dedication, "For Nelson, in the air," as well as through the unmitigated presentation of the sociopolitical hostility directed toward homosexuals in Cuba that resulted in the creation of the UMAP camps, "The Brightest Star" appropriates the tenets of the documentary novel to present a scathing attack of revolutionary homophobia. Yet while remaining faithful to the spirit of testimonial or documentary literature, Arenas's novel would never receive a prize in Cuba, for instead of presenting capitalistic exploitation, class struggle, or heroic episodes of the Cuban revolutionary struggle—all common and safe themes found in the most recognized documentary novels—it dismantles revolutionary expectations by examining those issues that illustrate the repressive nature and macho rhetoric of the revolution itself.

According to the Spanish novelist Juan Goytisolo, "The Brightest Star" is not a vehicle of propaganda or denunciation but rather a "beautiful revulsive poem":

> Avoiding the snares of politics, Arenas has written a beautiful revulsive poem of love which contains a force and authenticity superior to any propagandistic displays. The moral wound of the writer, transformed into a creative energy, has permitted him to elaborate a text that, like all authentic literary creations, will outlive and gain new readers even when the events and realities to which he refers rot in the dung heap of history.[23]

As Goytisolo eloquently points out, "The Brightest Star" is not political propaganda. It is much more than that. Arenas's novella is a defense of the individual's right to dream, to rise above the oppression that threatens to eradicate all expressions of difference. Like the original Spanish text, the English translation has neither paragraphs, blank spaces, nor periods. The protagonist's thoughts, memories, dreams, and fantasies shift and flow uninterrupted from one level of consciousness to another. Unlike the narrative in "Old Rosa," which is an entire flashback recounted chronologically, the narrative in "The Brightest Star" is elliptical, a combination of Arturo's memories, fantasies, and experiences in the UMAP camp that surface and resurface throughout the text with little respect for chronology. The novella begins with a rather ambiguous quotation that only becomes intelligible to the reader after he or she has finished the text:

> "I have seen a land of regal elephants, far, far away," he had written some years ago, not many really, when he was still convinced that a cluster of signs, a cadence of images perfectly described—*words*—might save him. ("Brightest Star," 49)

Many of the characters in Arenas's novels and stories find writing to be a refuge from the hate that surrounds them. As we saw in chapter 2, the child-narrator/Celestino, Fortunato, Hector, Gabriel/Reinaldo/the Tétrica Mofeta, among other characters in Arenas's oeuvre, embrace the written word as a source of vitality and freedom. These characters, identified by their search for self-expression through the written form, struggle to express themselves. However, doubt and uncertainty as to the practicality of the written word in the face of persecution often make these characters question their literary endeavors.[24] Such is the case with Arturo. The initial sentence of the novella points to the dilemma that Arturo faces throughout his captivity in the UMAP camp: To what extent does an individual's imagination or fictive flights of fantasy substitute for the very real pleasures of life? As the third-person narrator asks, can "a cluster of signs, a cadence of images perfectly described— *words*—" ("Brightest Star," 49) save Arturo from the very real threats that surround him? Yet on the other hand, what recourse does an individual like Arturo have but to imagine a better condition of existence that will allow him to forget, if only temporarily, the living hell that is his life? As Arturo states at one point in the novella: "[R]eality lies not in the terror one feels and suffers but in the creations that overpower that terror, and wipe it out, for those creations are stronger, realer, truer than the terror" ("Brightest Star," 53).

The first part of "The Brightest Star" provides narrative flashes of Arturo's memories of his life prior to his arrival at the UMAP camp: his life with Old Rosa before the fire, his mother's funeral, his move to town, his brother Armando's contempt and indifference, his sister Rosa's false concerns, the young gay men that he befriends at the library—his first refuge, his first escape—and finally, his memory of being captured one evening after a special concert by a Russian pianist, a rare cultural event on the island. Arturo remembers how he and his friends were picked up as they made their way out of the concert hall by the police:

> as they came to the exit there was a disturbance of some sort, there were shouts, someone started running down the street, there was a shot, but only when it was already too late did Arturo and his friends realize that this was one of the more and more frequent "roundups" of young men being carried out these days under the absurd pretext that one young man's hair was too long, or that another wore clothes of a certain cut or (more fatal) exhibited certain telling traits, had certain "mannerisms" . . . and so, one by one, as they passed through the doors, they were "selected," arrested—Arturo's friends were pulled in even before he was, and they gestured and gesticulated, they protested, they tried to get off, get out of it, get away, using the very voices and postures that had sentenced them beforehand in the other's eye, the eyes of the police, ("Brightest Star," 65)

This passage, while more concerned with the aesthetic representation of the events, indeed reproduces Carlos Alberto Montaner's previously stated words on the matter of how the Cuban revolutionary police arbitrarily and capriciously rounded up young men whose appearance somehow indicated or showed signs of difference (read homosexuality).

Once in the UMAP camp, Arturo tries to keep a low profile, to not draw too much attention to himself. Yet his isolation only fuels the verbal and subsequent physical attacks against him by the other homosexuals, "the girls" as they wanted to be called, who cannot tolerate his silence and indifference. Arturo, in order to survive, is then forced to adapt to his surroundings. And by adapting Arturo must portray an image of self that does not offend either the homosexuals imprisoned in the camp or the guards who watch over them: "[T]he ones that guarded, the ones that considered themselves superior, the elect, the pure, the high and mighty ones who prided themselves on never having had, never having (though it wasn't necessarily true), relations with anybody but women" ("Brightest Star," 52).

In the camp, Arturo must cope with the vulgar realities of daily survival: the forced slave-labor in the sugarcane fields, the horrific sanitary conditions, the extreme solitude, and the constant humiliations and abusive macho behavior on the part of the guards in charge who sadistically mistreat the homosexual inmates. Still, Arturo's oppression is not solely the result of the repressive political system that put him in the UMAP camp. Such a simplistic explanation would only convert "The Brightest Star" into political propaganda, a designation rejected by Juan Goytisolo. In the camp, oppression is also evident in the improper conduct of certain homosexual prisoners who create their own oppressive hierarchy of power, a "sistership" as they call it, that does not tolerate individuals who do not assimilate: "because at first he had tried not to have anything to do with them, . . . they began to want to get back at him" ("Brightest Star," 67). Already subjugated by the abuses of the guards, Arturo realizes that he must fit into this homosexual subculture if he wishes to escape further persecution. Thus, he begins to take on the dizzying slang, the poses, the cant of this imprisoned gay ghetto until he finally becomes the star of the transvestite spectacles performed at night in the barracks, "the Queen of the Captive Queers." Arturo discovers that he must destroy any expression of self that does not conform to the imprisoned homosexual world of the barracks, he must bury any authentic self-expression underneath a facade of burlesque and vulgar mockery in order to be accepted. Yet as time passes, the wild extravaganzas of the barracks nightlife begin to leave Arturo empty and unfulfilled. These feelings of frustration escalate after the tragic death of Celeste, one of the other stars of the transvestite shows. Thereafter, Arturo feels more and more desperate to escape his sordid surroundings, and consequently, in the notebooks that his sister, Rosa, brought to him in her one and only visit to the camp, Arturo begins to write a chronicle, a testimony of his prison life:

> [He] decided that to save himself he had to start writing, *now,* and so he started writing . . . [He] was going to fight, he was going to rebel, he was going to testify to the horror, tell someone, lots of people, tell the world, or tell even just one person, as long as there was one person who still had an uncorrupted, incorruptible capacity to think, he would leave this reality with that one person—and suddenly the notebooks, the common ordinary spiral notebooks with paper lined in blue, the notebooks Rosa had brought him, began to fill with, to be awash in, a sea of tiny tiny words, almost scribbled, fast, *fast,* and almost illegible, even to him, *hurry, hurry, keep on, fast.* ("Brightest Star," 71–72)

Like the child-narrator/Celestino in *Singing from the Well,* Arturo's urgency to write so overcomes him that when he runs out of paper he begins to use whatever he can find, blank pages of Marxist-Leninist manuals, political posters pasted up on the walls, the inside covers and spines of economics books stolen from the Political Section of the camp, and so forth, to frantically scribble the testimony of his intolerable reality. Concurrently, Arturo begins to create an imaginary theater in which he plays out the fantasies that are denied to him in life. At one point he takes on the creative task of dreaming/creating a fantastic and fabulous castle wherein he hopes to meet his ideal lover, an individual he refers to simply as *él* (he). (Arenas's refusal to name the imagined beloved, referring to him throughout the novella as simply *él* [he] reappropriates, as well as pays homage to, Gertrudis Gómez de Avellaneda's well-known pair of poems titled "A él" [To Him] in which the nineteenth-century Cuban poet also calls the man of her dreams *él*: "¿Qué ser divino era aquél? / ¿Era un ángel o era un hombre? / ¿Era un Dios o era Luzbel? / ¿Mi visión no tiene nombre? / ¡Ah! nombre tiene . . . ¡Era Él!" [What divine creature was there? / Was it an angel or a man? / Was it a God or Lucifer? / My fantasy has no name? / Oh! a name he has . . . It is He!]).[25] As the fantasy progresses and Arturo's constant state of oppression worsens, he begins, like other characters in Arenas's oeuvre (among others, the child-narrator in *Singing from the Well* and in the short story "Con los ojos cerrados" [With my Eyes Closed], Hector in *Farewell to the Sea,* and Juan in *The Doorman*), to dedicate his time to imagining and dreaming a better existence as a means of escaping his present asphyxiating situation. Yet while Arturo begins to (con)fuse reality with fantasy, the reader remains privy to both his imagined and UMAP camp existence and how each affects the other. Arturo's fictive flights of the imagination begin to take on, much in the same way as the sorcerer in Jorge Luis Borges's famous story "Circular Ruins," the task of dreaming a man. However, whereas in Borges's story it is a father who creates, by dreaming, a son to continue with the duties of the fire cult, in "The Brightest Star" the task that Arturo sets himself to is that of dreaming, as mentioned earlier, an ideal male lover.

> Arturo would have to . . . explore all the recesses of his imagination if he were going to bring to himself the real—definite, rounded—image of his lover . . . . [He] began to create anew, laboriously, in pain and suffering, and he started with the young man's hands—but what were his hands like? and his face? the smell of his body? . . . and what about his eyes? . . . he tried to reconstruct each individual part of his body, each gesture, each movement, yet the image wavered, flickered, and slipped away, it

faded, it became warped and disfigured, and it was impossible to pin it
down, reach it, hold it, as that ideal (real) boy dissolved (literally) into
memory; and so sometimes Arturo would spend one whole night on the
reconstruction—unsuccessful of a smile. ("Brightest Star," 87–88)

Arturo's labor of love, which requires all his passion and strength, is
constantly interrupted by the vile realities of the camp. To continue with
his work, what eventually becomes his only refuge, he begins to give up
sleep and meals, seizing every available moment. Yet, this time still is not
enough. In a last desperate attempt to complete his imaginary castle
Arturo decides to escape from the camp. As he throws his machete down,
he runs through the sugarcane fields until he reaches the vast esplanade
where he hopes to give shape to his wonderful castle. In the few minutes
(story time) before the soldiers reach him, Arturo is able to spend time
(discourse time, that is, imaginative time that is not limited by real
clocks) carefully building and lavishly furnishing his fantastic domain:

> and he made his way to the residential quarters, where he chose a large
> apartment in an angled corner with a view across the entire realm and a
> door that opened out onto a hanging terrace, and in the apartment
> Arturo set a curtained bed, a carpet, a table with a vase of roses, two can-
> delabra, and a mullioned window softly veiled and shuttered by a lattice,
> with an awning of fine canvas to protect them from the sun. ("Brightest
> Star," 100)

Precisely at the moment when Arturo completes his work, the squad of
soldiers advances toward him, pointing their rifles. Arturo, who sees a
choir of angels announcing the arrival of his lover (the reappearance of
the angel-destroyer figure first introduced in "Old Rosa"), eagerly runs
toward them. But as the "angels" get closer Arturo discovers "with
irrefutable, inarguable clarity" ("Brightest Star," 103) that these are not
angels, but a troop of soldiers who are led by none other than his
mother, Old Rosa, "boiling mad" who screams with gun in hand, *"Faggot faggot faggot, you won't get away from me this time"* ("Brightest Star,"
103). Perhaps even more painful, Arturo also realizes that among the
band of soldiers who have been chasing him is "the face of the divine
youth, the one for whom [his] castle had been built, . . . raising his rifle,
aiming it at him . . . *Faggot!*" ("Brightest Star," 103).
A reading of "Old Rosa" by itself might suggest that the abusive
authority of the main character, an obvious reflection of Cuba's prerevo-

lutionary social injustices, was able to be challenged and easily elimi-
nated by the revolution. In "The Brightest Star," however, we see how
this symbol of authoritarian oppression reappears, this time with far
more vengeance. Let us remember that "Old Rosa" was written when
the author was only 23 years old, that is, when his views on the subject
were rather limited by his inexperience. Moreover, "Old Rosa" was completed in 1966, that is, prior to the revolution's crackdown on homosexuals. On the other hand, "The Brightest Star" was finished in 1971
when the reality of the UMAP camps were indeed a very recent
reminder of the revolution's intolerance toward homosexuality. Thus,
"The Brightest Star" better reflects the sinister ambiguities, the devious
and insidious nature of oppression that can resurface and assert itself
under different forms and guises, as, for example, in a government's
decision to round up so-called deviants and lock them up while at the
same time presenting itself to the world as the champion of the under-
dogs and the downtrodden. "The Brightest Star" reveals that the
oppressor can indeed have many faces, as is the case with the sisterhood
of homosexuals within the UMAP camp. One might expect these individuals, themselves victims of intolerance and hate, to be more accepting of their fellow men. But such tolerance is not the case, and for this
reason the sistership practices perhaps the most nefarious form of
oppression.

Although "Old Rosa" and "The Brightest Star" can be read sepa-
rately for their respective literary singularity, it is apparent that a reading of both texts provides the reader with a far more penetrating look at
the issues of oppression than a separate reading of each text would allow.
Whereas oppression can clearly manifest itself in societies that suppress
ideological pluralism, as has been the case during both Cuba's prerevolutionary and revolutionary eras, it can also present itself on a more
restricted level, that is, in one person's intolerance to accept another's
expressions of difference, as is the case with Old Rosa, who is unable to
accept Armando's political beliefs, Rosa María's interracial marriage,
and Arturo's homosexuality; and as is also the case with the sistership of
homosexuals, intolerant of differences. Hence, the intertextual relation
between oppressor and oppressed that links these two stories goes
beyond the specific context of Cuban history to articulate a story of universal resonance.

In canto 3 of Arenas's *Farewell to the Sea,* a series of poetic INTERLUDES
(*Farewell,* 251–53) reveals the poet Hector's absolute disgust with
humanity:

Man

is without doubt the most alarming of all inventions—

made for thought, he never comes to

a definite conclusion which might save him;

made for pleasure, he persecutes and condemns

all those things which might

bestow it on him.

Man

is truly a thing which deserves

our most scrupulous condemnation—

having suffered every

manner of disaster

he does naught

but repeat them.

(*Farewell*, 252–53)

Hector is outraged by individuals who themselves have been oppressed and who then turn around and oppress others. The suggestion, also present in "Old Rosa" and "The Brightest Star," is that perhaps humanity, unable to accept or tolerate differences, is condemned to repeat this cycle of persecution. If such repetition is indeed the case, individuals who find themselves persecuted have only two alternatives: to give in to oppression, as do many of the homosexuals within the UMAP camp—"no insult seemed to touch them, they found such treatment logical, by now they were so mired in their disgrace, . . . that [it] was just a natural extension of themselves" ("Brightest Star," 71)—or to struggle against oppression in whatever form it exists. The latter is what Arturo chooses and thus he becomes a symbol of struggle in the war against intolerance.

Old Rosa, A Novel in Two Stories defends, as do all of Arenas's texts, human dignity and the individual's freedom to choose who he or she is or wishes to be, even in the face of humankind's propensity to discriminate against and maliciously persecute individual expression.

Chapter Four

Journey to the Source:
Viaje a La Habana

Viaje a La Habana (1990; Journey to Havana) was the last work Reinaldo Arenas saw published before his death.[1] The book, subtitled "Novela en tres viajes" or "Novel in Three Journeys," is a collection of three stories, or novelettes: "Que Trine Eva" (Let Eva Scream), "Mona," and "Viaje a La Habana" (Journey to Havana). Although each story has its own plot, characters, and action, the three are tied together by a central idea, or theme: the search for an emotional and/or physical space in which a homosexual *eros* can be acted upon freely, thus producing a personal liberation. This assertion is even true in "Mona," in which the search ends tragically with the destruction of the protagonist. *Viaje a La Habana* is unique in its frank articulation of the need for the homosexual man to accept and express himself freely in societies—the stories take place both in Cuba and New York City—that militate and censure his conduct.

Whereas the first story, "Que trine Eva," belongs to the writings Arenas produced in Cuba (the story is dated Havana, 1971), the last two are a product of the time the writer spent in exile ("Mona," Miami Beach, 1986; "Viaje a La Habana" is dated New York, October-November, 1983, and New York, September-November, 1987). The place and time in which each story was written is consistent with the thesis that Arenas became more audacious in his representation of homoerotic desire once he left Cuba. Although a clear camp sensibility is present in "Que trine Eva," the word "homosexual" is never mentioned and the story is purposefully ambiguous as to the nature of the relationship between the characters. On the other hand, in "Mona" and "Viaje a La Habana," homoerotic desire is not just openly discussed but is the motivation for the plot of both stories. Let us now move on to a separate analysis of each text.

"Que trine Eva"

In the introduction to Antonio Benítez-Rojo's interpretative study of Caribbean culture, *The Repeating Island: The Caribbean and the Postmodern*

Perspective,[2] the Cuban writer and critic states that if he had to pick one word to describe the culture of the Caribbean, that word would be *performance* (Benítez-Rojo, 11). Later, in a chapter titled " 'Viaje a la semilla' or the text as spectacle," which is an analysis of Alejo Carpentier's famous story "Viaje a la semilla" ("Journey Back to the Source"), Benítez-Rojo goes on to explain the *spectacular* nature of the literature of the Caribbean:

> I think that the novel written in the Caribbean is one of the most spectacular in the world. I should make it clear that in talking of spectacularity I don't refer to the use of certain experimental techniques which we see successfully employed in novels such as *Ulysses, In Search of Lost Time, Orlando, As I Lay Dying,* or, in Spanish America, in the works of Cortázar, Vargas Llosa, Fuentes, or Roa Bastos. When I mention the spectacular nature of the Caribbean's narrative, I mean to use the strictest definition of the word *spectacle* (my Larousse says "public entertainment of any kind"). I say this so definitely because I detect in the Caribbean novel a will to set itself up at all costs as a total performance . . . . [T]he characters in these novels often appear literally as singers, musicians, ballerinas, transvestites, etc., . . . But beyond these characters' virtuosity there is the text itself, the star of the show, the great performer. (Benítez-Rojo, 218)

"Que trine Eva" is indeed a spectacular text. More specifically, it is a camp performance that, while entertaining the reader on a discourse and plot/story level, also criticizes bourgeois hierarchies of value that attempt to silence representations of difference. As Moe Meyer argues in his essay "Reclaiming the Discourse of Camp," camp, or "queer parody," embodies a cultural critique that challenges all dominant labeling philosophies that attempt to limit or contain sex/gender identities.[3] Meyer's use of the term "queer" to designate what is generally referred to as "gay and lesbian" is part of an ongoing debate within the Anglo-American gay and lesbian community that questions the continuity and integrity of identity. (Although many male homosexuals and lesbians still see as an insult the hateful and aggressive nature of the word "queer" to refer to them, others within the gay and lesbian movement find that the appropriation of the word neutralizes its offensive value and provides a way of articulating a wide range of nonheterosexual sexualities. Furthermore, the word challenges the naive assumption that there is such a thing as a monolithic sexual identity.) Meyer sees the oppositional critique of gay and lesbian middle-class assimilation with its conformity to labels and classifications as one of the most valid aspects of the "queer" designation: "What 'queer' signals is an ontological challenge that displaces bourgeois notions of the Self as unique, abiding, and continuous while substituting instead a concept of Self as performative, improvisational, discontinuous, and processually constituted by repetitive and stylized acts" (Meyer, 2–3). Meyer's shift from a gay and lesbian identity based on a bourgeois epistemology, which stabilizes identity, to a performance paradigm based on camp, in which postures, gestures, costumes, dress, and speech acts become the elements that constitute identity, recasts camp not as an ironic moment or vague sensibility characterized by triviality, as first proposed by Susan Sontag in her now well-known 1964 article, "Notes on Camp,"[4] but as a representation of queer visibility in the social arena of everyday life. Meyer argues: "Camp, as specifically queer parody, becomes, then, the only process by which the queer is able to enter representation and to produce social visibility" (Meyer, 11).

"Que trine Eva" is the story of a Cuban couple, Evattt (at one point the character comments that she, who could also be a he dressed as a woman, has added three final "t's" to her name to make it more distinct) and Ricardo, who dress themselves in flamboyant and outrageous outfits and clothing resourcefully knit, considering the shortages on the island, by Evattt, a sort of Cuban Penelope. (Throughout the three stories of *Viaje a La Habana* mythological and religious figures and stories are appropriated, parodied, and recast.) Both characters are performers who are driven by a desire to be noticed, to stand out from the rest of society. Although Evattt and Ricardo love to be admired, and can even tolerate being hated or persecuted, what they cannot accept is being ignored. In fact, it is Ricardo's discovery that a mysterious "someone" remains indifferent to their exhibitionism that becomes the catalyst for the couple's odyssey across the island of Cuba in search of the indifferent one:

> Tú [Ricardo] fuiste el primero en sospechar que . . . aunque era cierto que causábamos todos esos aspavientos fabulosos, alguien, que todavía no habíamos podido localizar, dejaba de mirarnos siempre. Y ese alguien era más importante que todos los demás. Y ese alguien, ay, Ricardo, parecía estar en todos los sitios, acechándonos sin mirarnos, precisamente fastidiándonos por su poco interés en fastidiarnos; por su indiferencia. ("Que trine Eva," 32)

> You [Ricardo] were the first to suspect that . . . although it was true that we were causing such a fabulous fuss, someone, who we still had not been

able to locate, wasn't watching us. And that someone was more important than the rest. And that someone, oh, Ricardo, appeared to be all
over the place, threatening us by not watching us, bothering us precisely
by his very lack of not wanting to bother us; by his indifference. (my
translation)

Arenas's story is purposefully ambiguous as to the exact nature of the
relationship between Evatt and Ricardo: Is Ricardo homosexual? Is
Evatt a woman or a drag queen? If Evattt is indeed a woman, is this a
marriage or relationship of convenience? Is there love between Evatt
and Ricardo, or simply a rivalry between them? Although these questions remain unclear, what is clear is that both Evatt and Ricardo are
dedicated to their performances. They are willing to risk everything to
be noticed, to be visible and admired. "Que trine Eva" supports Moe
Meyer's assertion that camp, or queer parody, indeed produces social visibility. Although never labeled homosexual, lesbian, or bisexual, Evattt
and Ricardo demonstrate a queer sensibility; although marginalized and
disenfranchized, they ingeniously take existing structures of signification within the dominant order and transform them into alternative signifying codes. Evattt and Ricardo assign spectacular meanings to clothes;
they infuse clothing with what Moe Meyers calls a queer aura. In order
to keep up the appearances they have become famous for in Havana, the
couple become progressively more daring and provocative in the way
they dress. This outrageousness of course is not easy, given the rationing
and shortages on the island. Yet Evattt and Ricardo are not deterred by
these limitations:

> Por un tiempo desapareció hasta el hilo búlgaro y hasta el chino. Entonces
> le echamos manos a las tendederas del patio, a los cordeles de los vecinos,
> a los hilos de amarrar paquetes que tú regateabas en las ferreterías. Pero
> no desfallecimos. Cuando desaparecieron las agujetas, salimos una noche,
> varias noches, los dos muy cerrados de negro, con los slacks tejidos a punto
> remate, a robar rayos de bicicleta. Atravesamos en silencio las oscuras
> calles de la Quinta Avenida y, a riesgo de perder la vida (esta gente es
> capaz de llevar al paredón hasta a un infeliz ladrón de flejes), nos hicimos
> de una enorme colección de rayos que tú, con extraordinaria paciencia,
> transformaste en agujetas francesas . . . Y como si eso fuera poco, el gran
> acoso, la persecución constante. ("Que trine Eva," 36–37)

For a while even the Bulgarian and Chinese yarn disappeared. Then we
helped ourselves to the clotheslines from the backyard, the neighbors'

ropes, strings for wrapping package that you haggled over in the hard-
ware stores. But we didn't lose heart. When the knitting needles were no
longer available, we went out one night, various nights, both dressed in
black, with our slacks knitted with a finishing stitch, to steal bicycle
spokes. We silently crossed the dark streets of Fifth Avenue and, risking
our lives (these people are capable of taking even a poor common thief to
a firing squad), we got ahold of a huge collection of spokes that you, with
extraordinary patience, transformed into French knitting needles . . .
And if that weren't enough, the relentless harassment, the constant persecution. (My translation)

The last sentence of this quotation mentions the systematic persecution and harassment that Evatt and Ricardo are forced to endure. In the
text Evatt's and Ricardo's persecutors are never identified directly, but
the reader can infer that the revolutionary government is cracking down
on what it considers inappropriate and scandalous acts that undermine
revolutionary values. On one occasion, for example, after a successful
performance Evatt makes reference to "unos tipos forrados de verde"
("Que trine Eva," 18) (some guys dressed in green) before they flee, thus
alluding to the olive green fatigues of the revolutionary police. As I have
already presented in earlier chapters, the Cuban revolutionary government under which Arenas lived until he escaped from the island in
1980, although perhaps not bourgeois was nonetheless a system
grounded in uniformity that considered any type of extravagant behavior at variance with revolutionary morals. At the First National Congress on Education and Culture, for example, celebrated 23–30 April
1971, the following declarations were made in regard to fashion and
dress:

1. La revolución ha de tener en cuenta el fenómeno social de la moda
   dentro del marco de nuestras características económicas, ambientales
   e ideológicas.
2. Al estudiar este fenómeno de modas, costumbres, extravagancias,
   etcétera, ratificamos la necesidad de mantener la unidad monolítica e
   ideológica de nuestro pueblo, y el combate a cualquier forma de
   desviación entre los jóvenes.
3. Que es necesario el enfrentamiento directo para la eliminación de las
   aberraciones extravagantes. [5]

1. The revolution must take into account the social phenomenon of
   fashion within our particular economic, environmental, and ideological framework.

2. Upon studying this phenomenon of fashion, habits, extravagances, etc., we ratify the need to maintain the monolithic and ideological unity of our people, and to fight against all forms of deviation among our youths.

3. That the direct confrontation to eliminate extravagant aberrations is necessary. (My translation)

These declarations make it clear that the Cuban revolutionary government saw fashion as a potential threat to the building of a uniform revolutionary consciousness. Indeed, as Roland Barthes presents in his semiological study *The Fashion System,* clothes are not just functional or superficial items devoid of intent but rather a signifying system that creates meaning by differentiating garments, endowing details with significance, and establishing links between certain aspects of clothing and worldly activities.[6]

Ricardo's fear and obsession that there exists "someone" unmoved by his and Evatt's sensational and fabulous exhibitions ultimately leads the couple to embark on a journey—an odyssey reminiscent of Fray Servando's ill-fated peregrinations—that will have Evattt and Ricardo crisscrossing the island with their 27 suitcases ("al igual que las que llevó Rita Hayworth al festival de Cannes" ("Que trine Eva," 43) (just like the number Rita Hayworth took to the Cannes Film Festival). Evattt feels there is no reason to go, in fact, she fears leaving Havana, although she reluctantly agrees to the trip in order to please Ricardo. Tired and fatigued after performing and unsuccessfully searching for the "indifferent one" throughout the provinces of Cuba, the couple finally arrive in Baracoa, Cuba's most eastern tip. Under the most horrendous conditions, Ricardo continues to search, urging Evattt, bitching and bemoaning their odyssey, to continue to the Maisí lighthouse, an obvious phallic symbol as well as a symbol of possible personal illumination. The journey to the Maisí lighthouse is the most difficult of all. The couple must endure torrential downpours as they make their way on donkeys up and down mountains and across rivers. It is interesting that this remote and barren region, so far from the urban cosmopolitanism of Havana, is described through a textual performance that subtly but recognizably alludes to one of Latin America's most famous novels, *Pedro Páramo.*[7]

Juan Rulfo's *Pedro Páramo* addresses the tragedy of the Mexican revolution by presenting the story of Pedro Páramo, the *cacique,* or local ruler, of Comala, who as a result of his greed, ambition, and personal vendettas is responsible for the ultimate destruction of the town. Like

"Que trine Eva," Rulfo's novel is also the story of a quest; Juan Preciado, Pedro Páramo's illegitimate son, guided by an "arriero," or muleteer, journeys to Comala in search of his father. When he arrives at his destination he discovers that Comala is literally a ghost town. Later, in the middle of the novel, the reader discovers that Juan Preciado himself is also dead and that his story, the one the reader is reading, is being told after death to a fellow ghost. In "Que trine Eva," Ricardo, unsatisfied with his life in Havana, embarks on a journey motivated by a desire to find the "someone" who has remained indifferent. Like Rulfo's Comala, Baracoa is described as a region of death ("Pero seguimos andando por esa región de muerte" ("Que trine Eva," 47) (But we continued forward through that region of death). Also, like Juan Preciado, Evattt and Ricardo are being guided by a muleteer. Significantly, at one point (p. 46), Ricardo corrects Evattt's designation of the muleteer, whom she calls "mulero," as "arriero," the word used by Rulfo in his novel. At another moment, Ricardo protects Evatt from falling by taking her to a "páramo" with giant rocks ("Me tomaste por la cintura y me llevaste hasta un *páramo* con rocas inmensas donde el agua no caía directamente" ("Que trine Eva," 47, emphasis added) ("You grabbed me by the waist and took me to a high moor with giant rocks where the water was not falling directly). A *páramo* is a bleak plateau or high moor, yet it also means a wasteland; in Rulfo's novel the name is symbolic of the wasteland that Pedro has created. The echoes of Rulfo's novel that are introduced into Arenas's story appear intentional. Like *The Ill-Fated Peregrinations of Fray Servando,* with its explicit criticism of the lack of freedom that often accompanies the institutionalization of a revolution (a criticism that naturally implicated the Cuban revolutionary experience and thus was responsible for the book being censored in Cuba), "Que trine Eva" implicates, through its allusions to Rulfo's *Pedro Páramo,* in which a *cacique* figure is responsible for the destruction of a town, the Cuban revolution's own aggressive policing of any act, individual as well as artistic, not in keeping within revolutionary parameters. Through its use of camp, hyperbolic excess, and outrageous sense of humor, Arenas's story treats, albeit indirectly, the tragedy of a revolution recusant to accept expressions of difference.

After arriving at the Maisí lighthouse, Ricardo and Evattt learn that that very evening a celebration will take place to commemorate the landing of Antonio Maceo at Duaba beach, an important historical event that signaled the beginning of Cuba's War of Independence.[8] That evening the mysterious "someone," whom Ricardo had been searching

for, finally appears. He is identified as a young fisherman. Ricardo and
Evattt frantically try to out-perform each other to win the young man's
attention. For almost two pages the anaphoric structure "You" (wore
such-and-such a thing/danced such-and-such a dance), "I" (wore such-
and-such a thing/danced such-and-such a dance) is exploited:

> Tú saliste en short, botas, guayabera y abrigo mapache. Yo exhibí mi dis-
> fraz de jardinera. . . . Yo saqué el gran traje imperial a punto negro ilusión,
> la corona y el manguito. Tú, los pantalones de pana y la capa de super-
> mán. Yo, la casaca holandesa. Tú, el traje de faraón. Yo, la cartera a punto
> calado y el paraguas de seda fría. Tú, el camisón monacal. . . . Tú bailabas
> un pasodoble. Yo improvisé un zapateo. Tú bailaste el go-gó. Yo inventé
> ese mismo momento una danza exótica. Tú escandalizaste marcando el
> ritmo de una conga. Yo bailé una zamba. . . . ("Que trine Eva," 62–63)

> You came out in your shorts, boots, *guayabera* and raccoon coat. I showed
> off my gardening outfit. . . . I threw on my grand imperial suit decorated
> with black dreamy stitches, my crown and muff. You wore your corduroy
> pants and superman cape. I, my Dutch frock coat. You, your Pharaoh
> costume. I, my open worked handbag and cool silk parasol. You, your
> monastic gown. . . . You danced a *pasodoble*. I improvised a zapateo. You
> danced the go-go. I quickly invented an erotic dance. You caused a scan-
> dal moving to the beat of the conga. I danced a *zamba*. (my translation)

This "Yo/Tú" (I/You) structure parodies Afro-Cuban poet Nicolás Guillén's (1902–1989) well-known poem "No sé por qué piensas tú" ("Why
soldier, does it seem to you") in which revolutionary solidarity is
esteemed at the expense of individual differences. I will quote just a few
stanzas of Guillén's poem so that the reader can get a sense of the I/You
structure. (Let us recall that the Spanish "yo" is equivalent to both the
English nominative case "I" and the objective case "me"):

No sé por qué piensas tú	Why, soldier, does it seem to you
No sé por qué piensas tú,	Why, soldier, does it seem to you
soldado, que te odio,	that hatred is lurking in me,
si somos la misma cosa	if we are exactly the same,
yo,	me,
tú.	you.

Tú eres pobre, lo soy yo;   You are poor; just look at me.
soy de abajo, lo eres tú;   I come from below, so do you:
¿de dónde has sacado tú,   How did it occur to you,
soldado, que te odio yo?   soldier, that hatred is within me?

Me duele que a veces tú   It hurts me at times that you
te olvidas de quién soy yo;   tend to forget I am me
caramba, si yo soy tú,   caramba, since I am you,
lo mismo que tú eres yo.   the same way that you are me.

. . . .

Ya nos veremos yo y tú,   We'll soon see each other, me and you
juntos en la misma calle,   walking together in the street,
hombro con hombro, tú y yo,   shoulder to shoulder, you and me
sin odios ni yo ni tú,   without hatred, me or you
pero sabiendo tú y yo,   but knowing for certain, you and me
a dónde vamos yo y tú . . .   where we are going, me and you . . .
¡No sé por qué piensas tú,   Why, soldier, does it seem to you
soldado, que te odio yo!   that hatred is lurking in me![9]

Arenas pokes fun at Guillén's utopian vision of revolutionary camaraderie in which individuals, here specifically two men, do not compete
with each other but rather work together in solidarity. Ricardo and
Evattt, however, indeed compete; in fact, they fiercely do battle with
their clothes, and later with their bodies, in a war of seduction that
Ricardo, in the end, wins. The young fisherman extends his hand out to
the exhausted Ricardo and leads him toward the sea, which here, as in
many other texts by Arenas, is read as a symbol of freedom. Evattt
recounts the moment as follows:

> Vi al muchacho ponerse de pie, echar a andar con pasos viriles, atravesar
> todo el salón y dirigirse hasta el extremo donde tú estabas desfallecido.
> Lo vi llegar hasta ti, y mirarte. Lo vi extender una mano y ayudarte a
> incorporar. Y ahora vi a las dos (dos serpientes), caminado por sobre el
> promontorio de las rocas. "Que trine Eva", "Que trine Eva", cantaban
> con voces increíblemente claras mientras se perdían por entre los der-
> riscaderos y las tunas, rumbo al mar. ("Que trine Eva," 64)

I saw the young man get up and walk with virile steps across the entire
hall. He walked toward the far end of the hall where you now were, weak
and faint. I saw him come up to you, and look at you. I saw him extend
his hand to help you get up. And now I saw you two (two serpents), walking on the rocky promontory. "Let Eva scream," "Let Eva scream," they
sang with incredibly clear voices while they drew out of sight between the
ravines and prickly pear trees on route to the sea. (My translation)

In this scene Arenas subtly infuses homoeroticism into a number of religious allusions: the young fisherman, the serpent(s), Eva=Eve. The
young fisherman gives his hand to the dead Lazarus-Ricardo to help him
up; the serpent-Satan from the garden of Eden is split into two phallic
homoerotic symbols; and Eve, the first woman, Adam-Ricardo's mate, is
abandoned for another man. Symbolically, it is at this moment in the
text that a beam of light from the lighthouse hits Evattt and she understands, for the first time, how Ricardo has lied to her: "[C]omprendí que
no era yo precisamente quien tenía los ojos más hermosos del mundo"
("Que trine Eva," 64) (I understood that it wasn't just me who had the
most beautiful eyes on earth). The metaphoric allusion to the eyes, the
eyes seen as the window to a person's soul, reveals what perhaps has
been obvious to the reader all along but not to Evattt, who resisted and
denied the possibility of Ricardo having homoerotic desires. Ricardo is
very much like Hector in *Farewell to the Sea,* who, as a result of living
under a rigid and intolerant institutionalized revolution that believes
order is to be found in the preservation of an exemplary revolutionary
social consciousness, learns to hide and bury his homosexual desires. Yet,
whereas Hector creates a double, an imaginary wife, in order to survive,
Ricardo marries (or comes together with what appears on the surface to
be a "woman") in order to play the game, the so-called masculine/active
performance that his society demands that he play. Ricardo's dual performance—on the one hand, his exhibitionism with Evattt, and on the
other, his performance of husband/active partner to Evattt—leaves him
longing for something more substantial. Ricardo, who was unsatisfied
by his life in Havana, a picaresque existence impoverished by a system
that persecuted and hounded him for his difference, searched for and
finally found that "someone" who would take him to a liberating space.

As a final note, the Spanish title "Que trine Eva" is in itself a literary
performance, a parodic queer gesture, wink, or high sign. In Spanish the
verb "trinar" means to sing or warble (ornithology) but it also means to
be angry, hopping mad. That the title is repeated in the scene in which
Ricardo and the young fisherman abandon Evattt is rather telling. As I

have already established in previous chapters, the word "pájaro," or bird, is a pejorative label for male homosexuals in Cuba. Hence, the title can be read as follows: let Evattt or Eva (under a patriarchal and bourgeois logic, the quintessential first woman) scream from anger at being betrayed and abandoned by the "pájaro"/homosexual Ricardo. In the end, the reader learns that Evattt, defeated and abandoned, returns to Havana, where she dedicates herself, like Penelope (another parodic undermining of the myth of the faithful waiting wife), to knitting a regal black gown that she will wear to mourn her loss, a gown that she hopes to parade through the streets of Havana.

"Mona"

I analyze "Mona" using Tzvetan Todorov's as well as Ana María Barrenechea's theoretical work on the literature of the fantastic. This type of analysis provides a provocative way of approaching the theme of homoerotic desire. Although Todorov's book on the fantastic (*The Fantastic: A Structural Approach to a Literary Genre,* originally published in French in 1970 and translated into English in 1973)[10] is the most renowned in the study of this literary genre, Ana María Barrenechea has explored most extensively the literature of the fantastic in Latin American letters.[11] I would like to underscore from the outset that this type of analysis does not attempt in any way to pigeonhole "Mona," a text that allows for a variety of possible readings. Nonetheless, I do consider that "Mona" indeed enriches the fantastic in Latin American letters, a very fertile vein of writing that goes back to the end of the nineteenth century. Historically, the most recognized fantastic texts in Latin America have been from Argentina, yet Cuba, as Rogelio Llopis's collection *Cuentos cubanos de lo fantástico y lo extraordinario* (Cuban Stories of the Fantastic and Extraordinary) well attests to, has also produced a significant number of fantastic texts.[12]

Before highlighting those particular instances and features in "Mona" that demonstrate the presence of the fantastic, it is important to call attention to the assertion that Todorov makes at the beginning of his study with respect to Balzac's *The Magic Skin*; that is, to study a text in the context of the fantastic is not the same as studying that same text within the totality of a writer's oeuvre (Todorov, 3). In the specific case of Arenas, it would be useless, for instance, to conclude that the presence of fantastic elements in "Mona" signals some type of pattern that exists in the Cuban writer's other works, texts, which for the most part, are not fantastic but rather "alucinante," or hallucinatory, or to use Todorov's term, "marvelous."[13] Thus, this study of the fantastic is limited exclusively to the fictitious world that is represented in the novella "Mona."

In his study, Todorov affirms that homosexuality has been one of the recurrent themes in fantastic literature (Todorov, 131). This theme, however, has not been found in the Latin American version of fantastic literature, nor for that matter, in Latin American letters in general, which, until only very recently, have broken through the silence concerning homosexual and lesbian themes and motifs. Todorov goes on to propose that in modern times psychoanalysis has destroyed certain taboos such as, for example, homosexuality, that traditionally nurtured fantastic literature (Todorov, 157–62). Putting to one side the question of the silencing of homosexual desire in traditional Latin American letters, we might ask ourselves, if Todorov's statement that psychoanalysis has destroyed certain taboos like homosexuality is indeed true, why then does Arenas resort to the presentation of homosexuality in a clearly fantastic story when he already had presented the theme more directly in his other works, as for example, "The Brightest Star" and *Farewell to the Sea?* My analysis answers this and other questions.

I would like to define the fantastic as the contradictory coexistence (Todorov calls it hesitation; Barrenechea, problematization) of the rational and irrational order in a given literary representation. The fantastic operates according to a logical principal of opposition or confrontation, that is, unreal or unnatural actions and events are contrasted with real or natural actions and events. I am quite aware of the dangers of basing a definition of the fantastic on the opposition between the so-called natural and supernatural orders that apply to the world as we know it but not to literature. Barrenechea tackles this very issue when she states that in the world of literature:

> nothing is true or false, real or unreal, natural or supernatural [given the fact that] all is fiction. . . . However . . . fantastic literature has produced extraordinary examples in this era of pure "literariness." A good portion of these have been achieved by digging deeper into its own nature, that is, serving as a vehicle of rebellion of its own fictitious world, a world that violates the terrestrial order. (Barrenechea, 402, my translation)

In *The Fantastic: A Structural Approach to a Literary Genre,* Todorov presents a conceptual framework and systematic analysis of the fantastic that is based on a reader-response approach to the fantastic text:

[T]he text must oblige the reader to consider the world of the characters as a world of living persons and to hesitate between a natural and a supernatural explanation of the events described. (Todorov, 33)

Todorov goes on to explain that the reader who experiences doubt in his or her perception of what is narrated is not a real reader per se, but rather an implied reader, that is, the function of reader inscribed in or determined by the text. There are obvious problems with this type of focus. First and foremost, the abstract notion of an implied reader(s) runs the risk of confusing itself with the actual real reader(s). Moreover, to base a definition of a genre on the psychological reaction of readers constitutes a highly subjective and value-ridden judgment that is diffi-cult, if not impossible, to measure. In her own work on the fantastic, Barrenechea, while recognizing Todorov's contributions to the study of the fantastic, modifies his reader-response approach. The Argentine critic devalues Todorov's condition of hesitation affirming that adher-ence to this condition would in fact eliminate a great portion of contem-porary fantastic literature. In its place, Barrenechea proposes a defini-tion of the fantastic that eliminates the basic requirement of the reader's hesitation. For her:

Fantastic literature would be defined as that type of literature that pre-sents in the form of a problem abnormal, unnatural, or unreal actions and events. Those works that place at their center of interest the viola-tion of the terrestrial, natural, or logical order, either explicitly or implic-itly confronting one another within the text, would apply. (Barrenechea, 393, my translation)

For Barrenechea, if the unreal or supernatural can indeed coexist with the real or the natural without a problem, then we are in the realm of the *marvelous*; the world of fairy tales and fantasy with other-worldly settings; J. R. R. Tolkien's *The Lord of the Rings* (1954–1955) would be a good example. On the other hand, if coexistence is a difficulty or a problem, we would be in the world of the *fantastic*. Thus, for Barrenechea the fan-tastic is seen not as a question of hesitation or doubt on the part of the reader, as proposed by Todorov, but rather as an issue of coexistence. Where Barrenechea and Todorov do agree is in the concept of "ambigu-ous vision" (that is, the instability generated between the representation of referential or plausible actions and events that produce an effect of reality and those unstable or implausible actions and events that produce an effect of unreality). In addition, both critics coincide in their estimation that the fantastic operates according to a principle of opposition.

"Mona" recounts the fatal and extraordinary story of Ramón Fernández, a Cuban exile living in New York City, who is arrested and imprisoned for having attempted to destroy the Leonardo da Vinci masterpiece, the Mona Lisa. The text begins with a foreword and an editors' note that establish a series of different time lines. The foreword, dated New York, 1987, is written by Daniel Sakuntala, an alleged friend of Ramón Fernández, who claims to have received the testimony written by the protagonist while in jail. The editors' note, dated Monterey, California, May 2025, is a brief note written by the editors of Ramón Fernández's testimony in the distant future.[14] Here, the editors claim that Daniel Sakuntala was never able to publish the document during his lifetime. In fact, it first appeared in print in New Jersey in 1999, published by Ismaele Lorenzo and Vicente Echurre, editors of the magazine *Unveiling Cuba.* After the editors' note, "Ramón Fernández's Testimony" appears, to which the editors from 2025 have added, for purposes of clarification, a number of footnotes as a result of the printing errors in the first edition of 1999.

Daniel Sakuntala's foreword introduces an element of ambiguity (essential to fantastic literature) concerning Ramón Fernández's motives for his crime and mysterious death. For example, we learn that although the press reported that Ramón Fernández's death was a case of suicide, the entire matter, according to Daniel Sakuntala, was highly suspicious. Apparently Ramón Fernández was found strangled in his cell, although no object responsible for the so-called suicide was ever found. Even more odd, Ramón's body mysteriously disappeared from the jail before the forensic doctor and the district attorney ever arrived. Yet despite this serious information, Daniel Sakuntala's foreword also contains a number of unintentional (on the part of Daniel Sakuntala, yet intentional on the part of Arenas) humorous moments. For instance, at one point we read: "Two days later, while the front pages gave coverage to Mother Teresa's suicide, only a few newspapers reported that Ramón Fernández's body had mysteriously disappeared from the morgue" ("Mona," 551). Neither Todorov nor Barrenechea directly explore the relationship between humor and the fantastic in their respective studies. Nonetheless, it is important to consider the question, does humor invalidate the fantastic? As we recall, Todorov, whose definition of the fantastic is limited to a small number of nineteenth-century texts, sees the fantastic as closely connected to certain reactions on the part of the implied reader that provoke fear and horror (Todorov, 92).[15] Hence, we can assume that for Todorov the presence of humor would annul the fantastic because humor, as Freud and Bakhtin have so well pointed out, does not disturb or unsettle the reader but rather subverts seriousness, dismantling all persuasive and authoritarian discourses.[16] Barrenechea, as previously established, defines the fantastic as a question of problematization, that is, the coexistence of the natural and the supernatural, which produces an unstable confrontation. Unlike Todorov, her definition can accommodate the presence of humor. Thus, for example, Daniel Sakuntala's foreword, despite its humorous moments, still contains ambiguity, instability, and problematization about what is articulated. This problematization indeed awakens in the implied and/or real reader a desire to find a rational explanation for the actions and events.

"Mona" is constructed around a system of ambiguity that creates a favorable climate to actualize the fantastic. The three principle stylistic devices or procedures that most strengthen that system are "modalization;" the systematic repetition of the verbs "to think" and "to seem," which underscores subjectivity on the part of the speaker describing the actions and events; and the insistence on the part of the narrator-protagonist (Ramón Fernández) to find rational explanations for what appear to be strange and illogical actions and events.

In "Mona," Ramón Fernández's testimony, written from jail prior to his death, tells of how he first met and got to know the mysterious yet sensual and provocative Elisa. The use of modalization is already evident in the first four sentences of Ramón Fernández's testimony. According to Todorov, modalization consists "in using certain introductory locutions which, without changing the meaning of the sentence, modify the relation between speaker and his utterance" (Todorov, 38). Todorov gives the example of the two sentences "It is raining outside" and "Perhaps it is raining outside." Although both sentences refer to the same fact, the latter introduces uncertainty and ambiguity. In the case of "Mona," Ramón Fernández's testimony begins in the following way:

> This report is being written in a rush, and even so, I am afraid I won't be able to finish it. She knows where I am and any moment now will come to destroy me. I am saying *she,* and perhaps I should say *he;* though [*quizás;* perhaps that's not the best term to use.] to call *that thing.* From the beginning, she (or he?) ensnared me, confused me, and now is even trying to prevent me from writing this statement. But I must do it; I must do it, and in the clearest way possible. ("Mona," 553–54)[17]

We see the use of modalization in the repetition of the word "perhaps," which reveals an underlying ambiguity on the part of the speaker (Ramón Fernández) which in turn creates uncertainty for the reader in regard to what is about to be narrated. Moreover, ambiguity is further evident in the protagonist's indecision as to which pronoun he should use. Yet, at the same time Ramón Fernández recognizes his own state of confusion ("From the beginning, she [or he?] ensnared me, confused me"), he wants to write his "statement" in the clearest possible way, obviously something he does not accomplish in these first few sentences.[18] These initial sentences underscore Ramón Fernández's particular perception of strange events, a necessary element, according to Todorov, in a fantastic text: "The fantastic is defined as a special *perception* of uncanny events" (Todorov, 91).

In "Mona," the repeated use of the verb "to think" (whose definition, according to *The Merriam-Webster Dictionary* is "to form or have in the mind; to have as an opinion; to believe") and the verb "to seem" ("to give the impression of being; to appear") undermine certainty on the part of the observer (Ramón Fernández), thus producing ambiguity. Let me present just a few of the many examples that exist in the text: TO THINK—"I think I had a nightmare" (559); "Yes, I think that by daybreak I had managed to satisfy her completely" (559); "But with all I had seen, or thought I had seen . . . I had to find out who this woman really was" (560); "Once, instead of her face, I thought I saw the face of a horrible old man" (557); "I think I'd managed to do no harm at all to it" (570); TO SEEM—"I seemed to perceive an intense glow radiating from the tallest buildings" (556); "a warmish glow seemed to envelop everything" (557); "her beauty seemed to grow by the minute (559); "She seemed out of breath" (559); "The color of her hair seemed to have grown even more intense" (559–60); "it seemed as if I were back in Havana" (567).

Throughout his testimony, the narrator-protagonist is not altogether sure as to the interpretations of certain events that he himself classifies, on various occasions, as strange and peculiar. Before the decisive moment in the story when Elisa's true identity is revealed, Ramón Fernández's testimony is structured as a gradual presentation of strange and uncanny events that the protagonist attempts to explain rationally. This oscillation between the strange/the inexplicable and the rational creates a problematization that, according to Barrenechea, gives life to the fantastic. In the following chart I have represented the most obvious examples in the text. In the left column I have presented the strange or

peculiar event and in the right column, the rational explanation that
Ramón Fernández immediately reaches in order to logically explain the
event.

STRANGE OR PECULIAR EVENT	RATIONAL EXPLANATION
1. "I noted nothing strange in her that night, except for a peculiar pronunciation of certain words and phrases." (555)	1. "I supposed it was due to her lack of knowledge of the Spanish language." (555)
2. "[Elisa] was as if transported, looking at the strange luminosity and muttering unintelligible words." (556)	2. "I assumed [those words] were in her mother tongue." (556)
3. "A chill ran down my spine. One of her shoulders seemed to bulge out of joint in the shape of a hook." (557)	3. "Then I thought that surely I must have touched a safety pin or a shoulder pad, now back in place." (557)
4. "I kept glancing at Elisa in the rearview mirror; . . . Once, instead of her face, I thought I saw the face of a horrible old man." (557)	4. "I attributed this to our speed, which distorted images." (557)
5. "I opened my eyes slightly. Facing the early light, her back to me, was a beautiful naked woman . . . . Her bottom, her back, her shoulders, her neck, everything was perfect. Except that her perfect body had no head." (559)	5. "Since in the face of the most outlandish circumstances we always search for logical explanations, I rationalized what I had seen as purely an effect produced by the heavy fog so usual in that place." (559)

   Ramón's uncertainty comes to a head when he enters the Metropoli-
tan Museum and finds Elisa not among the people in the museum, but
rather on a canvas surrounded by a huge crowd. At this moment, the
naive Ramón believes he has finally discovered Elisa's true identity: that
she is a famous, exclusive artists' model. However, upon examining the
canvas, Ramón reads on the small placard next to the painting the title
"Mona Lisa," executed in 1505 by Leonardo da Vinci: "Stunned, I
backed up to take a good look at the canvas. My eyes then met Elisa's
intense gaze in the painting. I held her gaze and discovered that Elisa's
eyes had no eyelashes; she had the eyes of a serpent" ("Mona," 564).
Ramón resorts to his typical defense mechanism of searching for a rational explanation of an inexplicable event: "Of course, no matter how
much the woman in the painting resembled Elisa, it was impossible for

her to have been the model. So I quickly tried to find a reasonable explanation for the phenomenon" ("Mona," 564). From this moment on Ramón becomes obsessed with finding a rational explanation for the events surrounding the appearance and disappearance of Elisa. The answer finally arrives when Elisa, tired of being persecuted and hunted down by Ramón—let us recall that the theme of persecution is a constant one in Arenas's work; for example, the theatrical piece *Persecución,* or *The Ill-Fated Peregrinations of Fray Servando,* among others—reveals to him her true identity: "There is no difference between what you saw in the painting at the museum and me. We are the same thing" ("Mona," 568). In his testimony Ramón Fernández furnishes us with a supernatural explanation: Elisa is the incarnation of Leonardo da Vinci, who, through a mustering of genius and mental concentration, managed to paint himself onto the canvas thus ensuring his immortality. Moreover, when no one was present, he was able to step out of the painting to find the homosexual gratification that he had not been able to achieve during his own lifetime. After revealing her/his secret, Elisa/Leonardo has no other alternative but to kill Ramón. Yet Ramón manages to escape by once again having sex with Elisa/Leonardo:

> I am sure that in all my long erotic experience, never has my performance been so lustful and tender, so skilled and passionate—because in all truth, even knowing she intended to kill me, I still lusted for her. By her third orgasm, while she was still panting and uttering the most obscene words, Elisa had not only forgotten the dagger but become oblivious of herself. I noticed she apparently was losing her concentration and energy that, as she said, enabled her to become a real woman. Her eyes were becoming opaque, her face was losing its color, her cheekbones were melting away. Suddenly her luscious hair dropped from her head, and I found myself in the arms of a very old, bald man, toothless and foul-smelling, who kept whimpering while slobbering my penis. Quickly he sat on it, riding it as if he were a true demon. I quickly put him on all fours and, in spite of my revulsion, tried to give him as much pleasure as I could, hoping he would be so exhausted he would let me go. ("Mona," 570)

Ramón escapes but after a series of misadventures, most important of which is his failed attempt to destroy the painting of the Mona Lisa, he is imprisoned. "Mona" ends with Ramón fearing not so much that he is in jail, but that Elisa will come to destroy him. As we already know from the beginning of the story, Ramón Fernández indeed dies in his jail cell. As a result of all these accounts (i.e., Daniel Sakuntala's foreword, the

editors' note, Ramón Fernández's testimony), the reader—in this case
the implicit reader as defined by Todorov—is left with many questions:
Was it a case of suicide, or did in fact Elisa/Leonardo, wishing to maintain her secret, destroy Ramón? Or, rather, was it a case of paranoid
repressed homosexual feelings on the part of Ramón? Or did it all really
occur as the protagonist declares in his testimony? Todorov would define
this type of doubt on the part of the implicit reader as an example of the
fantastic. Finally, if one wishes to address the constant use of humor in
this story, which, in Todorov's model, debilitates the fantastic, then
"Mona" could perfectly be explained using Barrenechea's definition of
the fantastic in which the conflict or problematization of so-called natural and supernatural events coexist within a text.

I would like to make one last extratextual observation. At the beginning of this analysis I noted Todorov's observation that in modern times
psychoanalysis has destroyed certain taboos, like homosexuality, that
traditionally nurtured fantastic literature. If this is true, why then did
Arenas present a homosexual theme in a fantastic story? Perhaps we
might find a possible explanation in the foreword, in which Daniel
Sakuntala points out that upon receiving Ramón Fernández's testimony,
he went to see Reinaldo Arenas (fictionalized within the text) in order to
see if Arenas could help him publish the testimony in *Mariel,* an actual
magazine that Arenas founded with the help of other Cuban writers in
exile in the spring of 1982. Sakuntala states:

> But Arenas, with his proverbial frivolity and in spite of the fact that he
> was already sick with AIDS, the cause of his recent death, laughed at my
> suggestion, saying that *Mariel* was a modern magazine in which there
> was no room for this "nineteenth-century tale." ("Mona," 552)

The classification of Ramón Fernández's extraordinary testimony as a
"nineteenth-century tale," more than an example of Arenas's irreverent
humor, is quite telling for my particular analysis of "Mona" because,
according to Todorov, it is precisely this century in which fantastic literature flourished. Considering fantastic literature from a socio-historical
point of view, Todorov proposes that there "is a qualitative difference
between the personal possibilities of a nineteenth-century author and
those of a contemporary author" (Todorov, 159). According to Todorov,
the nineteenth-century writer, who lived in a repressive and conservative
environment, found a practical use for the fantastic: the ability to
describe certain censured themes, like incest, necrophilia, excessive sen-

suality, and so forth, without being accused of perversion. Todorov goes on to state that in modern times there has been a liberation of the human psyche that in turn has revoked social censorship, which at one point in time forbade dealing with certain taboo themes. Hence, the writer no longer has to avail him- or herself of the fantastic given the fact that he or she can treat these themes in a more direct fashion. Todorov affirms:

> There is no need today to resort to the devil in order to speak of an excessive sexual desire, and none to resort to vampires in order to designate the attraction exerted by corpses: psychoanalysis, and the literature which is directly or indirectly inspired by it, deals with these matters in undisguised terms. The themes of fantastic literature have become, literally, the very themes of the psychological investigations of the last fifty years. (Todorov, 160–61)

Perhaps Todorov's assertions were valid in the liberal environment of the 1970s when he was writing his book in France. However, much has changed in the world since then. In the United States, the 1980s initiated the beginning of a conservative era, an era in which Arenas lived, wrote, and suffered through. If homosexuals and lesbians won victories in their struggles for equal rights during the 1960s and 1970s, the 1980s ushered in a new era of hostility and discrimination toward these minority groups as a result of the AIDS epidemic. Seen from this perspective, we should not be surprised that Arenas, a victim of this discrimination, would write a fantastic tale that presents a homosexual theme as a case of repression: Leonardo da Vinci's inability to freely express himself as a homosexual during his lifetime as well as Ramón Fernández's possible homosexual inclinations. With this novella, Arenas has left behind the first example of a homosexual fantastic text in Spanish American letters.

"Viaje a La Habana"

The last story of the collection, "Viaje a La Habana" (Journey to Havana), was written in two stages: October-November 1983, three years after Arenas's arrival in the United States, and September-November 1987, three years prior to the author committing suicide. The story's title, which is also used for the entire collection, alludes to two well-known texts in Cuban literature: the Countess of Merlín's autobiographical account of her return voyage to Cuba, *Viaje a La Habana* (1844), and Alejo Carpentier's famous short story "Viaje a la semilla" (1944; "Journey Back to the Source"). Despite differences in their settings and concerns, these three texts do share a common narrative pattern: They all reconstruct a search for origins.

María de las Mercedes Santa Cruz y Montalvo (1789–1852), better known to Cuban readers as la Condesa de Merlín, or the Countess of Merlín, was born in Havana but sent to Spain as an adolescent. In 1809, at the age of 20, she married the French general Christophe Antoine Merlin, an officer and count in Joseph Bonaparte's army in Spain. Upon the fall of Joseph Bonaparte in 1810, the couple fled to France and settled in Paris, where the countess distinguished herself for her writings and musical performances in the Parisian salons. After the death of General Merlin in 1838, la Condesa de Merlín returned to Havana (1840) and in 1844 published a testimonial account of that return to her homeland titled *La Havane*. *Viaje a La Habana*, which appeared in Madrid the same year as the original French, is a significantly shorter and somewhat different version of the French edition. Whereas the French edition, three volumes long, is more a historical text chronicling the state of the Cuban colony in 1840, the Spanish edition, reduced to one volume, in Adriana Méndez Rodenas's words, reads more "as a personal memoir devoted to the lyrical reconstruction of origin."[19] Gertrudis Gómez de Avellaneda (1814–1873), who like la Condesa de Merlín abandoned Cuba at an early age and made her life abroad, was responsible for writing the prologue to the 1844 Spanish edition. In the prologue, Gómez de Avellaneda intuitively points out, even back then, the strange fate of Cuban writers who appear to be destined to live in exile. Adriana Méndez Rodenas in her carefully documented article, "Voyage to *La Havane*: The Countess of Merlín's Preview of National Identity," argues that both Gómez de Avellaneda, in her romance "La vuelta a la patria" (1860; "Return to the Homeland"), and la Condesa de Merlín, in *Viaje a La Habana* (1844), not only lyrically record their respective experiences of returning to Cuba but also contribute to the founding of a Cuban national identity. Grounding her argument on Cintio Vitier's sentimental concept of "lejanía" (a distanced perspective of seeing and yearning for "la patria," or homeland, nostalgically from afar)—what appears to be a unifying trait in Cuban literature since the writings of exiled poets José María Heredia (1803–1839) and José Martí (1853–1895)—Méndez Rodenas successfully argues that Gómez de Avellaneda and la Condesa de Merlín indeed inscribed their work within the search for a

Cuban national identity, yet, because they were women, their contributions in the symbolic process of inventing a national identity have been
played down and even denied in the past by Cuban critics not interested
in a feminine perspective "on the archeology of insular origins" (Méndez
Rodenas, 75).

Alejo Carpentier's famous story "Journey Back to the Source" inverts
the spatio-temporal continuum in order to present a character's life in
reverse order, from death to birth.[20] This flowing of time retrospectively
symbolizes a journey of discovery and self-knowledge through which the
character learns more about the significance of his origins. In *The Repeating Island: The Caribbean and the Postmodern Perspective,* Antonio Benítez-
Rojo reads Carpentier's story as a metaphorical search for the origins of
Caribbeanness: "Europe's sway over Carpentier's own ego . . . does not
disqualify him as a Caribbean man. The final measure of Caribbeanness
is the search for that which is Caribbean, independently of the port or
portal from which this search is undertaken. In reality, the Caribbean
Self must begin the utopian voyage toward its reconstitution from a cultural space that necessarily remains 'outside' " (Benítez-Rojo, 234).
While acknowledging Carpentier's own European (French) legacy,
Benítez-Rojo also points out two important aspects of this search for the
origins of Caribbeanness (Caribbeanness being the more general term
under which the concept of "lo cubano," or Cubanness, would fall): (1)
that the search itself is utopian in nature and (2) that the voyage or journey must be undertaken from a cultural space "outside" that which is
sought. We must be mindful of these two aspects throughout our discussion of Arenas's "Viaje a La Habana," a story that narrates the
utopian journey of a man who, marginalized for his homosexual desires
to the point that he is spiritually dead, struggles to understand and
come to terms with his sexual orientation, an act that symbolically
brings him back to life.

The protagonist of Arenas's story, Ismael, very much resembles his
biblical namesake, Ishmael, in that he is also disinherited, an outcast
who is lost and attempts to find his way. To articulate this story, Arenas
appropriates a number of Judeo-Christian religious allusions and
reframes them within a specific homosexual context. "Viaje a La
Habana" begins with a letter addressed to Ismael, now living in New
York City, from his estranged wife, Elvia, who has remained in Cuba.
(This beginning pays homage to la Condesa de Merlín's own distinct
epistolary style in *La Havane,* in which 36 interspersed letters appear
throughout.)[21] Elvia invites Ismael to return to Cuba to visit his son,

Ismaelito, who is now 23 years old and whom Ismael has not seen for 15 years: "Creo que para un hijo es siempre necesario ver a su padre aunque sea una sola vez en su vida" ("Viaje," 115) (I believe that it is necessary for a son to see his father at least once in his lifetime). This declaration gives impetus to Ismael's memories and retrospective ruminations of what occurred to him in Cuba and why he left. As a winter storm hits the city, Ismael, in his small New York City apartment, a protective space that he has created for himself, looks out his window and remembers; that is, he journeys back to the past, a past filled with painful memories that he once thought he had carefully buried, but now, like the copious snowflakes outside his window, overcome his very being. Ismael's feelings of frustration, anger, and confusion are not so much a consequence of Elvia's invitation but rather a result of the fact that he is forced to remember a life that he thought he had long ago laid to rest. It is through these memories that the reader learns of Ismael's past tragedy. We learn that in Cuba, feeling the pressure to assimilate and fit in despite his homosexual desires, Ismael—using the same logic as Hector in *Farewell to the Sea*—marries and has a child in order to place himself above suspicion. As a result of the homophobic repression surrounding him, Ismael desperately works at controlling and keeping his homosexual tendencies strictly in check. Although initially successful in projecting to his neighbors and colleagues an exemplary figure of moral rectitude, Ismael eventually stumbles. One day, while Elvia is away visiting her family in the interior of the island, the opportunity to feel, to experience what he long denied himself, is presented. Ismael meets the young and attractive Sergio and takes him back to his apartment where they have sex. The scene is described as one of bliss and mutual satisfaction. Yet the happiness Ismael finally feels after so many years of self-imposed homosexual abstinence is short-lived. Soon after Sergio leaves there is a knock on the door. Upon opening the door, Ismael discovers that the omnipresent national surveillance system, a tropical Big Brother, has indeed been doing its work; two militiamen, a police officer, and the president of the neighborhood C.D.R. or Defense Committee for the Revolution are all standing outside the door ready to arrest him for homosexual activities punishable by the state. (Whereas in *Farewell to the Sea* it is never clear whether the alluring figure of the young adolescent seduced in the end by Hector is indeed an agent of the security police attempting to set up and entrap so-called deviants, in "Viaje a La Habana" it is evident that Sergio is specifically brought in by the security police to seduce and entice Ismael.) After a humiliating trial, Ismael, unfairly convicted of corrupting a minor and sexual perversion, is sentenced to three years in prison. After serving his time he manages to escape from Cuba.

"Viaje a La Habana" is predominantly focalized through a third-person narrative voice that, instead of looking outward to external events and actions, looks inward toward Ismael, thus allowing the reader to (over)hear the character's interior monologues. In addition, as a way of underscoring and lending credibility to the third-person focalization, at various moments throughout the story, the text utilizes italicized sentences to switch the focalization back to a first-person narrative voice. At times this transition occurs rather deftly midway through a sentence as in the following example in which Ismael expresses his anxiety and guilt about his marriage to Elvia:

> Y no solamente sintió lástima por ella y, desde luego, por sí mismo, *sino que me sentí miserable y cobarde por haberle hecho participar en aquella farsa* de la cual ahora él ya no sabía cómo escapar. ("Viaje," 119)

> And he didn't only feel pity for her and, of course, for himself, *but I also felt miserable and cowardly for having made her participate in that farce* from which he no longer knew how to escape. (my translation)

Knowing Ismael's past is important for the reader in order to put the character's decision to return to Cuba into a meaningful context. Although logic and reason point to the fact that he should not return to the place that branded him an outcast, Ismael eventually does decide to return. This decision is lyrically articulated as a need to be physically back again in his homeland, the only space where his being can exist fully and be identified as such:

> Y se vio no entre esta blancura desolada que petrifica hasta la misma imaginación, sino allá, en medio de una tibieza y de un paisaje resplandeciente, junto a un mar y unos árboles que eran parte de su propia vida y que la distancia ennoblecía aún más. Se vio, no como realmente había vivido o creía sólo haber vivido, esclavo, humillado, mal vestido, insatisfecho y hambriento, sino joven y entusiasmado, aspirando desenfadadamente una atmósfera que no le era agresiva sino cómplice y protectora; aspirando, sintiendo, disfrutando una sensación de estar, de sentirse en su sitio, en el único sitio donde realmente su existencia puede tener ese nombre. ("Viaje," 136)

And he saw himself not in this desolate whiteness that petrifies even one's own imagination, but rather there, in the middle of a tepidness and a shining landscape, next to the sea and some trees that were part of his own life and that distance had dignified even more. He saw himself, not how he really had lived or only believed he had lived, a slave, humiliated, badly dressed, unsatisfied and hungry, but rather as a young man filled with enthusiasm, breathing in uninhibitedly an atmosphere that wasn't aggressive but rather a protective accomplice; breathing in, feeling, enjoying a sensation of being, of feeling in one's place, in the only place where one's existence can really have that name. (my translation)

What is interesting about these words is that Ismael, even after years of burying his desires and living with his grief, can still let himself *imagine,* that is, project himself into a space where he can feel he belongs both as a Cuban and a homosexual. Let us recall Benítez-Rojo's description of the search for the origins of Caribbeanness (which includes "lo cubano," or Cubanness) as being utopian in nature and undertaken from a cultural space "outside" that which is sought. In "Viaje a La Habana" Arenas lyrically and politically grafts homosexuality onto Benítez-Rojo's description of the utopian search for the origins of Caribbeanness from a position of outsider. By having Ismael decide to return to Cuba and face the ghosts of his past, Arenas inserts, as Benigno Sánchez-Eppler has so well illustrated in his essay, "Call My Son Ismael: Exiled Paternity and Father/Son Eroticism in Reinaldo Arenas and José Martí," issues of homosexuality and heterosexual homophobia into the discourse of Cuban national identity, a national identity shared both inside and outside of Cuba that continues to affirm that "real Cubans are not homosexuals [and] homosexuals are not real Cubans."[22]

There is a small visual break in the text (page 139) that separates the space of exile, New York City, from Ismael's arrival in Havana on 23 December 1994. That this part of the story is set in a distant future ("Viaje a La Habana," as mentioned earlier, was written in two stages, 1983 and 1987, and moreover, in his real life Arenas never again returned to Cuba after leaving through the Mariel exodus in 1980) places Arenas, the flesh-and-blood writer, in the same position as his character Ismael, that is, Arenas through the character of Ismael *imagines* a (utopian) space in Cuba, far away from the coldness of a New York City winter, where he can simply be homosexual and Cuban.

Upon arriving in Havana, Ismael does not go directly to his hometown of Santa Fe but rather stays the night in the Cuban capital. It is there that he meets a young guard, first identified as Carlos, with whom he falls in

love. Although the parallels with Sergio exist, and the possibilities of
being set up and humiliated present themselves again, Ismael, nevertheless, does eventually allow himself to feel, to act upon his homosexual
desires after so many years of abstinence. Since the moment of his arrest
and subsequent imprisonment, Ismael had chosen to lead a life of total
celibacy. In prison, and later on in the symbolic prison that is exile, Ismael,
recognizing his lack of freedom, consciously chose not to have sex. It is
only when he returns to Cuba, the space that initially prohibited and condemned his homosexual actions, that the character feels he can reclaim his
individual freedom to act and engage in what he wishes. Ismael's homosexual awakening is specifically and deliberately represented in the text as
both an emotional as well as a physical resurrection. At one point Ismael
tells the young guard: ¿No te das cuenta que yo estaba muerto y tú me
has resucitado? ("Viaje," 173) (Don't you realize that I was dead and you
have resurrected me?). Ultimately managing to outsmart the surveillance
at his hotel, Ismael spends the night of 24 December —for Cubans
Nochebuena, or Christmas Eve, is considered the most important family
gathering of the entire year—with the young guard. As if reliving a bad
nightmare, Ismael wakes up the next morning to discover that he has
been robbed. In addition to the gifts that Ismael was bringing his family,
also missing are the 20 thousand dollars (Ismael's *life* savings) that he had
unnecessarily but rather tellingly brought to Cuba. In a bold and provocative denouement intentionally charged with religious overtones, Ismael, in
a pair of old military shorts, the only article of clothing left in his hotel
room, must make his way to his hometown. The last four pages of the text
present the hardships and afflictions that Ismael—similar to Evatt and
Ricardo's odyssey in arriving at the Maisí lighthouse—must suffer in order
to make his way back on foot to Santa Fe, or Holy Faith (a name chosen
for its apparent symbolism), precisely on 25 December:

> Atravesó pedregales, terraplenes y arrecifes que le desgarraron los pies y
> hasta las manos, pues a cada rato se iba de bruces. . . . Ismael tomó un
> largo y pesado tronco lleno de clavos que las olas habían dejado en la
> costa y con él en hombros siguió andando. . . . [P]arecía un loco . . . [y]
> como loco fue tratado por la pandilla de delincuentes, quienes para
> entretenerse comenzaron a tirarle piedras y hasta golpearlo con estacas,
> correas y cabillas. Ismael se cayó varias veces, pero tomando el tronco se
> incorporó y siguió avanzando. ("Viaje," 177–78)

> He crossed rocky grounds, embankments and coral reefs that tore his feet
> and even his hands, for at every moment he would fall face down. . . . Ismael

took a long and heavy log filled with nails that the waves had washed up
onto the shore and placed it on his shoulders and kept moving. . . . He
looked like a madman and like a madman he was treated by gangs of delin-
quents who in order to amuse themselves began throwing rocks and even
hitting him with sticks, straps, and metal bars. Ismael fell many times, but
taking the log he got himself up and continued forward. (my translation)

As we see, Arenas inserts new possibilities of homosexual signification
into Christian religious episodes and symbols, thereby confronting the
moral sobriety and outright homophobia of Christianity.[23] Finally making his way home, Ismael is greeted by his wife, Elvia, and soon discovers that the young guard, Carlos, with whom he had made love, is in
fact Ismaelito, his son, who in turn confesses that he had known from
the very first time they met that Ismael was his father.

Ismael's physical and emotional *via crucis* is necessary for him to
achieve his resurrection, which in Catholicism represents the union of
the Father with the Son. In addition, the classical myth of Oedipus who
unknowingly killed his father, Laius, and married his mother, Jocasta, is
here recast as a homosexual incestuous triangle. (In Freudian analysis
homosexuality is seen as the inability of the male child to overcome the
Oedipal complex.) Yet unlike Oedipus who upon discovering the truth
of his acts gouges out his eyes, is banished from his home of Thebes, and
must spend the rest of his life wandering and begging, the story of
Ismael has a happy ending, something that is quite unique in Arenas's
literary oeuvre, which tends to present tragic endings. In the last sentence of the story we read: *"Luego, en silencio, los tres comenzamos a comer."*
(*Later, in silence, the three of us* [Elvia, Ismael, Ismaelito] *began to eat"*)
("Viaje," 153). The familial meal of *Nochebuena* is finally celebrated as a
final peace (silence) rains down on the united family.

Arenas infuses a political and humane message into "Viaje a La
Habana" by linking the searches for a homosexual and a national identity. It is Benigno Sánchez-Eppler's thesis that "Viaje a La Habana" can
be read as an attempt by Arenas to provocatively recast José Martí's book
of poems, *Ismaelillo* (1882)—a foundational text in the Cuban social
Imaginary that expresses a father's exilic pain for not having a space, that
is, a homeland in which he can live together with his son—into "an
explicitly incestuous and homoerotic narrative with a frank counter-
homophobic and counter-revolutionary political agenda" (Sánchez-Eppler,
70).[24] Arenas's text directly and boldly reflects on homosexuality, politics,
liberty, and exile.

There is no denying that "Viaje a La Habana" reads like a parable of sorts, the return of the prodigal father to his home(land), a utopian space of acceptance in which differences are respected. The story, although similar in circumstances to *Farewell to the Sea* (e.g., the idea of a marriage of convenience to hide homosexual desires, the potential setup by a national surveillance system out to entrap homosexuals, the suspense or detective story format in which the reader is anxious to find out the outcome of the events presented), also has much in common with Arenas's novel *The Doorman,* written in New York City during the same time as "Viaje a La Habana" (*The Doorman* was written between April 1984 and December 1986) and that likewise treats the theme of exile, albeit in a more universal way. *The Doorman* and "Viaje a La Habana" reveal Arenas's struggles with those common issues that face the exile, an outcast in a strange land who searches for a space in which he or she can feel, if not at peace, at least comfortable to live on his or her own terms. The two texts differ substantially, however, in the specificity of the exile condition and in their narrative approaches. Whereas "Viaje a La Habana" links the exile condition to issues of homosexuality and homophobia, *The Doorman* universalizes the theme. Also, "Viaje a La Habana" is a serious text, that is, it noticeably lacks the animated sense of humor that is a trademark of Arenas's body of writings. *The Doorman,* in contrast, is a very funny and festively intoxicating novel. I will briefly say a few words on *The Doorman,* Arenas's only novel set in the United States, to better establish its relationship with "Viaje a La Habana."

The main character of *The Doorman,* Juan, is a young exiled Cuban from the Mariel exodus who finds himself living in New York City and working as a doorman in an elegant building in Manhattan's upper West Side. Juan, who also embarks on a journey in search of meaning, is represented more as a symbolic caricature than is Ismael. The young doorman's search or journey for happiness in a world of absurdities, dehumanization, and excessive materialism transcends Ismael's personal homosexual experiences of "outsider" as well as his journey to understand these experiences. *The Doorman* presents how all men are spiritually exiled, their lives driven by an insatiable search for plenitude and satisfaction in a world beset by disappointment, ignorance, and brutality.

The Doorman is divided into two parts. Part 1 introduces the reader to the eccentric residents of the luxurious apartment building where the young man works. Arenas utilizes a combination of comic irony and pathos to present these peculiar characters, each obsessed by, and a prisoner of, his or her own fanaticism. (The first part of "Viaje a La Habana"

contains a segment in which Ismael talks of the fanaticism of various
political anti-Castro organizations in exile, groups motivated more by
demagoguery and a desire for power than by any authentic commitment
to the Cuban cause.) In *The Doorman,* Arenas presents the reader comical
and colorful sketches of a number of new-age zealots searching for happiness through their own personal and proselytizing philosophies. Thus,
for example, among the eccentric residents of the luxurious apartment
building in which Juan works we find: a Marxist professor of social sciences who ardently defends the Castro regime; two nearly identical gay
lovers who are devotees of the Hollywood Oscars and insatiable readers
of the New York Times (they call themselves Oscar Times One and
Oscar Times Two); an electro-technical wizard intent on replacing different parts of his body with more powerful mechanical replicas; and the
Supreme Pastor of the Church of Love of Christ Through Friendly and
Constant Contact (this last character is so driven by his messianic belief
of promoting the happiness of the human race through brotherly contact that he ties and glues together in pairs the animals in his home).
Each tenant introduced in this first part lives with a pet: a cat, a bird, a
fish, and even some rather exotic animals such as a rattlesnake, an
orangutan, and a polar bear (which, incidentally, belongs to the Marxist
professor, who proclaims to be repairing the injustices committed in cir-
cuses against bears by humans). But Juan himself is also somewhat of a
zealot. Besides the door that he opens and closes for the tenants, the
young man feels he has a sacred mission to lead the residents of the
building to "the true door of happiness." Early on we read: "Of course,
not even Juan himself knew what this door was or how to find it, much
less how to open it. But in his state of exaltation, or delirium or demen-
tia . . . he was sure this door really existed, and in some mysterious way
one might reach and open it" (*Doorman,* 6).

Part 2 of *The Doorman* presents a carnivalesque inversion of the hierarchy man/animal. In the tradition of fables, the tenants' pets begin to
talk and communicate with Juan. Gathering in the basement of the
building, they plan an escape from the abuses of their masters and elect
Juan to lead their mass flight to liberty. But when the tenants discover
Juan talking to their pets they have him admitted into Bellevue Psychi-
atric Hospital. At this point, the animals work together to rescue the
doorman, who in turn leads them, like a modern day Moses—as in the
stories of *Viaje a La Habana, The Doorman* utilizes a number of Biblical
allusions in its process of articulation—to the "true door to happiness."
In a final chapter titled simply "The Door" Juan sees the animals begin

to pass through the opening. After seeing them all pass through he comments: "All except me, the doorman, who on the outside will watch them disappear forever" (*Doorman,* 190). Juan will not pass through, he will remain outside, only imagining and dreaming how it would be to live in a world without fear, without sickness, suffering, or frustrations.

Whereas *The Doorman* presents a more universal and symbolic message that happiness is very much tied to the fact that all human beings need to find a space in which they can live life on their own terms, "Viaje a La Habana" takes on directly the homosexual issue and how the homosexual struggles for self and societal acceptance. In "Viaje a La Habana" Arenas provokes his readers not just with a story about homosexuality but also one of incest. Benigno Sánchez-Eppler proposes that among the possible readings of the story's recourse to incest, either as real incest or hyper-utopian sexual/national fantasy, is one that demands from the Cuban nation the creation of a space, a promised land of sorts, in which Cuban patriarchs in their nation-making discourses would "acknowledge, forgive, accept, celebrate a queerness somehow shared among Cuban fathers and sons" (Sánchez-Eppler, 92). This view would explain why in "Viaje a La Habana" the double taboo of homosexuality and incest is presented with such compassion and humanity. It is interesting that Arenas does not represent Ismael's homosexual lovemaking with graphic details, as we find in many of his later texts, for example, *El color del verano* and *Before Night Falls,* but rather with a suggestive and poetic language of elemental feelings of communion with another. The tone of "Viaje a La Habana" is not one of anger or heavy-handed propaganda demanding acceptance, but rather one of introspection and suggestive subtlety. In the end, what lies at the center of "Viaje a La Habana" is a story of deep compassion and commitment to human dignity and acceptance.

Chapter Five

Arenas's Poetry:
Politics and Sexuality

In December of 1987 I conducted an interview with Arenas in his New York City apartment. For the last question of the interview, I asked him to specifically comment on the poetic resonance and lyricism that exists in much of his prose writing. It was my estimation at the time, and still is, that the distinction between poetry and prose in much of Arenas's so-called prose texts is very difficult to discern. Arenas answered in the following manner:

> I believe that a writer should have a knowledge of poetry and from there get all the rest. Poetry is the source of everything. I read poetry. That is why I've always admired Borges, who is a great poet. Borges never abandoned poetry. Even when he wrote his last books of prose he always wrote poetry. One should never forget poetry or underestimate its power. Neither should one limit poetry to a genre, rather it should be a literary necessity. When a text requires a more poetic tone a writer should use one; if it isn't required then he or she should not use it. But a writer should always keep poetry in mind; if not, the text becomes journalistic, very arid. One of my aspirations is that after I'm dead some reader will remember me for the rhythm of some of my sentences. I'm obviously very optimistic. I can't help it. (Soto, 154)

Apart from Arenas's clear adoption of poetic tones and nuances into his prose writings, what he calls the rhythm of some of his sentences, the Cuban writer also composed a series of poetic texts, in the strict generic definition, during his lifetime. Perhaps his most accomplished endeavor in this field is the long poem *El central*.[1] This lengthy poetic composition, a lyrical and narrative hybrid written in prose and free verse, was Arenas's first published book of poetry in Spanish as well as one of his earliest translated English texts: *El Central: A Cuban Sugar Mill*.[2] Anthony Kerrigan's highly competent translation from the Spanish *El central* indeed supports the Mexican Nobel Laureate Octavio Paz's contention that poetry, because of its universality, can be translated—contrary to the admonition of many opposing theorists. Paz has written:

> The greatest pessimism about the feasibility of translation has been concentrated on poetry, a remarkable posture since many of the best poems in every Western language are translations. . . . Some years ago the critic and linguist Georges Mounin wrote a book about translation. He pointed out that it is generally, albeit reluctantly, conceded that . . . poetry is a fabric of connotations and, consequently, untranslatable. I must confess that I find this idea offensive, not only because it conflicts with my personal conviction that poetry is universal, but also because it is based on an erroneous conception of what translation is. [3]

If one expects a translation to be a literal equivalent of the original, then surely one would agree with Georges Mounin's position that proposes the untranslatability of poetry. On the other hand, if one sees a translation as a creative transformation of ideas and sensibilities from one language to another, an ongoing approximation, never quite finished, then Paz's words appear more accurate. Anthony Kerrigan's *El Central: A Cuban Sugar Mill* attests to the universality of Arenas's poetry regardless of the language in which it is delivered.

El Central: A Cuban Sugar Mill

Like *Singing from the Well* and *The Palace of the White Skunks,* which after they were written became part of a larger project (the *pentagonía,* both a writer's autobiography and a metaphor of Cuban history), *El central,* subsequent to its composition, became the first section of a poetic trilogy that presents the Cuban experience from the time of conquest to and including the Castro regime. The trilogy, titled *Leprosorio,* or Leper Colony, was published in its entirety in 1990.[4] (In the notes to the last poem of the trilogy [*Leprosorio,* 131], Arenas admits that the linguistically correct word, according to the Royal Academy for the Spanish Language, is in fact "Leprosería" and not "Leprosorio." In Spanish, the suffix "ería" is commonly used to denote a shop or store in which a specific product is sold; for example, "carnicería" is a store in which "carne," or meat, is sold; "heladería" is a shop in which "helado," or ice cream, is sold. With this logic in mind, Arenas notes that "Leprosería" would suggest to the average Spanish-speaker a store or shop in which "leprosos" or lepers are sold. Arenas's humorous and irreverent response is just

another indication of his undermining of hegemonic and dogmatic institutions; in this case, the Royal Academy for the Spanish Language.)

Leprosorio is composed of: *El central* (*El Central: A Cuban Sugar Mill*),
originally written by Arenas in the Cuban Sugar Mill Manuel Sanguily
in the province of Pinar del Río and dated May, 1970; *Morir en junio y con
la lengua afuera* (To Die in June, Gasping for Air), Havana, November,
1970; and *Leprosorio* (Leper Colony), Havana, 1974–1976, the title of
which is also used for the entire collection. In the Betania edition of *Leprosorio* each composition is subtitled as well: *El central,* "Fundación"
(Foundation); *Morir en junio y con la lengua afuera,* "Ciudad" (City); *Leprosorio,* "Exodo" (Exodus).

Leprosorio is Arenas's most political text. In it the poetic voice does
not hold back its anger and rage as it lashes out at the injustices and cruelties that have been committed in Cuba since the island was first settled
by Spaniards more than 500 years ago. The horrors of the sugarcane
fields of colonial Cuba, which turned the island into a prison first for
Indians and then for African slaves, are compared to the atrocities committed by the Castro regime that likewise have turned the "111,111
square kilometers" of island surface into a "cárcel, cárcel, cárcel" (*Leprosorio,* 106) (prison, prison, prison). The leper colony, infested with out-
breaks of epidemic virulent diseases, which are specifically enumerated
throughout the last poem of the trilogy, serves as a tragically grotesque
metaphor for what Cuba has become after successive periods of coloniza-
tion, military dictatorships, and socialist occupation. *Leprosorio* falls
within the tradition of that rare combination and balance of politically
and poetically committed verse that very few poets can achieve. In Latin
America the most noteworthy examples would be the Peruvian César
Vallejo (1892–1938)—*Poemas humanos* (1939) (*Human Poems*)—and the
Chilean Nobel Laureate Pablo Neruda (1904–1973)—*Tercera residencia*
(1947) (*Third Residence*)—whose socio-politically committed poetry is
recognized both for its aesthetics and its message of social justice. However, unlike Vallejo and Neruda, whose socio-political poetry defended
Marxism and socialism as viable options for Latin America, *Leprosorio*
indicts the Cuban socialist state for having defrauded—through censorship and repression, all in the name of the common good—the individual in his or her search for happiness. Moreover, in *Leprosorio* Arenas
gives voice to a homosexual discourse that does not appear in the works
of either Vallejo or Neruda. (Although Vallejo explores what we might
call brotherly love, Neruda is better known for his heterosexual compo-
sitions of love; the most renowned being *Veinte poemas de amor y una can-*

ción desesperada [1924; *Twenty Love Poems and a Song of Despair*]. Neruda and his love poetry were discussed in the Academy Award–winning Italian film *Il Postino*.) Arenas's *Leprosorio* technically and stylistically has more in common with the antipoems of the 1940s and 1950s of Chilean poet Nicanor Parra (b. 1914), who worked in the overwhelming shadow of fellow countryman Pablo Neruda. The Cuban poet's lyricism fits well within Parra's anguished vision of humankind. Although Parra himself was a left-wing writer, his anarchistic rebellion against society as well as his blatantly obscene remarks, satirical irreverence, and outrageous assertions into the poetic composition surely paved the way for Arenas's own rebellious poetic vision.

The first poem of Arenas's trilogy, *El Central: A Cuban Sugar Mill*, subtitled "Foundation," commences with the following dedication: "For my dear friend R. who made me a present of 87 sheets of blank paper." In the notes that appear at the end of the poem, Arenas identifies "R" as Reinaldo García-Ramos, a close friend who placed himself in jeopardy by smuggling in the blank pages to the writer, who was sent to the Manuel Sanguily Sugar Mill in Pinar del Río province to cut sugarcane. Various forms of "voluntary" work have been required of all Cuban citizens since the triumph of the revolution in 1959. In 1970, the year *El central* was composed, this voluntary work was significantly increased in order to achieve the goal set by Fidel Castro of attaining a record 10-million-ton sugarcane harvest that year. (The failure of this massive endeavor contributed much to Cuba's protectionist attitude and subsequent turn to the Soviet Union for economic assistance.) In a chapter of *Before Night Falls*, titled "The Sugar Mill" (*BNF*, 128–34), Arenas testifies of the horrific conditions that the so-called voluntary workers were forced to endure. At one point he states:

> To be sent to one of those places was like entering the last circle of hell. . . . I came to understand why the Indians had preferred suicide to working there as slaves; I understood why so many black men had killed themselves by suffocation. Now I was the Indian, I was the black slave, and I was not alone. I was one among hundreds of recruits. . . . The vision of all that enslaved youth inspired my long poem *El central*. I wrote the poem right there; I could not remain a silent witness to such horror. (*BNF*, 129)

Arenas's words attest to the testimonial or documentary function of *El central*, in which the poet becomes a channel of expression through which Indians, black slaves, and young adolescent recruits are allowed to testify of the repeated abuses and humiliations suffered under the Cuban sugarcane industry. Throughout the poem the voices of these slave hands are shuffled back and forth, thus fusing and confusing different eras of the Cuban experience and ultimately negating the reductionist notion of historical progress. *El Central: A Cuban Sugar Mill* presents Cuban history as a constant terror, a reiteration of abusive authoritarian systems under different names but with the same objective: to enslave and exploit, even when it is carried out under the name of the "common good."

In *The Repeating Island: The Caribbean and the Postmodern Perspective,* Antonio Benítez-Rojo proposes that the Plantation, "capitalized to indicate not just the presence of plantations but also the type of society that results from their use and abuse" (Benítez-Rojo, 9), is the most important historical phenomenon in the Caribbean basin. According to Benítez-Rojo, the Plantation has been responsible for producing: "imperialism, wars, colonial blocs, rebellions, repressions, sugar islands, runaway slave settlements, air and naval bases, revolutions of all sorts, and even a "free associated state" [that is, Puerto Rico] next to an unfree socialist state [Cuba]" (Benítez-Rojo, 9). Later in his study, Benítez-Rojo briefly mentions Arenas's *El central* as an example of a discourse of resistance to sugar, but, unfortunately, does not provide a closer examination of the text.

It is clear that Arenas was aware of the historical tragedies produced by Cuba's sugar industry. In the first section of *El Central: A Cuban Sugar Mill,* tellingly titled "Slave-Hands" (these words will become a leitmotiv throughout this first poem of the trilogy), the poetic voice chronicles successive stages of slave conditions on the island for Indians, black slaves, and so-called voluntary recruits of the Castro regime, all used as cheap fuel in the foundation of the Plantation machine that sucked in, according to Benítez-Rojo's figures, "no fewer than ten million African slaves and thousands of coolies (from India, China, and Malaysia)" (Benítez-Rojo, 9).[5] To these figures one must also add the untold numbers of adolescent recruits in revolutionary Cuba who, like the Indians and black slaves before them, have had no other choice but to participate in such grandiose projects as, for instance, the failed 1970 10-million-ton sugarcane harvest. In this first section of the poem, in addition to articulating the exploitation of slave hands in the Cuban sugarcane fields, a homosexual discourse is introduced through the figures of the Spanish Monarch Fernando of Aragon and Karl Marx, both portrayed as repressed homosexuals:

Beautiful is the figure of the
naked
Indian.
Beautiful is a body without down. Beautiful the
antipode's
piece
which hangs like a shining cylinder. Old (divine)
Isabella,

. . . . .

. . . kept her gaze,
imperturbable, riveted on the hanging piece so beautifully
shining.

. . . . .

Did Isabella's Fernando look? Did that great fairy look? Did that
grandson of a Jew, that piece of convert cuckold look?

(*Sugar Mill,* 10–11)

Behind all these public displays, behind all this
marching around, the hymns, the unfurling of flags, the
speeches, behind every
official ceremony,
lurks the intent of stimulating and raising your work
coefficient and
intensifying your exploitation.
It was Karl Marx who told me so, bursting into a laugh as
he wheeled
gracefully and set off at a trot behind the militarized
[asses] of the children who brought
up the rear guard.[6]

(*Sugar Mill,* 12–13)

The "outing," or accusations that certain individuals are homosexual,
should not be interpreted in Arenas's writing as an indication of self-
loathing, as some critics have proposed, but rather as a defiant stance
against Cuban homophobic hypermasculinity.[7] Arenas belittles the panic

of heterosexual masculinity, which, as a result of its patriarchal and phallocentric logic, relegates the homosexual to an inferior position in society.[8]
Therefore, it is quite irrelevant if indeed either Fernando of Aragon or
Karl Marx had homosexual inclinations or desires, but rather that both
men utilized their respective positions of authority to create and reinforce
respective homophobic ideological systems. Fernando of Aragon, through
his ardent defense of Catholicism and the establishment of the Inquisition,
furthered the intolerance of the Church toward any expressions of sexual
and gender differences. Karl Marx, for his part, proposed a totalizing theory of political economy based on a distribution of wealth achieved by
social ownership that produced a cult of production that ultimately
favored procreation and, thus, was antagonistic toward homosexuality. As
Michel Foucault posits in his writings, Marxism has not altered preexist-
ing power-knowledge mechanisms, but, ironically, has replaced one class
of exploiters for another. With specific regard to Marxism, Allen Young
argues in his book *Gays Under the Cuban Revolution* that the Cuban revolution's homophobic positions can indeed be traced to the antihomosexual
bias of the international Communist movement:

> I believe that the total elimination of homosexuality, as projected by the
> Cuban authorities, had an ideological basis which was derived not from
> within the Cuban political experience or the Cuban culture, as has often
> been alleged, but from the external tradition of European Marxism.
> (Young, 14–15)

Although in section 1 of *El Central: A Cuban Sugar Mill* the poetic
voice is unidentified, the first half of section 2, titled "The Good Consciences," utilizes the voice of the famous Dominican friar Bartolomé de
las Casas (1484–1566), who championed the cause of the indigenous
people of the Americas through his writings and actions. Known as the
"apóstol de los indios" or apostle of the indigenous, Bartolomé de las
Casas is an extremely controversial figure in Latin America given his
support for black slavery as a way of sparing the natives of the Americas
from ultimate extermination. In fact Bartolomé de las Casas repented
this racist position later in life, but section 2 of *El Central: A Cuban Sugar
Mill* nonetheless underscores the Dominican friar's twisted logic. The
irony of substituting one form of injustice for another is captured in the
very title of this section, "The Good Consciences." At one point in section 2 we hear Bartolomé de las Casas addressing an imaginary letter to
the Catholic Spanish Monarchs:

I dare propose to Your Most Serene Majesties . . . that since this slavish system is in accord with your needs to develop these lands, this system be applied to people more suitable for these tasks in this land made for dancing and diving. The Ethiopians of Africa are stronger, and they are black, as Your Highnesses know, and by reason of their strength and the blackness of their skin and the hard kinkiness of their hair, they are in better condition to carry out the regal plans of Your Majesties. The Africans would better be able to endure these violent travails. Besides, they are ugly. (*Sugar Mill,* 19)

Bartolomé de las Casas's "good conscience" drove him to propose black slavery as a solution to spare the natives of the Americas. Utilizing the same perverted logic, the second half of "The Good Consciences" presents the voice of the leaders of the new revolutionary regime. These leaders, again in the name of social justice and the good of the Cuban revolution, exploit young adolescent recruits who, precisely because of their youth, that is, their lack of commitment to any ideology except the ideology of self, can easily be manipulated to perform the physical tasks that others would never be able to tolerate. Hence, the decree is made:

> . . . I resolve:
> That all adolescents be called up, sought out, chased, and finally enlisted, and that they be sent off to farms, sugar mills and any other productive centers where they are needed. (*Sugar Mill,* 22)

What is resolved is the enslavement of adolescents needed to work the Cuban sugarcane fields. To achieve this end, the "Law of Obligatory Military Service" is promulgated so that all adolescents more than 15 years of age are ordered to provide mandatory service to the government. The section "The Good Consciences" ends with a series of stanzas that unite commentaries on the habits of the natives of early colonial Cuba with the habits of the new socialist regime. The following stanza is noteworthy because of its homosexual allusion:

> The Florida Indians were great sodomites and openly maintained male brothels where as many as a thousand gathered at nightfall. Last night, here, there was a "sweep" at Coppelia. (*Sugar Mill,* 24)

Coppelia, a popular ice cream parlor in Havana, was a well-known homosexual cruising area. In 1961 the revolution's Operation Three P's,

a round-up of pederasts, prostitutes, and pimps all with the aim of erad-
icating these so-called capitalistic ills, raided Coppelia in what has
humorously yet sadly been called "la cacería de locas" (faggot hunting).
In *El Central: A Cuban Sugar Mill* the Cuban revolution's persecution of
homosexuals is compared to the persecutions suffered in the past by
Indians and black slaves.

Sections 3 ("A Tropical Hunt"), 4 ("Vicissitudes en Route"), and 5
("The Night of the Negroes") all evoke the early black slave trade in
Cuba as well as the current enslavement of young recruits by the revolutionary government. In the face of so many injustices and atrocities the
poetic voice feels impotent to speak out: "I know that all these words
are merely useless artifices to delay inevitable decapitation" (*Sugar Mill*,
43). What can be articulated in the face of such repeated horrors?: "no
word at all, no matter how fine or noble, will lend more authenticity to
your poem than the cry of 'On your feet, you bastards!' at the edge of
every dawn" (*Sugar Mill*, 44). How can the poem express the hypocrisy
of having to applaud a system that enslaves?: "But one must / applaud, /
bend one's back and applaud / raise one's head and applaud. / One must
cut all the sugarcane and never stop / applauding" (*Sugar Mill*, 55). In
addition to denouncing the atrocities and oppression of Cuba's sugarcane industry throughout the ages, *El Central: A Cuban Sugar Mill* also
turns critically on itself to question the poem's own value and effective-
ness. In this way the poem, like history, cannot be idealized as a space of
ultimate truth. A repository of repeated frustrations, the poem becomes
a mere echo, faint words that desperately attempt to articulate the
abuses that have occurred and continue to occur in Cuba while all the
while conscious of its own impotence, its limited and fragmented vision:

no grand phraseology will do, nor complicated philosophical
speculations, nor hermetic poetry. In the face of terror there is the
simplicity of epic verse: simply *to tell*.)
One must tell.
One must tell.
A place where nothing can be told is a place where the most must be
told.
One must tell.
Everything must be told.

(*Sugar Mill*, 56)

Section 6 of the poem, entitled "Human Relations," narrates three short tales of corruption involving sexuality, power, and death. Reminiscent of, yet far more brutal than, the stories of *El conde Lucanor o el libro de Patronio* (Count Lucanor or the Book of Patronius) of Don Juan Manuel (1282–1349?), a foundational text in the Spanish literary tradition, the three tales in this section attest to the selfishness and hypocrisies of human relations, a common theme in many of Arenas's texts. Yet, unlike *El conde Lucanor,* there are no clear-cut moral lessons to be learned here.

The first story is that of Mr. Reeves, referred to as the Patriarch, who sets up a breeding farm in which he personally fathers hundreds of children with black women only to sell them to wealthy Brazilians. This story highlights the greed, ambition, and lack of human compassion that certain individuals are capable of. The second story is longer than the first but it too demonstrates the extent to which one person will go to control or enslave another. The nameless handsome blond man of this story, also a slave trader, becomes the sexual obsession of his wife who, jealous to the point of madness, will do anything to assure herself of her husband's fidelity. This story acquires a hyperbolic tone, typical in much of Arenas's fiction, as is evident from the following passage:

> Her fits of jealousy could not be allayed. Every afternoon she had the slave-girls paraded before her and she palpated their bellies. If one of them had an inch in girth, she had her beheaded at nightfall. She also kept rigorous records of their periods of menstruation: if one of them was a day late, she had a dagger driven through her belly. (*Sugar Mill,* 64)

Yet even after all her careful vigilance, one day the jealous wife discovers her husband with a blinded slave girl. After savagely killing the girl, the wife pickles her flesh and serves it to her husband who, after being told what he has eaten, shows no reaction to his wife. Desperate, in a final attempt to achieve the control she feels she must have, the wife plans to murder her husband. Yet at the very last moment, unable to actually commit the act, she turns the knife and kills herself. Unlike the tales of *El conde Lucanor,* which end with a rhymed couplet giving the moral of the story, the tale of the blond man does not have such a clear moral message. Rather, what is evoked is the nastiness of "human relations," the ironic title of the section, in which individuals either enslave others, both physically and emotionally, or are themselves enslaved by others.

The last tale of section 6 is that of Lieutenant Benito, an exemplary young military leader. With 300 recruits under his command, Lieu-

tenant Benito begins to feel a physical homosexual attraction for a
young sanitary corpsman, but as a result of his machismo, his anxious
hypermasculinity, he refuses to acknowledge such a taboo desire. One
night at a barrack party the lieutenant notices the young corpsman paying special attention to a distinguished visitor, "a young man with loose
gestures and a playful smile." (*Sugar Mill*, 67) Obviously jealous,
although unable to give a name to his feelings, the lieutenant proceeds
to order the sanitary corpsman to perform a number of meaningless
duties to hinder his contact with the visitor. The story ends in the following manner:

> The corpsman completed the task as fast as a phantom and returned to
> his post beside the distinguished visitor. Benito now ordered his man to
> stop serving and go to bed. The corpsman acted as if he had not heard
> the order. Benito repeated it. The corpsman announced that he was not
> tired and did not obey the order. Lieutenant Benito took out his revolver
> and sent five bullets into his orderly's head. . . . At the court martial, the
> case was treated as one of gross insubordination. Lieutenant Benito was
> absolved. (*Sugar Mill*, 68; the ellipsis points appear in the original)

Lieutenant Benito's repressed homoerotic desire leads him to commit a
brutal act of murder, which ultimately is absolved by a military judicial
panel that, likewise, is unwilling to entertain the existence of homosexual desire among so-called real masculine men. The poem's utilization of
ellipsis points after Lieutenant Benito fires his five bullets visually indicates the silence that cloaks homoerotic desire in the military, in which
homosexuality is seen as subversive to a nation's strength. As stated in
the introduction and again in chapter 1, immediately after its triumph,
the Cuban revolution institutionalized a systematic harassment and
incarceration of homosexuals all in the name of cleaning up the capitalist ills on the island. Male-male relations, and to a lesser degree female-
female relations, were seen as undermining the strength and ultimate
survival of the revolution. The very notion of homosexuality offended
the heroic sensibilities of the revolutionary leaders as is evident in the
following declaration published in 1965 in the newspaper *Revolución*:
"No homosexual represents the revolution, which is a matter for men, of
fists and not feathers, of courage and not trembling, of certainty and not
intrigue, of creative valor and not of sweet surprises."[9] Behind this simplistic binary opposition, which argues that heterosexual men are coura-
geous while homosexual men are frightened cowards, a clear homo-

phobic panic is evident. There has been no place within the Cuban army, which has fought hard and long for its national liberation, for males who do not reflect the ultra-virile values of Cuban machismo.

Sections 7, 8, and 9 (respectively titled "Uniquely, of One," "A Small Pretext for a Monotonous Discharge," and "The Monotonous Discharge"), although very short passages, begin to articulate the ire and fury of the poetic voice, who now begins to challenge the persecutions, high-sounding discourses, and obligatory and useless labor that befalls the young adolescent recruits on the island. History, that is, so-called official facts and figures that are manipulated by those in power to push forward particular agendas, is challenged by the poetic voice. History is presented as "a closed space" (*Sugar Mill,* 81) that only speaks to "what is now useless" (*Sugar Mill,* 81). Arenas is suggesting that historical facts or figures are incapable of capturing the vitality of the human experience because, by definition, they oversimplify and draw conclusions that dismiss the individual dimension of personal experience. Furthermore, historical discourses are deceptive in their attempts to present visions of totality.

The beginning lines of section 10 ("Finale 'Grandiose' ") make it apparent that the poetic voice is now that of a homosexual interned in a sugarcane plantation, perhaps an UMAP camp:

> O what a pessimistic queen this writer is, the up-to-date bourgeois will say (at ease in a wicker chair destined to keel over), himself won over by the optimistic wall-writing and slogans of the Marxist who know that without the holy faith of a cretin they would not be able to gobble up the earth before it explodes. (*Sugar Mill,* 85)

The idea that foreigners, living comfortably, sitting in their wicker chairs far away from the island, have assisted the revolution through their support is sarcastically derided. This theme is prevalent throughout *El Central: A Cuban Sugar Mill, Morir en junio y con la lengua afuera,* and *Leprosorio.* In all three poems the Cuban problem is seen as partially caused by individuals outside the island who both knowingly and unknowingly contribute to perpetuating the enslavement of the Cuban people. In section 1 of *El Central: A Cuban Sugar Mill,* for example, these individuals are the figures of the Spanish Monarchs but also those of bourgeois foreigners who consume the sugar produced by enslaved Cubans: "Slave-hands / have methodically constructed / this tiny square of sugar which you, notable / foreign consumer, so smartly dressed / in the open-air café / drop to the bottom of the modern / receptacle" (*Sugar Mill,* 12). In *Morir en junio y con la lengua afuera* (pp. 91–93), the poetic voice pokes fun at so-called progressive tourists who come to Castro's Cuba to enjoy themselves while ignoring the abuses that are committed against Cuban citizens who, unlike the tourists, cannot leave the island. Finally, in *Leprosorio* (pp. 15–116), after testifying of repeated horrors committed against the recruits, the poetic voice confronts with obvious irony the incredulous reader outside the island who refuses to believe what is going on: "no se inquiete: Usted no tiene porqué creerme" (*Leprosorio,* 116) (don't get upset: you have no reason to believe me).

In section 10 of *El Central: A Cuban Sugar Mill* the poetic voice serves as a witness to the abuses both of the past and of the present. Three stanzas, each commencing with the words "I see," blur the lines of official history to unite the plight of indigenous people, blacks, and armies of young recruits all presented as "enslaved and hungry." This "I see" is reminiscent of the recurrent use of the archaic predicate statement "yo vide" ("yo vi" = I saw) in Miguel Barnet's famous documentary novel, *Biografía de un cimarrón* (1966), in which Esteban Montejo revises (rewrites) history by presenting the black man's active participation in the struggle for Cuban independence.[10] Whereas in Barnet's text the direct voice of the witness, Esteban Montejo, is presented in the past tense, the "I see" of *El Central: A Cuban Sugar Mill* utilizes an epic present tense that encompasses 500 years of enslavement.

The last section of the poem ("The Introduction of the Symbol of the Faith") presents the poetic voice's incessant search for the fatherland despite the fact that "beyond death lies death" and "that there are no doors or exits from fright"—this last verse reminds the reader of Arenas's novel *The Doorman,* in which the main character searches for his own door to happiness. The voice of the poetic narrator is joined to a collective "we" who while searching for "the so-much desired land" are cognizant of the fact that it does not exist. The poem demythologizes any idealistic notion that literature can transcend human experience and find specific solutions. Still, the poem ends with the lines: "We continue to search for you [fatherland] / we continue / we continue" (*Sugar Mill,* 91).

El Central: A Cuban Sugar Mill challenges and undermines both past and present systems of power in Cuba that have attempted to establish themselves as absolute authority, as discourses of the highest truth, by enslaving individual expression. The poem's undermining of authoritative rules should not, however, be considered as pure anarchy. Rather, the poem's subversion is creative and directed toward affirmative and positive action, as is apparent in the final verse "we continue to search." This search for an ideal space in which the individual can feel free and safe is presented not just in this poem but in Arenas's entire oeuvre.

Morir en junio y con la lengua afuera

Morir en junio y con la lengua afuera (To Die in June, Gasping for Air) was written six months after *El central*.[11] It, like *El central,* is a poem of denunciation in which the poetic voice is marked by the immediacy of giving testimony of the constant threat and menace surrounding him. Dated November, 1970, the poem is not divided into sections or segments like *El central,* nor is it as long. Subtitled "Ciudad," or City, *Morir en junio y con la lengua afuera* once again casts the poetic voice in the role of critical observer, this time, riding in a Havana bus en route to the countryside, looking out the window at the world hoping to find some kind of distraction from the mediocrity and enslavement of city life, a life driven by "grandes teorías de metas y consumos" (*Morir en junio,* 75) (great theories of goals and consumption) in which everyone appears to be emotionally dead: "Todos estamos muertos" (*Morir en junio* 76) (We are all dead). The city is presented as a loud and obnoxious space filled with informers and volunteer teachers all blindly driven by the ideology of the revolutionary regime. It is in response to this excessive exemplary moral and physical loudness that the poet is driven to write:

> Por la noche los perros interfieren el *ta, ta, ta* de las
> musas divinas, ya en extinción.
> Por el día, un desafío de ollas, de cascos que se agitan,
> de latas, de piafantes maestras voluntarias,
> de esbirros disfrazados de bañistas,
> de bocinas con altoparlantes
> me impelen a tomar el artefacto.
>
> (*Morir en junio,* 76–77)

> During the evening the dogs interfere with the tap, tap,
> tap of the divine muses, already in extinction.
> During the day, a challenge of pots and pans, of
> agitating hard hats, of cans, of stamping voluntary

teachers, of informers dressed as ocean bathers,
of horns with loudspeakers
drive me to take the artifact.

(my translation)

In addition to the deafening noises of the city, the poetic voice presents
the fanatical figures of volunteer teachers and informers who uphold and
ardently defend the revolutionary party line. The mentioning of "maes-
tras voluntarias," or volunteer teachers, is a direct allusion to a well-
known Cuban documentary novel. The documentary-testimonial vein in
Cuban revolutionary literature can in fact be traced back to 1962 and
the publication of Daura Olema García's *Maestra voluntaria,* a work that
won the Casa de las Américas' novelistic prize that same year. *Maestra
voluntaria* relates, in documentary fashion, the experiences of a volunteer
teacher during the revolution's early campaign to eliminate illiteracy on
the island. In this book, which resembles a journalistic account of the
literacy campaign more than a work of fiction, the protagonist converts
to communism as a result of her training and subsequent dedication to
the teaching of Cuba's illiterates. This novel clearly illustrates the type
of literature that contributed to the shaping of a revolutionary consciousness and that was actively supported by the revolution's cultural
policy makers. *Maestra voluntaria* has no grey areas but rather presents
the experiences of the revolution as overly simplistic: either one ardently
defends the revolution or one is considered a traitor, that is, a counter-
revolutionary.

In *Morir en junio y con la lengua afuera* the adolescent youths are once
again presented as living in an inferno ("Una juventud que se corrompe
inútil y rápida" (*Morir en junio,* 75) (youths who are uselessly and quickly
corrupted) in which there is no hope whatsoever of divine intervention:
"Oh, dios, / estás postergado y silencioso, / estás muerto y vejado" (*Morir
en junio,* 75) (Oh, god, you disregard us and are silent, you are dead and
annoyed). Carefully watching is "el gran amo" or great master, an
Orwellian tropical Big Brother, constantly vigilant and always in complete control: "El gran amo está aquí; el amo vigila. / El gran amo dispon-
drá cuánto debes vivir, / para qué sirves, cuál es tu fin" (*Morir en junio,* 87)
(the great master is here; the master is vigilant. / The great master will
decide how long you should live, / what is your use, what is your purpose).

Near the end of the poem, the poetic voice identifies itself with Perceval, one of the more famous heroes in Arthurian legend.

Fue en Isla de Pinos
        (hoy "Isla de la Juventud").
Llovía y Percival lloraba sentado
en un arado de
tres esteras.

. . . .

Realmente tu historia y la mía son las mismas.
Tú en Munsalwashe,
dudando por piedad de Dios mismo.
Yo en Catalina de Güines revisando el marxismo.
Tú "admitido en la tabla Redonda."
Yo obligatoriamente concurriendo a la Asamblea.
                    (*Morir en junio*, 88–89)

It was on the Isle of Pines
        (Today called "Isle of Youth").
It was raining and Perceval was crying
as he sat on three grass mats
on the plowed ground.

. . . .

Truly your story and mine are the same.
You in Munsalvaesche,
doubting God for pity's sake.
I in Catalina de Güines reviewing marxism.
You "admitted to the Round Table."
I attending the obligatory Assembly.
                    (my translation)

The poetic voice goes on to present other valiant and heroic feats of the legendary Perceval that are compared to the meaningless and inane tasks that the poetic voice, representing Cuban youths on the island, is forced to perform. The poetic voice transports the intrepid knight of the Round Table to his cramped cell on the Isle of Pine, where the valiant Perceval is forced to perform endless "voluntary" manual labor and as a consequence becomes "acatarrado y hambriento" (*Morir en junio*, 89) (sick and hungry). Like the poetic voice, Perceval ironically becomes a "típica figura del hombre nuevo" (*Morir en junio,* 89) (typical figure of the new man).

The Arthurian legends have been a rich source of inspiration for writers throughout the ages. The Bretons passed the Arthurian lore on to the French. The first French writer of Arthurian romance was Chrétien de Troyes, a poet who lived in the latter half of the twelfth century and who was responsible for first inventing the name Perceval, previously known in Welsh sources as Peredur, and casting him as the hero of his romance *Perceval,* also known as *Le conte de graal* (The Story of the Grail). According to Chrétien de Troyes, Perceval was raised in the woods by his overprotective mother who wanted him to know nothing of knighthood. Yet after seeing some knights in the woods near his home, Perceval becomes determined to go to Arthur's court and become a knight of the Round Table. Recently, Arthurian scholars have begun to identify half-hidden homoerotic themes in many of the Arthurian texts.[12] Many of the special friendships and comradeship of knights described in these texts, while not being explicitly homoerotic, nonetheless do suggest a homosocial context. The clearly demarcated distinction between male bonding and homoeroticism that is quite prevalent today in fact did not exist prior to the eighteenth century, as Bruce Smith argues in *Homosexual Desire in Shakespeare's England.*[13] Thus, for example, male bonding (passionate friendship) and male homosexuality (homoerotic passion) were "aspects of the same psychological and social phenomenon" (Mieszkowski, 43). Among the many feats that the legendary Perceval performs and that are enumerated in *Morir en junio y con la lengua afuera,* a homosocial allusion is made when Perceval is presented "del brazo de Tristán" (*Morir en junio,* 90) (arm-in-arm with Tristan [a contemporary of King Arthur and a Knight of the Round Table]).

At the end of *Morir en junio y con la lengua afuera,* Arenas includes a rather lengthy footnote in which he presents information concerning Perceval, a character he describes as "sencillo de espíritu y puro de corazón" (*Morir en junio,* 98) (of natural spirit and pure heart). Out of all the information concerning this legendary character, Arenas focuses on two specific aspects. The first is Perceval's mother's isolation of her son in the woods to protect him from danger. Arenas reads this act as one of control and manipulation, which the son must escape in order to be free. (The idea of escaping from the mother in order to be free is a common motivation of many of Arenas's characters; they find themselves emotionally haunted by this dictatorial and tyrannical figure who at times is also presented as loving and caring.)[14] The second point that Arenas latches onto is Perceval's search, the search for his dead father, the search for the Grail, in sum, a search for some type of meaning in his life. Hence, breaking away from the overbearing mother is united to the idea of being able to search for meaning in one's life:

> La madre nos orienta hacia el terror.
> La madre se transforma en "virgen casta," la madre se
> disfraza de ofendida.
> La madre se disuelve entre los surcos para
> ser ya
> el hueco que enfanga nuestras manos.
> —La madre estimulando los espantos.
> Sí, nuestras historias son exactas. Sólo resta
> levantar el mosquitero y abrazarte.
>
> (*Morir en junio,* 91)

Mother directs us to the terror.
Mother transforms herself into a "chaste virgin," mother
disguises herself as the offended one.
Mother dissolves herself between the furrows in order
to be
the hole that covers our hands with mud.
—Mother prompting fears.
Yes, our histories are the same. What is only left is
to lift the mosquito net and embrace you.

(my translation)

The camaraderie that binds Perceval and the poetic voice is not one based on lionheartedly battling dragons and spirited enemies, but one in which the repressive figure of the mother is confronted. Arenas's story "Adiós a mamá" ("Goodbye Mother")[15] is particularly noteworthy in the treatment of this theme. In the story the death of the mother incites extravagant and delirious conduct on the part of the male protagonist's four sisters, whose fanaticism in not wanting to bury their mother's decomposing body leads them to commit suicide as a sign of solidarity with the deceased. The story ends when the protagonist, unconvinced of his slaughtered sisters' demented loyalty, rather than joining them in death, escapes to the sea declaring "I'm a traitor. A confirmed traitor. And happy" ("Goodbye Mother," 66).

Through his *burla,* or mocking attacks, the poetic voice of *Morir en junio y con la lengua afuera* creates a temporary safe space from which he challenges and keeps at bay those forces intent on destroying him. Unlike the fabled Perceval, whose mighty sword defended him from his attackers, the poetic voice only has his *lengua* (tongue), a word anaphorically repeated in a series of verses at the end of the poem (*Morir en junio,* 95 – 96). The Spanish title *Morir en junio y con la lengua afuera,* literally "To die in June and with one's tongue hanging out," implies not just the idea of gasping for air as a result of being beaten down by a system that brutally punishes disobedience but also the metonymical idea of tongue as speech that refuses to be silenced. Regardless of the many times he is beaten down, both physically and emotionally, the poetic voice continues to speak, to cry out.

Leprosorio

Leprosorio (Leper Colony), subtitled "Exodus," was written over a period of two years, 1974–1976.[16] In this last poem of the trilogy the poetic voice is desperately searching to escape from what has become an unbearable existence. Cuba is presented as an island-prison of "111,111 square kilometers" (a leitmotiv throughout the poem) infested with virulent germs, bacteria, and diseases. Reminiscent of Pablo Neruda's famous "The United Fruit Co.,"[17] in which the Chilean poet includes the names of such notorious Latin American dictators as Rafael Trujillo of the Dominican Republic, Tiburcio Carías Andino of Honduras, and Jorge Ubico of Guatemala, in *Leprosorio,* interspersed within stanzas that enumerate the names of pathological degenerative diseases are found the names of Cuban dictators:

> Endocarditis Lenta
> Weyler Valeriano Dictador
> Cefalea Avanzada
> Machado Gerardo Dictador
> Neuritis Periférica
> Batista Fulgencio Dictador
> Gangrena Orgánica
> Castro Fidel Dictador . . .
>   (*Leprosorio,* 114)

> Slow Endocarditis
> Weyler Valeriano Dictator
> Progressive Migraines
> Machado Gerardo Dictator
> Peripheral Neuritis
> Batista Fulgencio Dictator
> Organic Gangrene
> Castro Fidel Dictator . . .
>   (my translation)

This stanza first mentions the Spanish General Valeriano Weyler who was appointed to oversee the Spanish war effort in Cuba. Weyler, who arrived in Cuba in 1896 and was accompanied by some 50,000 Spanish troops, quickly and ferociously persecuted and imprisoned both Cubans and Spaniards who sympathized with Cuba's struggle for independence. The next three names, Machado, Batista, and Castro, represent the three longest periods of twentieth-century Cuban history in which one man has forcefully ruled with unquestionable power. Each of the three names has been altered by first mentioning the last name, the customary way in which Cubans refer to these individuals, followed by their first name, and finally ending with their unofficial yet recognized title of "dictator." Later in the poem each Cuban dictator—with the exception of Weyler who was Spanish by birth—is singled out in a stanza of his own in which one verse prominently displays the dictator's name. Let me cite the last example, that of Fidel Castro:

> Elefantiasis Compulsiva.
> Tularemia Virus.
> Sífilis Galopante.
> Cólera Morbo.
> Castro Comandante.
> Náusea y Diarrea . . .
>   (*Leprosorio,* 119)

> Compulsive Elephantiasis.
> Viral Tularemia.

Galloping Syphilis.
Morbid Cholera.
Commanding Castro.
Nausea and Diarrhea . . .
(my translation)

Despite the moral and spiritual disease on the island, the poetic voice vows to keep fighting, to not be defeated: "No podrán conmigo. No van a destruirme. Ya verán. Ya ven como los reto. Y al retarlos los burlo, los traiciono y derroto" (*Leprosorio,* 129) (They can't stop me. They can't destroy me. They'll see. They'll see how I'll challenge them. And challenging them I mock them, I betray and defeat them). In such an infested environment "partir" (to leave) or "correr" (to run) (*Leprosorio,* 129) becomes the only alternative. The last stanza of *Leprosorio* ends by stating:

Correr
entre el tiroteo y el azote del cielo,
burlando, traicionando, dejando atrás
la intransferible configuración de nuestros 111,111
    kilómetros
cuadrados
(cifra del ejército, naturalmente)
de leprosorio.

                  (*Leprosorio,* 129–30)

Running
in between the shooting and the heavenly scourge,
outmaneuvering, betraying, leaving behind
the untransferable configuration of our 111,111
    kilometers
squared
(naturally, a military number)
leper colony.

                  (my translation)

The only way to survive such monstrous conditions is to escape, to flee. *Leprosorio* was composed from 1974 to 1976, years that coincide precisely with Arenas's own imprisonment and anxious struggles to leave Cuba.

Voluntad de vivir manifestándose

In 1989 the editorial house Betania (Spain) published a collection of short poems by Arenas under the title *Voluntad de vivir manifestándose* (The Will to Live Manifesting Itself).[18] This collection, whose poems date from as early as 1969 to as late as 1989, is marked by the same intensity, fury, and seduction that characterize all of the writer's work. As a whole, *Voluntad de vivir manifestándose* is a poetic manifestation of the repression, persecution, loneliness, and general desperation that marked Arenas's life, a life scarred by Batista's tyranny, Castro's repressive regime, the United States's capitalist economy, and, finally, the AIDS epidemic. In the prologue to the collection Arenas writes:

> He contemplado el infierno, la única porción de realidad que me ha tocado vivir, con ojos familiares; no sin satisfacción lo he vivido y cantado . . . Sólo me arrepiento de lo que no he hecho. Hasta última hora la ecuanimidad y el ritmo. (*Voluntad*, 7)

> With familiar eyes, I have contemplated hell, the only portion of reality that I have lived; not without satisfaction have I lived and sang of it . . . My only regret is what I have not done. To the last second, equanimity and rhythm. (my translation)

The last line, "Hasta última hora la ecuanimidad y el ritmo" (To the last second, equanimity and rhythm), is identical to one of the last sentences in *Farewell to the Sea*. As Arenas explained to me during our conversation in 1987, equanimity is necessary for the poem to be created. Equanimity is imperative because "without it there is nothing, not even madness, that can be told or narrated. Up to the end, up to the last second, Hector can not lose his sense of rhythm or equanimity, without which he would lose his sense of creation" (Soto, 150). Even after having endured repeated tragedies, Arenas was well aware that without equanimity, the composure to withstand the disasters of life, the poem had no chance of being articulated.

Voluntad de vivir manifestándose is divided into four sections, titled: "Esa sinfonía que milagrosamente escuchas" (That Symphony Which You Miraculously Hear), "Sonetos desde el infierno" (Sonnets from

Hell), "Mi amante el mar" (My Lover the Sea), and "El otoño me regala una hoja" (Autumn Presents Me with a Leaf).

The nine poems of the first section (That Symphony Which You Miraculously Hear) were all written between 1969 and 1975 while Arenas still lived in Cuba. These poems articulate a profound sense of existential anguish as a result of a political system that prohibits the poet from expressing himself freely. The constant vigilance ("Carlos Marx / no tuvo nunca sin saberlo una grabadora / estratégicamente colocada en su sitio más íntimo" [*Voluntad,* 16] [Karl Marx / never had without knowing it a tape recorder / strategically situated in his most intimate spot]) as well as the enslavement of the revolutionary system ("Un millón de niños condenados bajo la excusa de 'La Escuela al campo' a ser no niños, sino esclavos agrarios" [*Voluntad,* 21] [A million children condemned with the excuse of School Camp to not be children but agrarian slaves]) are presented as being responsible for the poet's spiritual death. In the last poem of this first section, "Voluntad de vivir manifestándose" (The Will to Live Manifesting Itself), also used for the title of the collection, the poet, dead and buried, cries out:

> Me han sepultado.
> Han danzado sobre mí.
> Han apisonado bien el suelo.
> Se han ido, se han ido dejándome bien muerto y
> enterrado.
> Este es mi momento.
>
> (*Voluntad,* 24)

> They have buried me.
> They have danced over me.
> They have tamped the earth well.
> They have left, they have left me dead and well buried.
> This is my moment.
>
> (my translation)

This moment of spiritual death was precisely the reality Arenas was forced to endure after falling out of favor with the revolutionary establishment for his unorthodox writings and so-called improper conduct.

Still, the poet recognizes that it is precisely at this moment, when the malevolent forces believe that they have destroyed and silenced him, that he, like the phoenix, would rise up and rebel against the oppression.

The second section of the collection (Sonnets from Hell) is made up of 37 sonnets, all written between 1969 and 1980. In these sonnets, or antisonnets —although the formal aspects of the sonnet are respected the themes are far from traditional—death becomes an obsessive concern. For example, in the sonnet "También tenemos el Ministerio de la Muerte" (We Also Have the Minister of Death) we read:

> Hay muchas formas de aplicar la muerte.
> Tenemos la muerte por muerte sin muerte.
> También, la muerte y luego la másmuerte.
> Y la muerte que es muerte y sobremuerte.
>
> > *(Voluntad, 46)*

> There are many ways of applying death.
> We have death by death without death.
> Also, death and later moredeath.
> And death that is death and afterdeath.
>
> > (my translation)

Since Arenas's first novel, *Singing from the Well* (1967), the imaginative capability of the individual has been presented in his texts as something essential and vital that separates human beings from other beasts. In the sonnet "Todo lo que pudo ser, aunque haya sido" (All That Could Have Been, Although It Was) the possibilities of dreaming, that marvelous gift of the imagination, superior to any so-called objective reality, is underscored. In the end, it is the individual's unbridled fantasy that saves him or her from the repeated persecutions of life.

> Todo lo que pudo ser, aunque haya sido,
> jamás ha sido como fue soñado.
> El dios de la miseria se ha encargado
> de darle a la realidad otro sentido.

Otro sentido, nunca presentido,
cubre hasta el deseo realizado;
de modo que el placer aun disfrutado
jamás podrá igualar al inventado.

(*Voluntad,* 34)

All that could have been, although it was,
was never as one dreamed it.
The god of misery has made sure
of giving reality another meaning.

Another meaning, never predicted,
covers even fulfilled desire;
in such a way that enjoyed pleasure
will never equal invented pleasure.

(my translation)

Four sonnets in this section articulate clear homoerotic themes (pp. 40, 56, 58, 61). Of particular interest is the sonnet titled "De modo que Cervantes era manco" (And So Cervantes Was Maimed), in which an overview of the Western canon's most recognized homosexual artists is presented. The poetic voice first mentions some of the physical handicaps and emotional peculiarities of Western tradition's most celebrated artists (i.e., Cervantes, Beethoven, Luis de Góngora, and so forth) before proceeding to "out" homosexual artists throughout the ages.

De modo que Cervantes era manco;
sordo, Beethoven; Villon ladrón;
Góngora de tan loco andaba en zanco.
¿Y Proust? Desde luego, maricón.

Negrero, sí, fue Don Nicolás Tanco,
y Virginia se suprimió de un zambullón,
Lautrémont murió aterido en algún banco.
Ay de mí, también Shakespeare era maricón.

> También Leonardo y Federico García,
> Whitman, Miguel Angel y Petronio,
> Gide, Genet y Visconti, las fatales.

> Esta es, señores, la breve biografía
> (¡vaya, olvidé mencionar a San Antonio!)
> de quienes son del arte sólidos puntales.
>
> > *(Voluntad,* 40)

> And so Cervantes was maimed;
> Beethoven deaf; Villon, a thief;
> Góngora was so crazy he used stilts,
> And Proust? a faggot, of course.

> Don Nicolás Tanco, a slave trader, oh yes,
> and Virginia eliminated herself with one dive,
> Lautrémont died from some cold bench,
> Oh dear, Shakespeare was also a faggot.

> So were Leonardo and Federico García,
> Whitman, Michelangelo and Petronius,
> Gide, Genet and Visconti, those fatal queens.

> This is, ladies and gentlemen, the brief biography
> (Wait a minute, I almost forgot Saint Anthony)
> of art's most established artists.
>
> > (my translation)

Arenas lampoons the homophobic reader who perhaps would like to make the equation that homosexuality is a handicap or an emotional peculiarity. The sonnet ridicules, through irony, those homophobic readers who would be "surprised" to learn that many of Western tradition's most distinguished and established artists (the "sólidos puntales") were indeed "maricones." Here the term "maricón," or faggot, which Arenas uses throughout his writing with underlying affection, is purposefully deployed

with the pejorative connotation it holds when used by homophobic individuals intent on ridiculing and demeaning homosexual preferences. The
sonnet is dated Havana, 1971. Hence, while Arenas was still cautiously
veiling homosexual themes in his prose works of the period (for example,
in such texts as *The Palace of the White Skunks* and the stories of *Con los ojos
cerrados* [With My Eyes Closed]), he was, in his poetry, directly confronting
the theme of homosexuality, probably because the intensely personal tone
of lyrical poetry is often written with no intention of publication.

The third section of *Voluntad de vivir manifestándose* consists of only
one poem, titled "Mi amante el mar" (My Lover the Sea), dated 1973.
This prose poem, the longest single composition in the collection, utilizes chaotic enumeration to present the disillusionment of the Cuban
people, who have been reduced to simply surviving in a hostile environment. The repetition of the words "Yo veo" (I see) serve as a leitmotiv
that characterizes the degeneration and degradation that the poet wit-
nesses all around him. In order to free himself from the paltriness of life,
the poet addresses himself to his lover, the sea. Arenas purposefully uses
the masculine definite article "el" instead of the feminine definite article
"la," the more traditonal poetic choice, to denote the sea ("mar").

> Mi amante el mar me devolverá el niño que fui
> bajo la arboleda y el sol
> o con un susurro mecerá mis huesos.
> Mi amante el mar prolongará mi búsqueda y mi
> furia,
> mi canto, . . .
>
> (Voluntad, 79)

> My lover the sea will bring back the child I was
> under the grove and the sun
> or with a murmur he will rock my bones to sleep.
> My lover the sea will prolong my search and my fury,
> my song, . . .
>
> (my translation)

At the end of the poem, the male speaker unites with the lover, that is,
he commits suicide by drowning himself. Suicide, a constant in Arenas's

texts, often is the only escape for characters forced to live in an environment marked by cruelty, ignorance, and constant persecution.

The last section of the collection ("El otoño me regala una hoja") (Autumn Presents Me with a Leaf) contains 16 poems, all written in the United States. Now free from the fear of recrimination, the poetic voice allows itself to speak freely. In this section, the poem "Si te llamaras Nelson" (If You Were Called Nelson), previously discussed in chapter 3, appears. Still, the most moving poem of the entire section is the last, titled "Autoepitafio" (Self-Epitaph) and dated 1989, one year prior to Arenas's death. This poem, more than a morbid self-indulgence, is a celebration of the rebellious spirit that characterizes all of Arenas's work. The poem once again presents the indomitable spirit of the writer who refuses to surrender himself to mediocrity, an instinct that has served him as solace from "la prisión, el ostracismo, el exilio, [y] las múltiples ofensas típicas de la vileza humana" (*Voluntad,* 110) (prison, ostracism, exile, and the numerous typical offenses of human vileness). "Autoepitafio" ends with the poetic voice, speaking in the third person, recounting the poet's instructions of what to do with his body after death. These lines summarize, rather effectively, Arenas's indomitable spirit:

> Ordenó que sus cenizas fueran lanzadas al mar
> donde habrán de fluir constantemente.
> No ha perdido la costumbre de soñar:
> espera que en sus aguas se zambulla algún adolescente.
>
> (*Voluntad,* 110)

> He arranged for his ashes to be scattered into the sea
> where they would flow forever.
> Not having given up his habit of dreaming,
> he awaits a young man to dive into his waters.
>
> (my translation)

Chapter Six

Conclusion

We had not realized that what the public really loathes in homosexuality is not the thing itself but having to think about it.

—E. M. Forster, afterword to *Maurice*

Reinaldo Arenas would surely not have been so vehemently persecuted and censored by the Cuban revolutionary government had he not dared to speak out, that is, put into writing the brutal injustices committed in Cuba against homosexuals. As Andrew Hurley, translator of Arenas's work, has pointed out, the Cuban writer was not condemned so much for his homosexuality, but for his writing (making public) his homosexual experience; "If he had not written," Hurley tells us, "if he had not made a symbol of his experience, he would not have been in the situation he found himself with the Cuban government."[1] Hurley's assumption echoes E. M. Forster's words quoted at the beginning of this chapter; it is not so much that certain individuals detest homosexuality, but rather they detest the idea of making it public, of being forced to address that it indeed exists. From 1959 until 1980, the years in which Arenas lived in revolutionary Cuba, homophobia was institutionalized to the point that the mere identification of an individual as homosexual could land him or her in jail. Even today homophobia continues to permeate Cuban society; few Cubans are willing to be publicly identified as homosexuals. Ian Lumsden, for instance, for fear of reprisals, withholds the names of the homosexuals whom he interviewed for his book, *Machos, Maricones, and Gays: Cuba and Homosexuality* (1996). Lumsden makes clear that although homosexuals were historically oppressed in prerevolutionary Cuba (as they have been in other societies), after the triumph of the revolution, this primarily social oppression was replaced with a nationwide political agenda intent on regulating sexuality and gender. Lumsden's documentation of the revolution's homophobic campaigns of the 1960s and 1970s (i.e, the *redadas* [police raids] and *recogidas* [mass arrests] of homosexuals, the infamous UMAP concentration camps from 1965 to 1969, the homophobic resolutions of the 1971 Congress on Education and Culture, the 1979 Penal Code's prohibition

of "public ostentation" of any "homosexual activity," and so forth)
chronicles the systematic persecution of homosexuals in Cuba, in which
the traditional Cuban image of homosexuals hardly fits the paradigm of
revolutionary attributes as defined by Che Guevara's mythologized
"new man." The doctrinaire rigidity of the Cuban revolution made it
adopt Stalinist ideological tenets that saw homosexuality as a decadent
bourgeois phenomenon that had to be eradicated. (One has to keep in
mind that even in the homophobic pre-Stonewall days in the United
States, there was never a nationwide initiative supported by the government to wipe out homosexuals as was the case in Cuba.) It was precisely
within this hostile *machista* environment anathematic to homosexuality
that Reinaldo Arenas lived, wrote, loved, and struggled to survive.

Although both Ian Lumsden and the recent Cuban documentary film
"Gay Cuba" (1995, directed by Sonja de Vries) talk about an "unofficial" tolerance toward homosexuals in Cuban society since 1980, more
political changes are needed before such unofficial tolerance can indeed
become official. At the same time that Lumsden discusses so-called
unofficial positive changes for homosexuals in Cuba, he concedes that
actual governmental policies—such as Article 303 of the 1987 Penal
Code, which penalizes with prison sentences homosexual behavior that
causes "public scandal"—continue to discriminate against homosexuals:

> The Penal Code remains a central element in the homophobic environ-
> ment that has confronted Cuban homosexuals for much of the last three
> decades. The fact that some homophobic strictures have remained in the
> criminal code (and that a few were even strengthened in 1987) indicates
> that they exist because they serve the purposes of the Cuban state. Their
> purpose is to intimidate homosexuals and to contain homosexuality
> within a heterosexist if not *machista* social order. It would be ingenuous to
> believe otherwise. (Lumsden, 86)

Any current improvement for homosexuals in Cuba now or in the
future would do little for the thousands of individuals, like Arenas,
whose lives were destroyed by an authoritarian regime that persecuted
them for their sexual orientation. As homosexuals in the international
gay and lesbian liberation movement well know, one must always be on
guard; any unofficial tolerance that might exist today could easily be
reversed in the future. (If one thing can be said with certainty about
Cuban policies, it is their uncertain nature; such is the case, for example,
with U.S. dollars. Once considered illegal and their possession punish-

able by incarceration, they recently have become legal currency.) But most important, even as of this date, the Cuban revolutionary leadership has made no attempt to make amends for the immeasurable harm that was done to homosexuals in the past. For those critics and activists who hold up "El lobo, el bosque y el hombre nuevo" and *Fresa y chocolate* (Strawberry and Chocolate) as examples of more tolerance toward homosexuals in Cuba, Senel Paz's story as well as Tomás Gutiérrez Alea's cinematographic adaptation are but token gestures, flawed by their own excessive sentimentality and superficiality, that cannot make up for past brutalities. Equally unacceptable is Fidel Castro's repeated denials that homosexuals have ever been oppressed in Cuba. As Lumsden's book points out, the present Cuban leadership remains "instinctively homophobic" (Lumsden, 96).

Through his writing, Arenas brought the homosexual experience, a taboo subject not just in Cuba but in all of Latin America, out of the closet. By becoming more progressively daring in his representation of homoerotic themes and issues, Arenas took homoeroticism from its traditional private space of silence and self-censorship into the arena of public discourse, thus assigning it an ideological and political value. In such later works as *Farewell to the Sea, El color del verano, Viaje a La Habana,* and *Before Night Falls,* homoerotic themes are not merely encoded or *entendidos* (understood), but are boldly and aggressively represented in an in-your-face attitude that challenges machismo, the Latin American variant of patriarchal sexism, as well as its scripted gender roles that cast the homosexual as weak, cowardly, dependent, and passive, both sexually and emotionally. For challenging machismo, Arenas was and still is criticized, not just in Cuba, but also in the equally homophobic Cuban exile community in the United States. Yet for making the traditionally private discourse of homosexuality quite public, Arenas must be considered revolutionary and avant-garde; truly to date no other writer has been so outspoken and daring in his or her representation of homoeroticism in Latin American letters.

Some Anglo-American readers perhaps might be offended or turned off by Arenas's representation of homosexuals in his work. Surely the writer's portrayal of homosexuality in no way can be considered positive in the way that much of contemporary Anglo-American gay literature strives to represent gay relationships based on mutual respect and equality. Yet despite what some readers might see as Arenas's casting of homosexual characters as *locas,* screaming queens who parody stereotypical female mannerisms for lack of alternative ways of defining themselves, these *locas* (literally, crazy women) are anything but crazy. In *El color del verano,* for example, the *locas* are presented as imaginative and highly resourceful individuals who manage to survive under a repressive political system that is bureaucratically insane. Throughout the novel, the *locas* ironically demonstrate a quixotic spirit of turning the ugly and crass into the marvelous and beautiful. Their zany antics, sexual conquests, and ingenious solutions to the most trying circumstances demonstrate an indomitable spirit of survival that indeed makes them, as one of the characters of the novel eloquently points out, "the heroes of all time":

> La tesis de Oliente Churre era sencilla y profunda: Se había perdido el sentido de la vida porque se había perdido el paraíso y se había perdido el paraíso porque se había condenado el placer. Pero el placer, perseguido, execrado, condenado, esquilmado y casi borrado del mundo, aún tenía sus ejércitos; ejércitos clandestinos, silenciosos y siempre en peligro inminente, pero que no estaban dispuestos, de ninguna manera, a renunciar a la vida, esto es, a hacer gozar a los demás. Ese ejército . . . [estaba] formado por los maricones . . . , los héroes de todos los tiempos, los sostenedores de la ilusión del paraíso y los que a toda costa pretenden recuperarlo. (*El color,* 388)

> Oliente Churre's thesis was simple and profound: The meaning of life had been lost because paradise had been lost and paradise had been lost because pleasure had been condemned. But pleasure, persecuted, abominated, condemned, impoverished and almost erased from the face of the Earth, still had its armies; clandestine armies, silent and always in imminent danger, but, nonetheless, adamant not to renounce life, that is, giving pleasure to others. That army . . . was made up of faggots . . . , the heroes of all time, the supporters of the dream of paradise and who, at all cost, seek to regain it. (my translation)

Reinaldo Arenas has left the international gay community an important literary legacy. His writings, passionate, rebellious, and irreverent, fascinate the reader as well as provoke further dialogue and discussion concerning the homosexual's problematic relationship with society.

Notes and References

Chapter One

1. Reinaldo Arenas, *Before Night Falls,* trans. Dolores M. Koch (New York: Viking Penguin, 1993), 317; hereafter cited in text as *BNF.*

2. Although homophobia in Cuba is clearly tied to its Spanish and Catholic cultural heritage, there is no denying that after 1959 homophobia became politically institutionalized. For detailed accounts of the problematic relationship between the Castro regime and homosexuals, see Allen Young's *Gays under the Cuban Revolution* (San Francisco: Grey Fox Press, 1981), hereafter cited in text; Marvin Leiner's *Sexual Politics in Cuba: Machismo, Homosexuality, and AIDS* (Boulder, Colo.: Westview Press, 1994), hereafter cited in text; and Ian Lumsden's *Machos, Maricones, and Gays: Cuba and Homosexuality* (Philadelphia: Temple University Press, 1996), hereafter cited in text.

3. Reinaldo Arenas, *Avant la nuit* (Paris: Julliard, 1992).

4. Reinaldo Arenas, *Antes que anochezca* (Barcelona: Tusquets, 1992).

5. Other works by Arenas that appeared first in French before appearing in their original Spanish edition include: *Le monde hallucinant,* 1968 (Spanish edition, *El mundo alucinante,* 1969); *Le palais des très blanches mouffettes,* 1975 (Spanish edition, *El palacio de las blanquísimas mofetas,* 1980); *Le portier,* 1988 (Spanish edition, *El portero,* 1989); *Adiós a mamá* (1993), (Spanish edition, *Adiós a mamá,* 1995).

6. Roberto González Echeverría, "An Outcast of the Island," review of *Before Night Falls, New York Times Book Review,* 24 October 1993, 33.

7. Philippe Lejeune, "The Autobiographical Pact," trans. Katherine Learyis, in *On Autobiography* (Minneapolis: University of Minnesota Press, 1989), 4; hereafter cited in text.

8. Robert Richmond Ellis, "The Gay Lifewriting of Reinaldo Arenas: *Antes que anochezca," A/B: Auto/Biography Studies* 10, no. 1 (Spring 1995): 127; hereafter cited in text.

9. David Unger, "The Archetypal Misfit," letter to the editor in *New York Times Book Review,* 28 November 1993, 35.

10. The favorable reviews of *Before Night Falls* clearly outweigh the negative reviews that have appeared. A sampling of favorable reviews would include: Guillermo Cabrera Infante, "La destrucción del sexo," *El País,* 29 May 1992, 15–16, hereafter cited in text; Juan Goytisolo, "Caído en el campo de honor," *El País,* 6 June 1992, 13–14; Mario Vargas Llosa, "Pájaro tropical," *El País,* 15 June 1992, 15–16, hereafter cited in text; Alastair Reid, "Troublemaker," *The New York Review,* 18 November 1993, 23–25; Alfred Corn, "Where We Stand," *The*

Kenyon Review 16, no. 4 (Fall 1994): 158–60. The negative and discrediting reviews of *Before Night Falls* are limited to: Manuel Pereira, "Reinaldo antes del alba," *Quimera* 111 (1992): 54–58; Miguel Riera, "El mundo es alucinante," *Quimera* 111 (1992): 58–59, hereafter cited in text; Eliseo Diego, "Eliseo Diego habla sobre Reinaldo Arenas," *Enlace* 1, no. 1 (1994): 1–4; Clemmer Mayhew III, "Sentenced to Tell the Truth," *Christopher Street* 210 (1994): 13–16; Abilio Estévez, "Between Nightfall and Vengeance: Remembering Reinaldo Arenas," *Michigan Quarterly Review* 33, no. 4 (1994): 859–67, hereafter cited in text. Let me briefly comment on the negative reviews. Both Manuel Pereira and Miguel Reira, similar to David Unger but not as spiteful, accuse Arenas of indulging in hyperbole and vindictive gossip. In addition, both reviewers are particularly troubled by what they perceive to be Arenas's exaggerated number of sexual encounters. The Cuban writer Eliseo Diego states that after coming to the United States Arenas became an enemy of the revolution: "cosa que me parece lógica; además estaba en todo su derecho (something that is logical to me; besides he had every right to)" (p. 4). Yet Diego adds that after coming to the United States Arenas "mintió mucho" (lied a lot). Clemmer Mayhew's review attacks Arenas's autobiography indirectly by undermining Dolores M. Koch's English translation. Estévez's review will be discussed at length later in this chapter.

    11.   Achy Obejas, "The Exiles' Exile," *The Nation,* 21 March 1994, 387; hereafter cited in text.

    12.   Sylvia Molloy, *At Face Value: Autobiographical Writing in Spanish America* (Cambridge: Cambridge University Press, 1991).

    13.   Paul de Man, "Autobiography as De-facement," *MLN* 94, no. 5 (1979): 922.

    14.   See Michael Sprinker, "Fictions of the Self: The End of Autobiography," in James Olney, ed., *Autobiography: Essays Theoretical and Critical* (Princeton: Princeton University Press, 1980), 321–42.

    15.   Paul John Eakin, foreword to *On Autobiography* (Lejeune, ix). Eakin has written two books on autobiography: *Fictions in Autobiography: Studies in the Art of Self-Invention* (Princeton: Princeton University Press, 1985), in which he argues that the self articulated in autobiography can be read as a fictive construct; and *Touching the World: Reference in Autobiography* (Princeton: Princeton University Press, 1992), in which he explores the issues of language, referentiality and the contexts of historical and biographical fact.

    16.   Philippe Lejeune, *Moi aussi* (Paris: Seuil, 1986).

    17.   Reinaldo Arenas, *The Ill-Fated Peregrinations of Fray Servando,* trans. Andrew Hurley (New York: Avon Books, 1987), xvi.

    18.   Eduardo C. Béjar, *La textualidad de Reinaldo Arenas: Juegos de la escritura posmoderna* (Madrid: Editorial Playor, 1987), 32–33; my translation; hereafter cited in text.

    19.   Liliane Hasson, "Le mémoire aiguisée. Entretien avec Reinaldo Arenas," in *Autrement* 35 (1989): 62–70. Jana Bokova's "Havana" was produced by the BBC in London in 1990; the historical and literary investigation for the

movie was done by Gualberto Ferrari. Arenas's meeting with his father is also recounted in Roberto Valero's *El desamparado humor de Reinaldo Arenas* (The Forlorn Humor of Reinaldo Arenas) (North Miami: Hallmark Press, 1991), 12; hereafter cited in text.

20. Reinaldo Arenas, *The Palace of the White Skunks,* trans. Andrew Hurley (New York: Viking Penguin, 1990); hereafter cited in text as *Palace.*

21. Arenas's novels contain many instances of breaks with typographical conventions as a desire to challenge the limitations of linearity. The use of different size letters and types; blank spaces, and even blank pages; off-centered, vertical, and slanted writing are all typographical transgressions that exploit the many possibilities of the blank page and promote the palpability of the texts, emphasizing them as *texts,* that is, linguistic artifices and not neutral transcriptions of reality.

22. Nedda G. de Anhalt, "Reinaldo Arenas: *aquel* mar, una vez más," in *Rojo y naranja sobre rojo* (México: Editorial Vuelta, 1991), 153–54; my translation.

23. Reinaldo Arenas, *La Vieja Rosa* (Caracas: Editorial Arte, 1980), 108; my translation.

24. James Goodwin, *Autobiography: The Self Made Text* (New York: Twayne, 1993), 15.

25. José Quiroga, "Fleshing out Virgilio Piñera from the Cuban Closet," in *¿Entiendes? Queer Readings, Hispanic Writings,* eds. Emile L. Bergmann and Paul Julian Smith (Durham: Duke University Press, 1995), 178; hereafter cited in text.

26. Alastair Reid, in his review of *Before Night Falls* (*New York Review of Books* 40, no. 19 [18 November 1993]: 23–25), comments that although Arenas "had every reason in the world to write his book of 'vengeance against most of the human race,' as he promised the photograph of Virgilio Piñera; . . . the tone of the book, while not without its sardonic asides, is calm, dispassionate, spare" (p. 23).

27. Alain Robbe-Grillet explains eroticism in the following way: "Eroticism is what differentiates man from beast, precisely because it comes about through the imagination: it is the sexual act, but only to the extent that it is picked up by the imagination, which enhances the sexual act, which starts a sort of exchange all over again. It's typically man's; it's his greatest glory: man is an animal with imagination" (p. 90). See Alain Robbe-Grillet, "What Interests Me Is Eroticism," in *Homosexualities and French Literature,* eds. George Stambolian and Elaine Marks (Ithaca: Cornell University Press, 1979), 87–100.

28. Roberto Valero, " 'Ay, qué lindo tienes el pelo.' Un testimonio de los últimos tiempos de Arenas," in *La escritura de la memoria,* ed. Ottmar Ette (Frankfurt: Vervuert Verlag, 1991), 29–32; my translation. This article was first published in *Diario las Américas,* 29 March 1991, p. 6-A.

29. Reinaldo Arenas, *The Doorman,* trans. Dolores M. Koch (New York: Grove Press, 1991); hereafter cited in text as *Doorman.*

30.   Paul Julian Smith in *The Body Hispanic: Gender and Sexuality in Spanish and Spanish American Literature* (Oxford: Clarendon, 1989) observes that "For Sontag, camp was the sign or symptom of the collapse of the moral or political into the aesthetic. Thus sexual object choice (for example) was removed from the sphere of ethics or religion and transplanted to a realm of pure affect, pure 'taste.' But if camp itself claimed to be apolitical, this did not mean it was 'outside' politics: just as Jewish liberalism was an act of prolepsis, an attempt to anticipate and disable the illiberalism of the gentiles, so the camp of the homosexuals served as self-defense against the attacks of moralizers. Thus the very apoliticism of camp can be read as a political strategy, albeit of a highly oblique kind" (pp. 175–76).

31.   Quoted in Leiner, p. 26.

32.   Lillian Manzor-Coats, *Latin America Writers on Gay and Lesbian Themes,* ed. David William Foster (Westport, Conn.: Greenwood Press, 1994), xv-xxxvi; hereafter cited in text.

33.   David William Foster, "Latin American Literature," *The Gay and Lesbian Literary Heritage,* ed. Claude J. Summers (New York: Henry Holt, 1995), 426.

34.   David William Foster, *Gay and Lesbian Themes in Latin American Writing* (Austin: University of Texas Press, 1991); Emile L. Bergmann and Paul Julian Smith, eds., *¿Entiendes? Queer Readings, Hispanic Writings* (Durham, N.C.: Duke University Press, 1995); Elena M. Martínez, *Lesbian Voices from Latin America: Breaking Ground* (New York: Garland Press, 1996); David William Foster, *Sexual Textualities: Essays on Queer/ing Latin American Writing* (Austin: University of Texas Press, 1997).

35.   Guillermo Cabrera Infante, "The Death of Virgilio," in Virgilio Piñera's *Cold Tales,* trans. Mark Schafer (Hygiene, Colo.: Eriadnos Press, 1987), xiii.

36.   Mikhail Bakhtin, *Rabelais and His World,* trans. Helene Iswolsky (Bloomington: Indiana University Press, 1984); hereafter cited in text.

Chapter Two

1.   *Celestino antes del alba* (1967) and *Cantando en el pozo* (1982) are the same novel, but with different titles. When *Celestino antes del alba* was reissued in 1982, it was published under the new title *Cantando en el pozo* because of copyright issues. For Arenas's own comments concerning this change of title, see my interview with him in the appendix of *Reinaldo Arenas: The Pentagonía* (Gainesville: University Press of Florida, 1994), 141; hereafter cited in text.

2.   See the interview with Reinaldo Arenas that appears in the appendix of *La Vieja Rosa* (Caracas: Editorial Arte, 1980), 109–10; my translation.

3.   In an interview with Franz-Olivier Giesbert of the *Nouvel Observateur,* no. 880 (19–25 September 1981): 64–68, later translated into English in *Encounter,* 58, no. 1 (January 1982): 60–67, Arenas recounts the vicissitudes he experienced (re)writing and publishing *Otra vez el mar.* In my conver-

sation with Arenas, he states that he conceived of *Otra vez el mar* in 1966 and completed the first version in 1969. See Soto, *Reinaldo Arenas: The Pentagonía*: p. 204.

4. Severo Sarduy, "Carta privada a Reinaldo Arenas," *Unveiling Cuba,* no. 3 (New York: April 1983), 4; my translation.

5. Viking Press has under contract the English translation of *El color del verano.* Andrew Hurley is currently working on the translation.

6. Andrew Hurley, in his translation of *The Assault,* renders the Spanish "el Reprimerísimo Reprimero" (literally, "The Very Repressive, Very First One") as the "Represident."

7. Over the years Arenas repeatedly stated his intentions to complete the *pentagonía.* Yet, after the publication of *Otra vez el mar* (*Farewell to the Sea*) he published four other texts: *Arturo, la estrella más brillante* ("The Brightest Star") (1984), *La loma del ángel* (*Graveyard of the Angels*) (1987), *El portero* (*The Doorman*) (1989), and *Viaje a La Habana* (Journey to Havana) (1990).

8. Although I do mention the issue of homosexuality in my book *Reinaldo Arenas: The Pentagonía,* the monograph restricts itself to the study of the five novels of the *pentagonía* through the general framework of the Cuban documentary novel tradition, a specific vein within the state-sanctioned literature of the revolution. This chapter builds on my previous work by focusing critical attention on the articulation of homoerotic desire, which in each novel of the quintet becomes more progressively bold.

9. Reinaldo Arenas, *Singing from the Well,* trans. Andrew Hurley (New York: Viking Penguin, 1987), hereafter cited in text as *Singing.*

10. In *The Ill-Fated Peregrinations of Fray Servando,* which was written immediately after *Singing from the Well,* Arenas changes his subversive tactics and uses multiple beginnings; the novel contains three separate chapter 1s.

11. Eliseo Diego, "Sobre *Celestino antes del alba,*" *Casa de las Américas* 7, no. 45 (1967): 163. I am also reminded of Paul de Man's declaration concerning Jorge Luis Borges's work: "The creation of beauty thus begins as an act of duplicity. The writer engenders another self that is his mirror-like reversal. In this anti-self, the virtues and the vices of the original are curiously distorted and reversed" (Paul de Man, "A Modern Master," *The New York Review of Books,* 19 November 1964, 8).

12. Mikhail Bakhtin, *Problems of Dostoevsky's Poetics,* trans. Caryl Emerson (Minneapolis: University of Minnesota Press, 1984), 117.

13. See Ernesto Méndez y Soto, *Panorama de la novela cubana de la revolución (1959–1970)* (Miami: Ediciones Universal, 1977); George R. McMurray, *Spanish American Writing since 1941* (New York: Ungar, 1987); Kessel Schwartz, *A New History of Spanish American Fiction* (Coral Gables, Fla.: University of Miami Press, 1971), among others.

14. Despite his homophobic panic, there is sufficient cause to warrant a homosexual reading of Borges's work. See, for example, Daniel Altamiranda, "Jorge Luis Borges," in Foster, pp. 72–83; Daniel Balderston, "The 'Fecal

Dialectic': Homosexual Panic and the Origin of Writing in Borges," in Bergmann and Smith, pp. 29–45; Herbert J. Brant, "The Mark of the Phallus: Homoerotic Desire in Borges' 'La forma de la espada,' " in *Chasqui* 25, no. 1 (May 1996): 25–38.

15. Emir Rodríguez Monegal informs us that this poem first appeared in the literary magazine *Sur* (December 1936, pp. 71–72) and was later included in the 1943 edition of *Poemas* (Buenos Aires: Editorial Losada, 1943). See Emir Rodríguez Monegal, *Jorge Luis Borges: A Literary Biography* (New York: E. P. Dutton, 1978), 274–75.

16. Federico García Lorca, *Libro de poemas* (Madrid: Maroto, 1921).

17. Reinaldo Arenas, "Celestino y yo," *Unión* 6, no. 3 (1967): 119; my translation.

18. Ian Gibson, *Federico García Lorca: A Life* (New York: Pantheon Books, 1989), 468.

19. For more information on Lorca's life as well as the homosexual themes in his writing, see my entry, "Federico García Lorca," in *The Gay and Lesbian Literary Heritage*: 303–5.

20. Perla Rozencvaig, "Entrevista," *Hispamérica* 10, no. 28 (1981): 47–48; my translation.

21. This deconstruction of gender is not a case of metamorphosis, like it is, for example, in Virginia Woolf's *Orlando* (a character who incidently makes a brief appearance in Arenas's *The Ill-Fated Peregrinations of Fray Servando*). Also, in Argentine novelist Julio Cortázar's masterpiece *Rayuela* (*Hopscotch*) (trans. Gregory Rabassa [New York: Avon Books, 1966]), a novel in which the use of the *doppelgänger* is central to the story, the double is limited to the same-sex combination La Maga-Talita and Oliveira-Traveler.

22. Jorge Olivares, "Carnival and the Novel: Reinaldo Arenas' *El palacio de las blanquísimas mofetas*," *Hispanic Review* 53, no. 4 (1985): 474.

23. Reinaldo Arenas, *Farewell to the Sea*, trans. Andrew Hurley (New York: Viking Penguin, 1986); hereafter cited in text as *Farewell.*

24. Reinaldo Arenas, *El color del verano* (Miami: Ediciones Universal, 1991); hereafter cited in text as *El color.*

25. Perla Rozencvaig, "Reinaldo Arenas's Last Interview," *Review: Latin American Literature and Arts* 44 (January-June 1991): 79; hereafter cited in text.

26. Reinaldo Arenas, *The Assault*, trans. Andrew Hurley (New York: Viking Penguin, 1994); hereafter cited in text as *Assault.*

27. Carlos Espinosa Domínguez, "La vida es riesgo o abstinencia," *Quimera* 101 (1990): 56; my translation.

28. For Arenas's own comments on the presentation of the mother figure in his novels, see my conversation with the author in *Reinaldo Arenas: The Pentagonía,* pp. 206–8.

29. The cultivation and popularity of the detective genre in revolutionary Cuba is studied at length in Tzvi Medin's *Cuba: The Shaping of Revolutionary Consciousness* (Boulder: Lynne Rienner Publishers, 1990).

30. Tzvetan Todorov, "The Typology of Detective Fiction," in *The Poetics of Prose,* trans. Richard Howard (Ithaca: Cornell University Press, 1977); hereafter cited in text.

31. Milan Kundera, *The Art of the Novel,* trans. Linda Asher (New York: Grove Press, 1988).

Chapter Three

1. Reinaldo Arenas, *Con los ojos cerrados* (Montevideo: Editorial Arca, 1972).

2. Also see *Before Night Falls, pp.* 287–88.

3. Reinaldo Arenas, *Termina el desfile* (Barcelona: Seix Barral, 1981); hereafter cited in text as *Termina.*

4. Four of these stories have been translated into English: "The Parade Ends," trans. Andrew Bush, *The Paris Review* 23, no. 80 (Summer 1981): 96–122; "In the Shade of the Almond Tree," trans. Suzanne Jill Levine, *Fiction* 6, no. 3 (1982): 74–78; "The Wounded," trans. Andrew Bush, *Latin American Literary Review* 8, no. 16 (1980): 173–82; "Bestial Among the Flowers," trans. Andrew Hurley, *A Hammock Beneath the Mangoes,* ed. Thomas Colchie (New York: Plume Books, 1992), 321–47.

5. For a full account of the Peruvian Embassy episode as well as the Mariel exodus see José Luis-Llovio Menéndez, *Insider: My Hidden Life as a Revolutionary in Cuba,* trans. Edith Grossman (New York: Bantam Books, 1988), 382–89.

6. To date, only one published article studies the stories of *Termina el desfile* in their entirety: Elio Alba-Bufill, "Constantes temáticas en *Termina el desfile*" (Recurrent Themes in *Termina el desfile*), eds. Julio Hernández-Miyares and Perla Rozencvaig, *Reinaldo Arenas: alucinaciones, fantasías y realidad* (Glenview, Ill.: Scott, Foresman/Montesinos, 1990), 38–44; hereafter cited in text. Alba-Bufill, however, makes no mention whatsoever of homosexual allusions or homoerotic encoding in these stories.

7. Reinaldo Arenas, *La Vieja Rosa* (Caracas: Editorial Arte, 1980); hereafter cited in text as *Vieja Rosa.*

8. Reinaldo Arenas, "Old Rosa" and "The Brightest Star," in *Old Rosa, A Novel in Two Stories,* trans. Ann Tashi Slater and Andrew Hurley (New York: Grove Press, 1989); hereafter cited in text as "Old Rosa" and as "Brightest Star."

9. I am using the most restricted acceptation of the term "intertextuality," that is, the relation(s) between one text and another to which it is directly linked. In this case, "Old Rosa" is the intertext on which "The Brightest Star" is (re)written.

10. In "El Cometa Halley" (Halley's Comet, 1986), from the collection *Adiós a mamá* (Goodbye Mother), Arenas presents a comical and carnivalesque intertextual adventure involving Bernarda Alba's five daughters, who

find themselves living in Cuba when Halley's Comet appears in the spring of 1910.

11. Great Big Mama in turn serves as a precursor of the decrepit tyrant El Reprimerísimo Reprimero (the Represident) of Arenas's last novel of the *pentagonía, The Assault*. Old Rosa, Great Big Mama, and the Represident can all be studied within the dynamics of the literature of the dictator, a well-established genre within Spanish American letters. See my article, *"El color del verano*: innovaciones temáticas y aportaciones ideológicas a la novela del dictador" (*The Color of Summer*: Thematic Innovations and Ideological Contributions to the Dictator Novel), in *Apuntes Postmodernos/Postmodern Notes*, 6, no. 1 (Fall 1995): 59–65.

12. Nelle Morton, "Patriarchy," in *A Feminist Dictionary*, eds. Cheris Kramarae and Paula A. Treichler (Boston: Pandora Press, 1985), 323.

13. William L. Siemens, "Treinta años de soledad: 'La Vieja Rosa' " in Hernández-Miyares and Rozencvaig, 51–55.

14. Lisa Tuttle, *Encyclopedia of Feminism* (London: Longman Group Limited, 1986), 199.

15. The image of Rosa ordering the men of the farm to tear down a hut to be made into charcoal serves as an ironic foreshadowing of her own final destruction. In "The Brightest Star" Arturo, still haunted by his mother's funeral, remembers walking behind "that gleaming black contraption bearing the singed remains, that forked charcoal *thing* [the burned body of his mother]" ("Brightest Star," 57).

16. I have used Tzvetan Todorov's distinction between *énonciation* (the narrative process, that is, the telling and the ordering of events) and *énoncé* (the story, that is, the history or tale communicated by means of the narration). See Tzvetan Todorov, *Litterature et signification* (Paris: Larousse, 1967).

17. Reinaldo Arenas, "Pourquoi j'ai fui Fidel Castro." Interview with Franz Olivier-Giesbert. *Le Nouvel Observateur* no. 880 (19–25 September 1981): 64–68. Later reprinted as "Dangerous Manuscripts: A Conversation with Reinaldo Arenas," *Encounter* 58, no. 1 (January 1982): 60–67; hereafter cited in text.

18. Carlos Alberto Montaner, *Fidel Castro y la revolución cubana* (Barcelona: Plaza & Janés Editores, 1985); hereafter cited in text.

19. In *Before Night Falls* (pp. 147–50) Arenas provides a more complete account of Rodríguez Leyva's failed attempt to hijack a Cubana de Aviación plane.

20. Reinaldo Arenas, "Si te llamaras Nelson," *Voluntad de vivir manifestándose* (Madrid: Editorial Betania, 1989), 86–89; hereafter cited in text as *Voluntad*.

21. Roberto González Echevarría, *"Biografía de un cimarrón* and the Novel of the Cuban Revolution," *The Voice of the Masters* (Austin: University of Texas Press, 1985), 110.

22. Miguel Barnet, "Testimonio y comunicación: una vía hacia la identidad," *Unión*, no. 4 (1980): 131–43.

23. Juan Goytisolo, "Apuntes sobre *Arturo, la estrella más brillante* (Some Notes on "The Brightest Star") in Hernández-Miyares and Rozencvaig, 181; my translation.

24. For a more thorough study of this very idea in the novels of the *pentagonía,* please refer to part 2, chapter 7, "The Mistrust of Literary Forms," in my book, *Reinaldo Arenas: The Pentagonía,* pp. 116–28.

25. Gertrudis Gómez de Avellaneda, *Obras de Doña Gertrudis Gómez de Avellaneda* (Madrid: Ediciones Atlas, 1974), 253–54; my translation.

Chapter Four

1. Two Spanish editions of *Viaje a La Habana* exist: Ediciones Universal (Miami, 1990) and Narrativa Mondadori (Madrid, 1990). My source is the Narrativa Mondadori edition because it is more carefully edited and does not suffer from the excessive amount of errata and typos that the Ediciones Universal edition does. For the English translations of these stories, or novelettes, Grove Press has purchased the rights to contract for and publish the English translation of *Viaje a la Habana.* However, Dolores M. Koch has already translated "Mona" for *The Penguin Book of International Gay Writing,* ed. Mark Mitchell (New York: Viking Penguin, 1995), 550–76. I shall quote from her translation; hereafter cited in text as "Mona." The English translations for "Que trine Eva" (Let Eva Scream) and "Viaje a La Habana" (Journey to Havana) are my own; hereafter cited in text as "Que trine Eva" and "Viaje."

2. Antonio Benítez-Rojo, *The Repeating Island: The Caribbean and the Postmodern Perspective,* trans. James E. Maraniss (Durham and London: Duke University Press, 1992); hereafter cited in text.

3. Moe Meyer, "Reclaiming the Discourse of Camp," *The Politics and Poetics of Camp,* ed. Moe Meyer (London and New York: Routledge, 1994), 1–22; hereafter cited in text.

4. Susan Sontag, "Notes on 'Camp' " in *Against Interpretation* (New York: Farrar, Straus & Giroux, 1966), 275–92.

5. Quoted in Néstor Almendros and Orlando Jiménez-Leal's *Conducta Impropia* (Madrid: Editorial Playor, 1984), 180. Fashion was not the only item discussed at the First National Congress on Education and Culture. Art and literature were also topics of discussion. Specific declarations were made that accorded value to art and literature in terms of their service to the revolution. That is, reality described by works of art/literature would have legitimacy only in terms of the revolution; all reality would receive its meaning within the context of the revolutionary struggle. See Fidel Castro's closing speech before the First National Congress on Education and Culture, printed in full in the March-June issue of *Casa de las Américas* nos. 65–66 (1971): 21–33.

6. Roland Barthes, *The Fashion System,* trans. Matthew Ward and Richard Howard (New York: Hill & Wang, 1983).

7. Juan Rulfo, *Pedro Páramo* (México: Fondo de Cultura Económica, 1955); trans. Margaret Sayers Peden (New York: Grove Press, 1994). Arenas was very familiar with Rulfo's work. In 1969, two years before completing "Que trine Eva," Arenas published an article, "El páramo en llamas," in a book that compiled essays by Cubans on the Mexican writer's work, *Recopilación de textos sobre Juan Rulfo,* ed. Antonio Benítez-Rojo (Habana: Casa de las Américas, 1969), 60–63. Arenas wrote: "[En *Pedro Páramo*] palpita constantemente el hombre, con todas sus tragedias, sus temores, su soledad ancestral y su desgarrado intento por encontrar el significado de su existencia (la dicha)" (p. 62) (At the heart of [*Pedro Páramo*] lies man; man with his tragedies, his fears, his ancestral solitude and his brazen attempt to find the meaning of his existence [happiness]).

8. The landing of Antonio Maceo and other distinguished generals at Duaba Beach on 1 April 1895 is an important historical event of Cuba's War of Independence. Curiously enough, after making landfall the expedition was immediately attacked by the Spaniards and had to make its way to safety in the town of Guantánamo. When independence for Cuba was won in 1901, the United States Naval Base at Guantánamo was established with a 99-year lease. Today Guantánamo remains both a symbol of freedom for many Cubans who have risked their lives to reach the base (Arenas himself one of them; see *Before Night Falls,* pp. 163–65) and a constant bitter reminder to Fidel Castro of U.S. presence in Cuba.

9. Nicolás Guillén, *¡Patria o Muerte! The Great Zoo and Other Poems,* trans. and ed. Robert Márquez (New York and London: Monthly Review Press, 1972), 184–85.

10. Tzvetan Todorov, *The Fantastic: A Structural Approach to a Literary Genre* (Ithaca, N.Y.: Cornell University Press, 1980); hereafter cited in text.

11. To blindly apply Todorov's theoretical framework—a framework specifically developed within and for a European literary tradition—to a Spanish American story could not possibly take into account the singularity and fecund production of fantastic texts in Spanish America. Therefore, I will mediate Todorov's work with Ana María Barrenechea's notions of the fantastic in twentieth-century Spanish American narrative. The Argentine critic's ideas are best summarized in her well-known essay "Ensayo de una tipología de la literatura fantástica" (A Typological Essay on Fantastic Literature), *Revista Iberoamericana* 80 (1972): 391–403; hereafter cited in text.

12. *Cuentos cubanos de lo fantástico y lo extraordinario,* ed. Rogelio Llopis (San Sebastián: Equipo Editorial, 1968). This collection contains stories from Alejo Carpentier, José Lezama Lima, Virgilio Piñera, Eliseo Diego, and Antonio Benítez-Rojo, among others. Also, Arenas's story "Con los ojos cerrados" (With My Eyes Closed) is published here under the heading of "Magical Realism."

13. The "marvelous" refers to a category of literature in which magical, supernatural, or other astonishing impossibilities are accepted as normal within an imagined world clearly separated from our own reality. Such is the case, for

instance, in the appearance of goblins and witches in *Singing from the Well* or in the science fiction setting of *The Assault.*

14.   The fact that the editors' note is dated 2025 does not allow the contemporary reader to identify directly with the story, a necessary element, according to Todorov, of fantastic literature. Still, despite the fact that there might not be a direct identification on the part of the reader with a world that exists far into the future, there does exist a "confrontation" between a natural/logical world and supernatural/illogical one. This confrontation of course creates problematization, the necessary ingredient in Barrenechea's definition of the fantastic. Future readers, that is, after the year 2025, of Arenas's "Mona" will be faced with the same problem that faces today's readers of Jorge Luis Borges's classic fantastic tale "Tlön, Uqbar, Orbis Tertius." Borges's famous story ends with the date 1940 immediately followed by a postscript from 1947. Although today's readers do not even pay attention to this detail, the story, with its postscript of 1947, actually first appeared in the magazine *Sur* in May of 1940.

15.   Other scholars of the fantastic (Roger Callois, Louis Vax, H. P. Lovecraft, among others) coincide with Todorov in establishing as an essential element the capacity of the fantastic to awaken fear or horror in the reader. In *Busca del unicornio: los cuentos fantásticos de Julio Cortázar; elementos para una poética de lo neofantástico* (In Search of the Unicorn: Julio Cortázar's Fantastic Stories; Elements for a Neofantastic Poetics) (Madrid: Gredos, 1983), Jaime Alazraki introduces the designation of "neofantástico," or "neofantastic," to distinguish those texts, like Borges's and Cortázar's, that contain fantastic elements but whose function is not to assault the reader through fear or terror. According to Alazraki, the Spanish American "neofantastic" differs considerably from the conception and practice of the fantastic genre of the nineteenth century. The "neofantastic" assumes that the so-called real world is only a referential mask that hides a second reality, which in fact is the more authentic message of the story. This second reality is alluded to obliquely and/or metaphorically because it cannot be named directly by a referential, scientific, and patriarchal language. As I later establish, in "Mona" Arenas carnivalizes, in his familiar hallucinatory fashion, the (neo)fantastic genre in order to obliquely and/or metaphorically allude to the repression (silencing) of homosexual desire in contemporary society that continues to resist such manifestations and that has become more intolerant as a direct result of the AIDS crisis.

16.   See Sigmund Freud, "Jokes and the Species of the Comic," *Jokes and Their Relation to the Unconscious,* trans. and ed. James Strachey in collaboration with Anna Freud (Great Britain: Butler & Tanner LTD., 1960), 181–236. In *Rabelais and His World,* Bakhtin states: "The principle of laughter destroys . . . all pretense of an extratemporal meaning and unconditional value of necessity. It frees human consciousness, thought, and imagination for new potentialities" (Bakhtin, 49).

17.   I have included a bracket in Dolores Koch's English translation in order to be able to render a more literal translation of the original Spanish. In

Spanish, Arenas makes a point of using both the expressions *"tal vez"* ("perhaps") and *"quizás"* (also translated as "perhaps").

18.   The original Spanish uses the word "alegato," from the verb "alegar," that is, to establish the proof of some fact. Dolores Koch translates "alegato" as "statement."

19.   Adriana Méndez Rodenas, "Voyage to *La Havane*: The Countess of Merlín's Preview of National Identity," in *Cuban Studies 16,* ed. Carmelo Mesa-Lago (Pittsburgh, Pa.: University of Pittsburgh Press, 1986), 83; hereafter cited in text.

20.   Considering Carpentier's own background, it is not surprising that he too would write a text about a search for origins. Like la Condesa de Merlín, Alejo Carpentier (1904–1980) was born in Havana but spent most of his life living abroad. Carpentier's father was French and his mother was of Russian immigrant descent; at home the family always spoke French. In 1914 the family resettled in France. It was not until the early 1920s that the young Carpentier returned to Cuba to study music and architecture. After being arrested for a brief time for his opposition to the Machado dictatorship, Alejo Carpentier once again returned to France, where he stayed until 1939. Afterward, the Cuban novelist would spend the rest of his life living in and out of Cuba. In 1966, Carpentier settled definitively in Paris, where he was posted as cultural attaché to the Cuban consulate until his death in 1980. In *Alejo Carpentier: The Pilgrim at Home* (Austin: University of Texas Press, 1990), Roberto González Echeverría proposes that the question of Carpentier's own quest for identity persistently comes into play in all his writings (p. 31). González Echeverría's ironic subtitle, "The Pilgrim at Home," suggests Carpentier's peregrinations throughout the world, with Cuba always remaining the spiritual home to which he would continuously return.

21.   Only 10 letters were left in the much shorter Spanish edition of *Viaje a La Habana.* That Arenas had la Condesa de Merlín in mind when he wrote his own story is evident by a quote from the Countess that he chooses for the epigraph of his tale: "¡Sólo encuentro un montón de piedras sin vida y un recuerdo vivo!" (I only find a heap of lifeless rocks and a living memory).

22.   Benigno Sánchez-Eppler, "Call My Son Ismael: Exiled Paternity and Father/Son Eroticism in Reinaldo Arenas and José Martí," in *Differences: A Journal of Feminist Cultural Studies* 6, no. 1 (1994): 69; hereafter cited in text.

23.   This scene is not the first time that Arenas reappropriated Judeo-Christian symbols and biblical episodes. In the "Play" section (pp. 313–42) of *The Palace of the White Skunks,* for example, verses from the "Song of Songs" are appropriated and counterpoised to the direct speech of Adolfina and the chorus of princes who attempt to adopt the style of the biblical text. The difference between the lofty elegance of the "Song of Songs" and Adolfina's depravation and vulgarity results in an ironic text marked with what the Russian critic Mikhail Bakhtin called elements of folk humor that produce a carnivalesque spirit of renewal.

24. Perhaps delving more into the story of Genesis than Arenas ever intended, Sánchez-Eppler provides a well-documented account and interpretation of the biblical sources of Ishmael, son of the Egyptian slave Hagar and the sojourning Abraham, as well as of the intertwining biblical narratives about Abraham's parenting and nation-making paternity. What he reveals is "that within the Judeo-Christian inaugural narrative of a migrant/exiled family in search of a place to settle, at the very moment when a group of people assert their way of defining that special relationship with Yahweh which will make them a nation, we find parents and children transacting the nature and future of their peoplehood in stories foundationally anxious about incest and homosexuality" (Sánchez-Eppler, 91).

Chapter Five

1. Reinaldo Arenas, *El central* (Barcelona: Editorial Seix Barral, 1981); hereafter cited in text as *El central*.
2. Reinaldo Arenas, *El Central: A Cuban Sugar Mill,* trans. Anthony Kerrigan (New York: Avon Books, 1984); hereafter cited in text as *Sugar Mill*.
3. Octavio Paz, "Translation: Literature and Letters," trans. Irene del Corral, in *Theories of Translation,* ed. Rainer Schulte and John Biguenet (Chicago: University of Chicago Press, 1992), 155.
4. Reinaldo Arenas, *Leprosorio* (Madrid: Editorial Betania, 1990); the poems contained herein are hereafter cited in text as *Morir en junio* and *Leprosorio*.
5. In his novel *La loma del ángel* (*Graveyard of the Angels;* trans. Alfred MacAdam [New York: Avon Books, 1987])—a parodic rewriting of Cirilio Villaverde's solemn nineteenth-century Cuban novel *Cecilia Valdés*—Arenas literally exploits the idea and image of the black slave being sucked into the Plantation machine. In chapter 24 of the novel, titled "The Steam Engine," the impact of technology and its effects on black slaves in early nineteenth-century Cuban sugar production is sarcastically ridiculed when an English manufactured steam engine is acquired by don Cándido with the hope of grinding sugarcane more quickly and thus rendering obsolete the old grinding machines powered by horses, mules, and sometimes slaves. However, because it is a new machine, no one knows exactly how to work it. Thus, when the engine becomes clogged, a black slave is sent into the engine to unblock the machine. While the slave is inside the machine, the pressure finally builds to such a point that the machine explodes, hurling the slave through the air by the force of the compressed steam. Arenas's narrative now takes on a hyperbolic and satirical tone as other black slaves frantically throw themselves into the engine with the hope of fleeing from the plantation. Afraid of losing all his slaves, don Cándido yells out: "Stop that machine or all my slaves will disappear! I should have known you can't do business with the English! That's no steam engine, it's an English trick to send the blacks back to Africa!" (*Graveyard,* 81)

6. I have slightly modified Anthony Kerrigan's translation to account for the sexual innuendo of the Spanish original, which reads: "Esto me lo dijo Karl Marx, haciendo un gracioso giro, soltando una carcajada y marchándose apresurado tras los fondillos de los niños-militares que integraban la retaguardia" (*El central,* 14). The Spanish word "fondillos," literally the "seat or bottom of trousers," in the Cuban vernacular is synonymous to "rear end" or "ass."

7. Both Manuel Pereira in "Reinaldo antes del alba" (*Quimera* 111 [1992]: 54–58) and Miguel Riera in "El mundo es alucinante" (*Quimera* 111 [1992]: 58–59) see Arenas's accusations that certain individuals are homosexual as an indication of self-loathing.

8. I use the term "panic" as proposed by Eve Kosofsky Sedgwick in her studies *Between Men: English Literature and Male Homosexual Desire* (New York: Columbia University Press, 1985) and *Epistemology of the Closet* (Berkeley: University of California Press, 1990).

9. Samuel Feijoó, "Revolución y vicios" [Revolution and Vices], *El Mundo,* 15 April 1965, 5. As quoted in Lois M. Smith and Alfred Padula, *Sex and Revolution: Women in Socialist Cuba* (New York: Oxford University Press, 1966), 172–73.

10. For a more detailed study of the Cuban documentary novel and Arenas's subversive response to this genre promoted and actively supported by the revolutionary cultural policy makers, see my book *Reinaldo Arenas: The Pentagonía.*

11. All translations of *Morir en junio y con la lengua afuera* are mine. Page numbers refer to the Spanish edition of *Leprosorio.*

12. See, for example, Gretchen Mieszkowski, "The Prose *Lancelot's* Galehot, Malroy's Lavain, and the Queering of Late Medieval Literature," *Arthuriana* 5, no. 1 (1995): 21–51; hereafter cited in text. Mieszkowski studies two late-medieval Arthurian works: the Prose *Lancelot* (thirteenth-century Old French romance written by an anonymous writer) and Malory's fifteenth-century portrayal of Lavain in the story of Elaine le Blanke, the Fair Maid of Astolat. The critic discusses and convincingly argues for second levels of homoerotic meanings in these texts. Although Mieszkowski does not specifically treat the character of Perceval, other Arthurian scholars have mentioned homosocial connotations in the Perceval stories in their Internet discussions (see http://www.mun.ca./lists/arthurnet). In one example, a critic cites the German Wolfram von Eschenback's Parzival (a thirteenth-century text based on Chrétien's romance) in which, in one episode, Parzival's (Perceval's) "erect lance" is presented as a challenge to the other knights.

13. Bruce Smith, *Homosexual Desire in Shakespeare's England: A Cultural Poetics* (Chicago: University of Chicago Press, 1991).

14. During our conversation in 1987, I asked Arenas to comment on the fact that in many of his texts the mother figure is presented as tyrannizing and oppressing the son, who she wishes to destroy. He answered: "It's a dual relationship. There's this type of relationship in all my novels. It's not com-

pletely a tyrannical relationship. The mother is destructive, but at the same time she is affectionate. She can destroy, but also love. It's a relationship of power and control that she has with her son. She dominates him, but also cares for him; she destroys him, but also loves him. To a certain extent I see in this the tradition of the Cuban mother, a tradition that is the result of our Spanish heritage. The son loves his mother but also realizes that he must get away from her. I believe that Cuban mothers have had a negative and positive influence on our writers. For example, Lezama Lima publishes *Paradiso* after his mother's death. Perhaps he wouldn't have dared to publish that novel beforehand, which, among other things, pays homage to his mother. We don't dare reveal our true selves to our mothers, much less if we're homosexual. Mothers see that as absolutely taboo, completely immoral and prohibited; at least the majority of mothers see it that way. That love/hate, rejection and rapprochement of the mother is a contradictory relationship, but very real. In *El asalto* at the same time the protagonist destroys his mother he does it by possessing her. Therefore, there isn't total hate, but rather obsession and passion." See Soto, 143–44.

15. The story, which appears in the collection that bears the same title, *Adiós a mamá* (Miami: Ediciones Universal, 1996), has been translated by Jo Labanyi as "Goodbye Mother" and published in *The Faber Book of Contemporary Latin American Short Stories,* ed. Nick Caistor (London: Faber and Faber, 1989), 53–66; hereafter cited in text as "Goodbye Mother."

16. All translations of *Leprosorio* are my own. In 1987 Andrew Hurley, responsible for translating a number of Arenas's novels, translated and published the first five pages of *Leprosorio.* See "Leprosorio, Leprosarium, The Leper Colony," *The World and I* (July 1987): 242–47.

17. Pablo Neruda, *Canto general* (México: Talleres Gráficos, 1950). Translated and edited by Ben Belitt in *Pablo Neruda, Five Decades: Poems 1925–1970* (New York: Grove Press, 1974).

18. All translations of the poems from *Voluntad de vivir manifestándose* are my own.

Chapter Six

1. "Entrevista con Andrew Hurley," *Apuntes Postmodernos/Postmodern Notes* 6, no. 1 (Fall 1995): 47; my translation.

Selected Bibliography

PRIMARY WORKS

Spanish Editions

NOVELS

Celestino antes del alba. La Habana: Ediciones Unión, 1967.
Cantando en el pozo. Barcelona: Editorial Argos Vergara, 1982.
El mundo alucinante. Caracas: Monte Avila Editores, 1982.
Otra vez el mar. Barcelona: Editorial Argos Vergara, 1982.
El palacio de las blanquísimas mofetas. Barcelona: Editorial Argos Vergara, 1982.
La loma del ángel. Málaga: DADOR/ediciones, 1987.
El portero. Málaga: DADOR/ediciones, 1989.
El asalto. Miami: Ediciones Universal, 1991.
El color del verano. Miami: Ediciones Universal, 1991.

NOVELLAS

La Vieja Rosa. Caracas: Editorial Arte, 1980.
Arturo, la estrella más brillante. Barcelona: Montesinos, 1984.
Viaje a La Habana. Madrid: Narrativa Mondadori, 1990.

SHORT STORY COLLECTIONS

Con los ojos cerrados. Montevideo: Editorial Arca, 1972.
Termina el desfile. Barcelona: Seix Barral, 1981.
Adiós a mamá. Barcelona: Ediciones Altera, 1995.

POETRY

El central. Barcelona: Seix Barral, 1981.
Voluntad de vivir manifestándose. Madrid: Editorial Betania, 1989.
Leprosorio (Trilogía poética). Madrid: Editorial Betania, 1990.

DRAMA

Persecución (Cinco piezas de teatro experimental). Miami: Ediciones Universal, 1986.

OTHER

Lazarillo de Tormes (lecturas fáciles). New York: Regents, 1984.
Necesidad de libertad (Mariel: testimonios de un intelectual disidente). México: Kosmos-Editorial, 1986.

Un plebiscito a Fidel Castro. Madrid: Editorial Betania, 1990.
Final de un cuento. Huelva: Diputación Provincial de Huelva, 1991.
Antes que anochezca. Barcelona: Tusquets Editores, 1992.

English Translations

NOVELS

Hallucinations (translation of *El mundo alucinante*). Trans. Gordon Brotherson. New York: Harper and Row, 1971.
Farewell to the Sea (translation of *Otra vez el mar*). Trans. Andrew Hurley. New York: Viking Penguin, 1986.
Graveyard of the Angels (translation of *La loma del ángel*). Trans. Alfred MacAdam. New York: Avon Books, 1987.
The Ill-Fated Peregrinations of Fray Servando (new translation of *El mundo alucinante*). Trans. Andrew Hurley. New York: Avon Books, 1987.
Singing from the Well (translation of *Celestino antes del alba / Cantando en el pozo*). Trans. Andrew Hurley. New York: Viking Penguin, 1987.
The Palace of the White Skunks (translation of *El palacio de las blanquísimas mofetas*). Trans. Andrew Hurley. New York: Viking Penguin, 1990.
The Doorman (translation of *El portero*). Trans. Dolores M. Koch. New York: Grove Press, 1991.
The Assault (translation of *El asalto*). Trans. Andrew Hurley. New York: Viking Penguin, 1994.

NOVELLAS

Old Rose. A Novel in Two Stories (translation of *La Vieja Rosa* ["Old Rosa"] and *Arturo, la estrella más brillante* ["The Brightest Star"]). Trans. Andrew Hurley and Ann Tashi Slater. New York: Grove Press, 1989.
"Mona" (translation of "Mona"). Trans. Dolores M. Koch. In *The Penguin Book of International Gay Writing,* ed. Mark Mitchell, 550–76. New York: Viking Penguin, 1995.

SHORT STORIES

"The Wounded" (translation of "Los heridos"). Trans. Andrew Bush. In *Latin American Literary Review* 8, no. 16 (1980): 173–82.
"The Parade Ends" (translation of "Termina el desfile"). Trans. Andrew Bush. In *The Paris Review* 23, no. 80 (Summer 1981): 96–122.
"In the Shade of the Almond Tree" (translation of "A la sombra de la mata de almendras"). Trans. Suzanne Jill Levine. In *Fiction* 6, no. 3 (1982): 74–78.
"The End of a Story" (translation of "Final de un cuento"). Trans. E. A. Lacey. In *My Deep Dark Pain is Love: A Collection of Gay Fiction,* ed. Winston Leyland, 103–14. San Francisco: Gay Sunshine Press, 1983.

"Traitor" (translation of "Traidor"). Trans. Helen Lane. In *Unveiling Cuba* 5 (October 1983): 5–6.

"Goodbye Mother" (translation of "Adiós a mamá"). Trans. Jo Labanyi. In *The Faber Book of Contemporary Latin American Short Stories,* ed. Nick Caistor, 53–66. London: Faber and Faber, 1989.

"Bestial Among the Flowers" (translation of "Bestial entre las flores"). Trans. Andrew Hurley. In *A Hammock Beneath the Mangoes,* ed. Thomas Colchie, 321–47. New York: Plume Books, 1992.

"Traitor" (new translation of "Traidor"). Trans. Dolores M. Koch. In *Index on Censorship,* eds. Alberto Manguel and Craig Stephenson, vol. 25, no. 6 (November/December 1996): 19–25.

"The Glass Tower" (translation of "La torre de cristal"). Trans. Dolores M. Koch. In *Grand Street 61* 16, no. 1 (Summer 1997) 7–17.

POETRY

El Central: A Cuban Sugar Mill (translation of *El central*). Trans. Anthony Kerrigan. New York: Avon Books, 1984.

"Leprosorio, Leprosarium, The Leper Colony" (partial translation of "Leprosorio"). Trans. Andrew Hurley. *The World and I* (July 1987): 242–47.

OTHER

Before Night Falls (translation of *Antes que anochezca*). Trans. Dolores M. Koch. New York: Viking Penguin, 1993.

SECONDARY WORKS

Books

Béjar, Eduardo C. *La textualidad de Reinaldo Arenas.* Madrid: Editorial Playor, 1987. One of the earliest book-length studies of Arenas's work. A thorough poststructural analysis of the writer's early novels. Does not include, however, many later works.

Ette, Ottmar, ed. *La escritura de la memoria.* Frankfurt am Main: Vervuert, 1992. Collection of articles, informative interviews, and extracts from Arenas's autobiography. Contains an extensive and well-documented bibliography.

Hernández-Miyares, Julio, and Perla Rozencvaig, eds. *Reinaldo Arenas: alucinaciones, fantasía y realidad.* Glenview, Ill.: Scott, Foresman, 1990. Twenty-two articles by different scholars on diverse aspects of Arenas's novels, short stories, and poetry.

Nazario, Félix Lugo. *La alucinación y los recursos literarios en las novelas de Reinaldo Arenas.* Miami: Ediciones Universal, 1995. Studies four of Arenas's novels from the perspective of hallucination, an organizing principle that represents reality as a series of illusions and reflections. Although recently published, it fails to take into consideration the more recent scholarship on Arenas's work.

Paulson, Michael G. *The Youth and the Beach.* Miami: Ediciones Universal, 1993. A comparative study of Thomas Mann's *Death in Venice* and Arenas's *Farewell to the Sea.* Not very convincing.

Rozencvaig, Perla. *Reinaldo Arenas: narrativa de transgresión.* México: Editorial Oasis, 1986. Relatively early study of four novels. Chapter 4 provides an excellent analysis of Arenas's use of the double in *Singing from the Well.*

Sánchez, Reinaldo, ed. *Reinaldo Arenas: recuerdo y presencia.* Miami: Ediciones Universal, 1994. Excellent collection of essays by some of the most respected critics of Arenas's work. Also contains personal testimonies by Arenas's friends.

Soto, Francisco. *Conversación con Reinaldo Arenas.* Madrid: Editorial Betania, 1990. General introductory essay provides an overview of Arenas's work. The interview is especially useful in presenting the genesis of the novels of the *pentagonía.*

——. *Reinaldo Arenas: The Pentagonía.* Gainesville: University Press of Florida, 1994. First major book-length study in English of the *pentagonía.* The five novels are studied within the historical context of the Cuban documentary novel tradition.

Valero, Roberto. *El desamparado humor de Reinaldo Arenas.* North Miami: Hallmark Press, 1991. An analysis of the themes of humor and desolation in Arenas's writings. Comprehensive in its study of novels, novellas, and poetry. Moreover, contains many personal anecdotes on Arenas that provide a wealth of biographical information.

Articles, Interviews, and Parts of Books

Barnet, Miguel. "Celestino antes y después del alba." *La Gaceta de Cuba* 6, no. 60 (1967): 21. Early interview conducted in Cuba that reveals Arenas's playful nature and unwillingness to be pinned down on any matter.

Beaupied, Aida. "De lo anecdótico a lo conceptual en *El mundo alucinante* de Reinaldo Arenas." *Revista de Estudios Hispánicos* 11 (1984): 133–42. An excellent essay that demonstrates how, in *The Ill-Fated Peregrinations of Fray Servando,* the text does not hide but rather lays bare its mode of production (that is, it presents itself as what it is, fiction) thus forcing the reader to move from a passive anecdotal reading to an active conceptual involvement with the text.

Borinski, Alicia. "Re-escribir y escribir: Arenas, Menard, Borges, Cervantes, Fray Servando." *Revista Iberoamericana* 41, nos. 92–93 (1975): 605–16. A study of rewriting as a parodical destruction of the original in Borges and Arenas. This early and insightful essay studies Arenas's shifting narrative voice in *The Ill-Fated Peregrinations of Fray Servando* as one that decenters discourse and cancels out any final validity.

Bush, Andrew. "The Riddled Text: Borges and Arenas." *MLN* 103, no. 2 (1988): 374–97. A Lacanian study of the riddle-structure of Borges's and Arenas's short stories, whose denouements often provide no solutions to the riddles they pose.

Diego, Eliseo. "Sobre Celestino antes del alba." *Casa de las Américas* Año 7, no. 45 (1967): 162–66. Early praise and discussion of Arenas's first novel, *Singing from the Well*, from within the Cuban revolutionary literary establishment.

Ellis, Edwin E. "Reinaldo Arenas and His 'Act of Fury': A Writer in Exile Documents Repression in *El central*." *The Advocate* 398 (10 July 1984): 38–40. A profile of Arenas and Cuba's repression of homosexuals.

Ellis, Robert Richmond. "The Gay Lifewriting of Reinaldo Arenas: *Antes que anochezca*," *A/B: Auto/Biography Studies* 10, no. 1 (Spring 1995): 126–44. An excellent and thorough analysis of *Before Night Falls* as both a political (homosexual) gesture and a means of survival.

Espinosa Domínguez, Carlos. "La vida es riesgo o abstinencia." *Quimera* 101 (1990): 54–61. One of Arenas's final interviews. Here the writer talks at length on many of his later texts: *The Doorman, El color del verano* (The Color of Summer), *The Assault*.

Foster, David William. "Critical Monographs, Dissertations, and Critical Essays about Reinaldo Arenas." In *Cuban Literature: A Research Guide*, 89–91. New York: Garland Publishing, 1985. Early yet thorough bibliography on Arenas's work.

———. Study of *Arturo, la estrella más brillante*. In *Gay and Lesbian Themes in Latin American Literature*, 66–72. Austin: University of Texas Press, 1991. Insightful analysis of homosexual themes in Arenas's novella. Especially noteworthy for the English reader.

———. "Consideraciones en torno a la sensibilidad gay en la narrativa de Reinaldo Arenas." *Revista chilena de literatura*, no. 42 (1993): 89–93. Interesting discussion of what is meant by a gay or homosexual sensibility in a text. Also, a very convincing argument of how *The Palace of the White Skunks*, despite the fact that it does not articulate a clear and open homosexual thematic, does present a homosexual sensibility through its resistance to a bourgeois heterosexist understanding of the world.

G. de Anhalt, Nedda. "Reinaldo Arenas: *aquel* mar, una vez más." In *Rojo y naranja sobre rojo*, by Nedda G. de Anhalt, 133–67. México: Editorial Vuelta, 1991. Frank and insightful interview in which Arenas talks at length about his literary craft as well as his own homosexuality.

Gordon, Ambrose. "Rippling Ribaldry and Pouncing Puns: The Two Lives of Friar Servando." *Review* 8 (Spring 1973): 40–44. Early essay that discusses the use of humor and play in the English translation *Hallucinations*.

Méndez Rodena, Adriana. "*El palacio de las blanquísimas mofetas*: ¿narración historiográfica o narración imaginaria?" *Revista de la Universidad de México* 39, no. 27 (1983): 14–21. The answer to the title question is that it is both. An excellent study of *The Palace of the White Skunks* that examines both the novel's testimonial as well as its poetic moments.

Molinero, Rita M. "Donde no hay furia y desgarro no hay literatura." *Quimera* 17 (1982): 19–23. Provocative interview in which Molinero gets Arenas to speak about his "creative furies."

Montenegro, Nivia. "El espejismo del texto: reflexiones sobre *Cantando en el pozo*." *Revista canadiense de estudios hispánicos* 13, no. 2 (Winter 1989): 276–84. An excellent discussion of the creative activity as a paradigmatic action central to *Singing from the Well*.

Olivares, Jorge. "Carnival and the Novel: Reinaldo Arenas' *El palacio de las blanquísimas mofetas*." *Hispanic Review* 53, no. 4 (1985): 467–76. A study of the use of the carnivalesque in *The Palace of the White Skunks*.

Olivier-Giesbert, Franz. "Pourquoi j'ai fui Fidel Castro." *Le Nouvel Observateur* no. 880 (19–25 September 1981): 64–68. Reprinted as "Dangerous Manuscripts: A Conversation with Reinaldo Arenas." *Encounter* 58, no. 1 (January 1982): 60–67. Arenas recounts the vicissitudes he experienced in Cuba (re)writing *Farewell to the Sea*.

Ortega, Julio. "The Dazzling World of Friar Servando." *Review* 8 (Spring 1973): 45–48. Brief essay on Arenas's unrestrained verbal recreation of the life of Friar Servando.

Oviedo, José Miguel. "Reinaldo Arenas, *Termina el desfile*." *Vuelta* 7, no. 74 (1983): 43–46. Discussion of Arenas's short stories in *Termina el desfile* (The Parade Ends).

Rodríguez Monegal, Emir. "The Labyrinthine World of Reinaldo Arenas." *Latin American Literary Review* 8, no. 16 (1980): 126–31. One of the first studies to praise Arenas's unique and subversive literary voice in response to the official ideology of the Cuban revolution.

Rozencvaig, Perla. "Entrevista." *Hispamérica* 10, no. 28 (1981): 41–48. Recommended interview for the valuable insights it provides concerning the structure and narrative discourse of *The Palace of the White Skunks*.

———. "Reinaldo Arenas's Last Interview." *Review: Latin American Literature and Arts* 44 (January–June 1991): 78–83. Important for being the last interview Arenas granted.

Sánchez-Eppler, Benigno. "Call My Son Ismael: Exiled Paternity and Father/Son Eroticism in Reinaldo Arenas and José Martí." *Differences: A Journal of Feminist Cultural Studies* 6, no. 1 (1994): 69–97. Excellent study of the representation of homosexuality in "Viaje a La Habana" (Journey to Havana) and its significance to the discourse of Cuban national identity.

Sánchez-Grey Alba, Esther. "Un acercamiento a *Celestino antes del alba* de Reinaldo Arenas." *Círculo: Revista de Cultura* 10 (1982): 15–24. Good general analysis of Arenas's first novel.

Santí, Enrico Mario. "Entrevista con Reinaldo Arenas." *Vuelta* 47 (1980): 18–25. Arenas presents his views on literature and Cuba shortly after his

arrival in the United States. Provides a wealth of biographical information.

———. "The Life and Times of Reinaldo Arenas." *Michigan Quarterly Review*
23, no. 2 (Spring 1984): 227–36. Introductory study of Arenas's life and
writings. Especially informative for the English reader.

Schwartz, Kessel. "Homosexuality and the Fiction of Reinaldo Arenas." *Journal
of Evolutionary Psychology* 5, nos. 1–2 (March 1984): 12–20. Despite
being the first study to focus on homoerotic moments in Arenas's writings, the essay is rather misguided in its presentation of homosexuality as
a fear of women and as an identification with female roles.

Soto, Francisco. "*Celestino antes del alba, El palacio de las blanquísimas mofetas,* and
Otra vez el mar: The Struggle for Self-Expression," *Hispania* 75, no. 1
(March 1992): 60–68. A study of how the protagonists of *Singing from
the Well, The Palace of the White Skunks,* and *Farewell to the Sea* struggle to
express themselves through the written form.

———. "*Celestino antes del alba*: escritura subversiva/sexualidad transgresiva,"
Revista Iberoamericana 154 (January–March 1991): 345–54. Studies the
epigraphs to *Singing from the Well* to reveal an encoded homosexual discourse.

———. "*El color del verano*: Innovaciones temáticas y aportaciones ideológicas a
la novela del dictador." *Apuntes Postmodernos/Postmodern Notes* 6, no. 1 (Fall
1995): 59–65. Studies *El color del verano* (The Color of Summer) within
the dynamics of the Spanish American literature of the dictator.

———. "Mona" de *Viaje a La Habana*: hacia una lectura fantástica." In
Reinaldo Arenas: recuerdo y presencia, ed. Reinaldo Sánchez, 169–82.
Miami, Fla.: Ediciones Universal, 1994. A reading of "Mona" as an
example of fantastic literature.

———. "The Palace of the White Skunks." *Masterplots II: American Fiction,* ed.
Frank N. Magill, 2518–23. Pasadena, Calif.: Salem Press, 1994. A pre-
sentation of themes, characters, and structure in *The Palace of the White
Skunks*. Good for the English reader.

———. "*El portero*: una alucinante fábula moderna." *INTI* 32–33 (Fall
1990–Spring 1991): 106–17. A study of *The Doorman* as a subversive
fable.

———. "Reinaldo Arenas." In *The Gay and Lesbian Literary Heritage,* ed.
Claude J. Summers, 58–59. New York: Henry Holt, 1995. A brief sum-
mary of homosexual themes in Arenas's major works.

———. "Reinaldo Arenas." *Latin American Writers on Gay and Lesbian Themes.
A Bio-Critical Sourcebook,* ed. David William Foster, 24–36. Westport,
Conn.: Greenport Press, 1994. A discussion of homosexual themes and
motifs in Arenas's major works.

———. "Reinaldo Arenas's Literary Legacy." *Christopher Street Magazine* 156
(May 1991): 12–16. Arenas's literary legacy is reviewed for an international homosexual reading audience.

————. "Reinaldo Arenas: The *Pentagonía* and the Cuban Documentary Novel." In *Cuban Studies 23,* ed. Jorge Pérez-López, 135–66. Pittsburgh: University of Pittsburgh Press, 1993. A study of the first three novels of the *pentagonía* within the tradition of the Cuban documentary novel.

————. "La transfiguración del poder en "La Vieja Rosa" y *Arturo, la estrella más brillante." Confluencia* 8, no. 1 (1992): 71–78. A intertextual reading of Arenas's "Old Rosa" and "The Brightest Star."

Volek, Emil. "La carnavalización y la alegoría en *El mundo alucinante* de Reinaldo Arenas." *Revista Iberoamericana* 51, nos. 130–131 (1985): 125–48. A Bakhtinian study of carnivalesque mechanisms used in *The Ill-Fated Peregrinations of Fray Servando.*

Special Issues of Journals Dedicated to Arenas

Apuntes postmodernos/Postmodern Notes 6, no. 1 (Fall 1995). Excellent collection of essays on Arenas's work as well as insightful interviews with four of Arenas's translators.

Círculo: revista de cultura 20 (1992). Contains five articles especially noteworthy for their analyses of Arenas's novels, short stories, and drama.

Index

The Author

Francisco Soto received his doctorate in Latin American Literature from New York University in 1988. He has taught at the University of Michigan–Dearborn and is currently professor of Spanish and Latin American Literature at the College of Staten Island, City University of New York. He is widely published, having contributed articles to several leading journals: *Hispania, Revista Iberoamericana, Confluencia: Revista Hispánica de Cultura y Literatura, INTI: Revista de Literatura Hispánica, Utah Foreign Language Review, Review: Latin American Literature and Arts, Linden Lane Magazine,* and *The Americas Review.* In 1990 he published *Conversación con Reinaldo Arenas* (Madrid: Betania), a critical essay on and interview with Reinaldo Arenas. *Reinaldo Arenas: The Pentagonía* (Gainesville: University Press of Florida), the first book-length study to examine Arenas's quintet in its entirety, appeared in 1994. In 1991 he was awarded first prize for translation from the *Instituto de Escritores Latinoamericanos de Nueva York* (New York Latin American Writers Institute).

The Editor

David William Foster is Regents' Professor of Spanish and director of Spanish graduate studies at Arizona State University, where he also chairs the publications committee of the Center for Latin American Studies. He is known for his extensive contributions in the field of Latin American literary bibliography and reference works. In addition, he has published numerous monographs on Latin American literature, with emphasis on theater and narrative, the most recent of which is *Violence in Argentine Literature: Cultural Responses to Tyranny* (University of Missouri Press, 1995).